Helping Children with Ill or Disabled Parents

of related interest

Group Work with Children and Adolescents
Edited by Kedar Nath Dwivedi
1-85302-157-1

Interventions with Bereaved Children
Susan C. Smith and Sisiter Margaret Pennells
1-85302-285-3

Child Play
Its Importance for Human Development
Peter Slade
1-85302-246-2

Parenting Teenagers
Bob Myers
1-85302-366-3

Meeting the Needs of Ethnic Minority Children
Edited by Kedar Nath Dwivedi and Ved P Varma
1-85302-294-2

Child Welfare Services
Developments in Law, Policy, Practice and Research
Edited by Malcolm Hill and Jane Aldgate
1-85302-316-7

Helping Children with Ill or Disabled Parents

A Guide for Parents and Professionals

Julia Segal and John Simkins

Jessica Kingsley Publishers
London and Bristol, Pennsylvania

First published in the United Kingdom in 1996 by
Jessica Kingsley Publishers Ltd
116 Pentonville Road
London N1 9JB, England
and
1900 Frost Road, Suite 101
Bristol, PA 19007, U S A

Copyright © 1996 Julia Segal and John Simkins

Library of Congress Cataloging in Publication Data
Segal, Julia, 1950-
[My mum needs me]
Helping children with ill or disabled parents : a guide for parents and professionals
Julia Segal and John Simkins.
p.   cm.
Includes bibliographical references and index.
ISBN 1-85302-409-0 (pbk.)
1. Parent and child. 2. Sick--Family relationships. 3. Parents-
-Death--Pscyhological aspects. 4. Family psychotherapy.
I. Simkins, John. II. Title.
BF723.P25S44   1996
362.1--dc20   96-13485
                                               CIP

British Library Cataloguing in Publication Data
Segal, Julia, 1950-
Helping children with ill or disabled parents : a guide for
parents and professionals
1. Children of handicapped parents - Services for
2. Handicapped parents - Services for 3. Sick - Family realtionships
I. Title II. Simkins, John III. My mum needs me
362.7

ISBN 1-85302-409-0

Printed and Bound in Great Britain by
Athenaeum Press, Gateshead, Tyne and Wear

Contents

Introduction

'I haven't got time to be ill, not with two small boys.'

'I don't mind being ill myself, it only ever lasts a few days, I feel it's time off. But my husband hates it if I'm ill. He gets really bad-tempered. It's not that he can't cope, he's perfectly happy cooking and shopping when I'm well, but he just hates me being ill.'

'My father is always saying he's ill: I don't believe him. I think he just wants to be the centre of attention. I never let on when I'm ill – I *hate* saying it.'

guilt —['If I had a serious illness I think I'd be worried most about the effect on the family: whether I'd be a burden.']

'I wouldn't mind him being ill if he wasn't so selfish and negative all the time; it's the way he shouts at me and the children that I can't bear. He thinks he's the only person who counts because he's ill and we aren't.'

'I sometimes wish I could be ill in an ordinary way, just 'flu or something, without having to be afraid of what it's going to do to me. I never know how my multiple sclerosis will be affected. When I'm ill like that I can't cope with Jody and I just want someone to take her away. I feel really bad about that: I never thought a mother could want their baby to be taken away.'

It is clear from these quotations that the way people feel about their own and their parents' illnesses are enormously mixed. There is a sense of illness as indulgence; as 'time off'; as a holiday from the stresses of real life; to be taken only by the weak-willed and selfish and scorned by the strong and good. There are strong beliefs about how people ought to behave and feel when they are ill, and reality may not match up. Illness can be seen as inflicting a burden on other people: or it can be used in emotional blackmail: 'Do as I say or I'll be ill and *then* you'll be sorry.'

Any parent can be ill. 'Flu, arthritis, minor or major illnesses or injuries may affect anyone. Mothers hospitalised for tuberculosis in the 1940s and 1950s left many children unmothered at crucial stages in their development: some of these children are now adults and parenting their own children. Cancer may cause at best periods of worry and treatment; at worst, the loss of a parent entirely, with all the disruption that accompanies a major family trauma. Many of the neurological conditions such as motor neurone disease and multiple sclerosis as well as lesser known ones may cause slow deterioration and loss of faculties. With many illnesses there is the added struggle of living with uncertainty, not knowing the outcome. Some illnesses leave no physical trace, although the children's lives may have been affected in subtle or less subtle ways; others leave dramatic scars, both physical and emotional; losses or disabilities which require many years of hard struggle before the changes they bring can be taken for granted. The pain of the loss caused by an illness or accident may never entirely go away.

How do parents handle these conditions? Ignore them in the hope that they will go away? Make a big fuss? Keep quiet but let everyone know you are suffering in silence? Immediate bed rest? Keep going regardless? Major illnesses may be treated at first as if they were minor ones; minor ones exaggerated. Whichever of these parents choose, their children are watching, assessing, making up their own minds about the reality or otherwise of the condition, and making their own decisions, conscious and unconscious, about the ways they are going to be ill or healthy when they grow up.

> 'My mother's mother always seemed to be ailing: not really ill, just "not very well". I think my mother really didn't want to be like her; she wanted to be like her father who never let on if he was in pain at all. I knew when she talked about painkillers she must be having a bad time and sometimes you could see it, though we never said anything. She'd go upstairs quietly to rest and you knew she was in terrible pain, the sort that painkillers don't touch. I felt I had to remember it without being told, and sometimes I forgot and that was awful. I just felt so guilty and bad. I used to bully my brothers to behave, out of terror of what it would do to my mother if they were naughty.'

Illnesses often cause separation from parents for children.

> 'When my mother had to have a minor operation in London, my two little brothers were about two and four. I remember the trouble she went to to make sure they were looked after by a motherly friend: "Mummy Liz" they called her by the time my mother came back. My mother took them to see her many times, both before and after she went to hospital. She made sure they knew each other well and kept in contact afterwards.'

This mother was able to plan a separation between herself and her small children. Some illnesses allow for such planning; other situations happen quite suddenly, leaving the children without a parent from one day to the next, with no affectionate 'Mummy Liz' to look after them.

When the mother described above returned from hospital, her children did not seem in any hurry to come home with her. Another child described her mother's homecoming, in a wheelchair, after a stay in hospital when the child was two. She greeted her mother with 'You're not my mummy, this is my mummy,' showing her a photograph of her mother standing up which she had cherished throughout the separation. The child was a teenager when she spoke and she said she still felt guilty at 'what she had done to her mother'.

Professionals in many situations have to work with people who are ill or disabled parents. Social workers, nurses, doctors, occupational therapists and counsellors may all find themselves confronted with clients or patients who have children. Very often the concerns of the children have to take second place to the concern of the ill parent. If a parent worries about their child in a counselling session, the counsellor has to choose between picking up the worries in terms of the children or in terms of more hidden worries belonging to the parents. 'I'm fine but I'm worried about how my daughter is coping' may well alert a counsellor to wondering just how fine the mother is. A doctor may see their role as primarily reassuring an ill and anxious parent 'not to worry' about the children: 'children are tough, they'll be all right'. In both of these situations the actual concerns of the children, and how 'all right' they are, may not be addressed.

Exactly where can these issues be addressed? Under normal circumstances it is difficult to answer this question. If the children are showing overt problematical behaviour teachers, psychologists or Child Guidance may be called in: but many of the children of ill parents show no signs of difficulty. Parents, teachers, doctors or even social workers may hesitate to raise the question of how the children are coping for fear of upsetting the parents 'who have enough to cope with as it is'. They may equally hesitate to raise the question with the children for fear of drawing unwelcome attention to a child who is coping by pretending nothing is wrong. This can be exacerbated by uncertainty about how to approach children, and whether attention drawn to their situation will fail to help and will actually make things worse.

Looking at the painful feelings which parents and children have to bear if a parent becomes ill or disabled is disturbing. It is disturbing for professionals who have to struggle between seeing their patient or client as someone in need of care while simultaneously being someone who has to provide care for their children. And raising disturbing issues with an ill or vulnerable patient is not to be undertaken lightly. Even if the patient is well at the time, raising questions about the children may give serious offence.

In addition, it is extremely painful to consider what the children are in fact feeling. Having a mother or father ill or suddenly disabled, or different in any way from other people's parents, raises all kinds of painful conflicts for children. Many professionals will have experienced these themselves as children. Many paramedics have in fact had ill parents themselves, and have experienced 'mothering their mother' at some time in their lives. This experience can make it very hard to tolerate thinking about how a child may feel about not being mothered themselves. It is only when a mother is in some way failing to mother their child (for example, by not being there for a time; by being alcoholic; by being so preoccupied with her own life that there is no room for the child; by being worryingly ill) that the child starts mothering them. It is unlikely that the child will have been given an opportunity to grieve the loss of mothering and far more likely that moving into parenting mode is a form of denial of the loss. A similar process takes place, I think, when people assert that they were independent from a very early age. When such children become professional adults they may find it very painful really to consider what the effect on children is of losing some aspect of parenting. They may be tempted to see the children involved as requiring no attention at all.

Professionals as well as parents have been known to expect teenage girls to provide personal care to their mothers at weekends; or to assume that the presence of a ten-year-old in the house means that the parent will be fed. These are problems of children who live with only one parent. However, many children with two parents may still be expected to take care of an ill or disabled parent. Girls have been kept off school to keep their housebound mothers company in order that their father could go to work. A father may refuse to help his wife, leaving a child the only source of assistance; a mother may hide the extent of her disability from her husband, using her children to help cover it up. Sometimes these things happen because nobody has thought sufficiently about the situation. A teenage boy whose divorced mother was alcoholic as well as physically ill said he would never have managed continuous assessment at school because he was always thinking about whether the bills were paid and whether there was any food in the house. For a short period, a social worker would sometimes take him and his sister to her house for a meal, but then she left and there was nobody again. Most children, whether their parents are disabled or ill or not, are well looked after, but some are not.

Mental illness (including alcoholism) in a parent may be particularly destructive of children's peace of mind, but it may be very difficult for any other adult to decide whether, how or when to intervene. It can be very disturbing for children to be brought up by parents whose state of mind is very unpredictable, sometimes quite unrealistic or possibly dangerous. Such parents may be able to prevent any action being taken to protect the children; but it may also not be clear if action could be taken, and if it were, whether the child would be better off. Whether action is taken or not, the child has to live with the effects of their parent's mental state. *Parents ill /effect on child*

    In looking at the painful feelings which parents and children have to bear when a parent is ill or becomes disabled, some of the observations we make and some of the questions we raise will be disturbing. Ill health and some disabilities are disturbing in many ways. They disturb relations between people and feelings people have about themselves. They disturb relations between family members and relations between the family and the professionals who are supposed to be helping them. However kindly a GP tells a patient they have a seriously damaging condition, relations between the GP and the patient's family are likely to be strained afterwards.

    Part of the disturbance involves a very common and natural reluctance to talk about distressing things within the family, which may make talking about anything impossible. In our experience, many of the difficulties arising between parents and children as a result of illness or disability stem from a desire to protect each other, which in fact separates and isolates members of the family from each other. Equally, many of the difficulties arising between patient and doctor arise from a similar reluctance of the doctor to be the bearer of bad news. Social workers and occupational therapists are generally given more training in handling distressing issues, but the particular issues addressed in this book may not have been the focus of much consideration. Teachers are highly unlikely to have been helped to think about children with ill parents: yet these are the people who are in the front line, perhaps playing a very important role in maintaining normality for children in an abnormal situation.

    This book aims to help two kinds of professionals: those who have ill or newly disabled clients or patients who have children themselves; and those who work directly with children who have ill or disabled parents. Originally it was written for parents and family members: this edition has been modified to focus more on the needs of those involved as a function of their job, paid or unpaid. A new Chapter 15 has been added to discuss issues which can arise for health and care workers of all kinds, faced with clients or patients who have disabilities or chronic illnesses. However, it is still suitable for parents and family members. This chapter may be of particular interest to families which are having difficulty with a professional or other worker.

    We also raise questions about the role of a parent who is ill or disabled in some way. Some illnesses prevent parents from fulfilling some of the functions of parents; others simply change the way it must be done. The role of 'helper of others' does not belong simply to the able-bodied and the well. In our experience not only professionals but also parents and children themselves sometimes need reminding that an ill parent is an adult and a parent, with parental responsibilities for their children. Some of these responsibilities may not be carried out while they are ill or disabled, but it is important to distinguish between those aspects of parental responsibility which have to be given up when a parent is ill and those which can be held onto or gained. Parents and children cannot exchange roles without serious loss to the children: a loss which may be overlooked by those (including many children) who devalue parenting and idealise independence in the young.

Since this book was first published there have been considerable developments nationally in regard to children identified as 'young carers'. Conferences, studies, projects and reports have all made more visible this group of children who take a significant role in caring for their parents. Their numbers have been estimated at 15,000–40,000. Awareness has been raised amongst professionals, some of the obstacles to provision of help have been removed and Young Carer's Projects around the country have provided a new source of support for about 700 of these children to date. The Carer's National Association has been a prime mover in this work, and can be contacted for up-to-date information.

We hope this book will be of help to those involved in these projects, as well as to those concerned about the many more children who are not in any sense 'young carers' but who are, perhaps more subtly, affected by a parent's illness.

✠   ✠   ✠   ✠

Our interest in this subject stems from our work with people with multiple sclerosis (MS). MS is a chronic condition which affects the Central Nervous System and which has extremely varied and unpredictable symptoms. Diagnosis is most common between the ages of 25 and 35, the ages at which many people are having children. It therefore affects many parents with young children.

People with MS are ordinary people facing a difficult situation. How they handle their condition throws some light on the ways ordinary people face other illnesses and health problems. Working with people with MS has forced us to consider general issues about the meaning of illness for people, in particular for parents, for children and for those involved with them professionally.

Most parents with MS are not disabled, but some are. Working with these people and their families raises questions about the ways people with other disabilities manage their lives. Being disabled by MS is not the same as being disabled either at birth or after an accident, or by some other condition, but some of the issues are common and some of the experiences we describe will be familiar to people in these different situations.

Counselling adults whose parents were mentally or physically ill when the clients were children has given us some insight into the impact a parent's illness can have on children. It has also provided something of a child's eye view of adult behaviour in such circumstances.

Counselling people whose own parents died when they were children has also given us some insight into the kind of issues which affect children who lose a parent. They have also raised our awareness of the difficulties adults have in helping children through such painful bereavements. We have kept for a separate chapter issues around the death of a parent.

As we have been writing this book an increasing number of children have begun to be faced with the problem that their parents have AIDS. Such children are going to need help, and so are the adults who look after them. We hope this book will contribute something to the lives of these children and their caretakers.

Mostly, however, we are concerned with families *living* with illness or disabilities, rather than with parents dying. We are interested in the rewards and pleasures of parent–child relationships as well as the difficulties.

Chapter 1 looks at the issues mainly from the point of view of parents and their own concerns, leaving on one side their concerns for their children.

In Chapters 2–4 we describe some of the children we have met who have parents with Multiple Sclerosis. We then discuss the issues from the point of view of the children involved. We look at how children interpret the world and at the way a parent's health can affect children's developing sense of themselves.

After much discussion we decided to use minimal disguises throughout the book in order to allow readers to test their own ideas in a way impossible with fictionalised case histories. The children themselves are all now several years older and would probably not recognise their younger selves. Most of the interviews took place with parents in the room and we have omitted anything we think or know the children did not want their parents to know. The children and their parents knew we were talking to them both for their own sake and to help others. We are extremely grateful to these children and to their parents for allowing us to talk with them about such painful issues.

In Chapters 5–7 we pick up some issues which can cause difficulty in families. We look at housework and at aggression and control.

Chapters 8–13 are about attempts to help. We look first at ways parents who are ill or have a disabling condition can help their children. We then look at some of the issues that arise when other people want to help. In Chapter 10 we discuss the role of schools and teachers.

In Chapter 14 we take up the issues which can arise for families if a parent dies.

Chapter 15 looks at some of the issues which arise for professionals, volunteers or other paid or unpaid workers involved with families where a parent is ill or disabled.

Finally, we list some of the sources of help and information, both practical and emotional, which we have found.

Acknowledgements

The writings of the psychoanalyst Melanie Klein and her co-workers and followers have provided a theoretical framework. Maggie Cohen gave helpful advice and encouragement, as did Isobel Menzies, John Steiner, Jon Stokes and members of Dorothy Judd's seminar at the Tavistock Clinic, London. Sylvia Heal at the Carer's National Association brought us up to date with new developments and resources. Vic Finkelstein of the Open University provided some of the references. We would like to thank all of these for their time and the stimulation of their conversation.

We are most grateful to all the parents who brought their children to see the Counsellor, and to the children who came. We are also grateful for the contribution of our own families and aware of the price they have paid for the authors' present state of understanding. A great debt is owed to Ruth Malcolm.

Without the support of Action and Research for Multiple Sclerosis (ARMS) and the ARMS Clinical Research Unit at the Central Middlesex Hospital, London, this book would never have been written. We are grateful to Margaret Bluman for her initial encouragement and her excellent editing, and very grateful to Jessica Kingsley for coming to our aid in a time of need.

The authors

John Simkins has two children and one step-child, all of whom had a parent with MS. For sixteen years he was the Chief Executive of Action and Research for Multiple Sclerosis (ARMS); since then he has been working as an Executive with the charity Multiple Sclerosis Research Centre. Over the whole of this time he has listened to many people with MS talking about their lives, their troubles, their worries and their triumphs.

Julia Segal trained with the Marriage Guidance Council (now Relate) and has been counselling people with MS, their relatives and their children for the past ten years, first as Research Counsellor for Action and Research for Multiple Sclerosis and presently as Counsellor for the CMH MS Unit, Central Middlesex Hospital, London. She has three children and is the author of *Phantasy in Everyday Life: a psychoanalytical approach to understanding ourselves* (Karnac 1995) and *Key Figures in Counselling and Psychotherapy: Melanie Klein,* (Sage 1992). Her interest in the subject of this book, like John Simkins', is personal as well as professional.

PART I

Issues and Views

CHAPTER 1

How Parents See It

Stress
- ignorance
- violence

When parents are ill for a short time <u>tempers may become frayed</u>. Perhaps the children become more clinging or more considerate or more quarrelsome than they were before, but this is unlikely to seem very serious to the parents. The parents recover and they generally expect their children to recover.

If a parent does not recover fully, however, the situation is different. Parents may become preoccupied with their own or their partner's health to the exclusion of all else. On the other hand, one or both parents may be concerned about how they can continue being good parents to their children. Sometimes children are seen as a threat to their parent's health and it is the ill parent's suffering which takes priority.

> John's mother died of cancer when he was fifteen and he was told it was because she had such a hard time looking after him and his two brothers. He always felt her illness was more important than anything else: the whole family had to think of her first. When he became ill he was afraid he would find his own children too much and arranged for them to attend boarding-school to keep them out of his way. He felt his needs and wishes should take priority over his children's. It seemed he had never felt taken care of as a child, but that it was his right now, as an adult, to be taken care of.

Healthy partners, who may have their own problems, may be worried about the children or may themselves have other priorities: their partner's state of health, or perhaps their own and what the partner's illness means for them. Often relations between parents are strained in these circumstances, and parents may worry about the effect of this on their children.

The children may be assumed to be managing all right, and be forgotten or thoughts about them put on one side 'until things settle down.' During short-term crises children often seem to behave exceptionally well and may allow themselves to be put on one side and temporarily ignored. If a long-term or disability or repeated or long-term stays in hospital are involved, s may have more time for thought about the effects of this upon their ren.

'I don't think it's made much difference to my son really. He's just the same as he would have been. I've had to cope with it, but he hasn't. I still went to everything at school; I still do everything for him, now he's 20. He's always had lots of friends round, he's an only child like I was, and my parents did it too: the house was always full of teenagers... They accept things as they are...

I'm in a wheelchair now, I was diagnosed when he was eight, and I've been permanently in a wheelchair for the last two years. It doesn't seem to make any difference. All his friends come and talk to me; all teenagers are like that, they find it easier to talk to someone else's mother than their own. I can't get anything out of mine, but I was the same with my parents...

He's very shy, like me: I was always shy... The thing I've noticed is he doesn't like change, he doesn't expect things to change; he expects and wants things to stay the same...I think all teenagers are like that.

I was talking to someone on the phone the other day and she said her children wouldn't walk down the street with her because she's using sticks now. I asked how old they were and she said 12 and 14, so I laughed and said 'no teenagers want to walk in the street with their mother, whatever she looks like.'... I think it's your attitude that makes the difference, not the condition. Perhaps I was lucky, I was older when it happened to me, I think it might be harder for younger women.'

❈   ❈   ❈   ❈

'We tried hard not to let it affect them, but you can't help it. I was lucky, my husband was really supportive. I used to say "I'll leave, you'd all be much better off without me" and he would say "well, you can leave if you want to, but I don't want you to go". We're all saved by a sense of humour I think. The boys would tease me about the wheelchair; they used to scoot down the hall in it, playing in it. They didn't hate it like I did. They've grown up into lovely boys, I don't have any complaints really.'

'I think the children have grown up with a better idea of the value of money because we didn't have any [because both parents were disabled and unable to work.] They had me and my wife at home to teach them right and wrong. They had a much better upbringing than we did, much

more loving. We all care about each other; my parents and
parents didn't care about anybody.'

'When the Social Worker came round (he was very young and he saiu
things that we had been terribly careful not to say), he asked my daughter
what her daddy had been like... She said "he made me laugh...he got
cross when I was naughty...he loved me very much..."...I took him on
one side afterwards and said, "Look, what you won't have got from that
is that for the last five years of his life, since she was four, he wasn't able
to speak at all..."'

'I don't want it to affect them, I think I try to make it up to them by
being a "Supermum"...I *have* to go to all the school meetings, I'm always
making cakes for school fetes and things... I know the other mothers
don't do it, but I don't look disabled and I think they know I'm at home,
I ought to be doing those things... I do get so tired, sometimes my eyes
go completely and I know it's because I've been doing too much... I
suppose if I hadn't got MS I wouldn't have done half the things I do for
the children; I'd have got a job and been out most of the time...'

wrong

Many parents with disabilities or illnesses say that their condition does not
harm the children. Some feel their condition may have affected the children
but if so they show little or no sign of it, or of any damage. Some feel they
have paid a high price to maintain the normality of life for their children, but
it was a price well worth paying.

The question of what difference it makes being a parent with a chronic
illness or a stable or progressive disabling condition, is a real one. Different
does not necessarily mean better or worse, though it might. Different might
mean difficult.

'What I hate most about MS is my children growing up with me like this
[paralysed in all four limbs]...'

'I felt that they were deprived. That's the thing that stands out. What
they were deprived of was the normal activities; if they wanted a cuddle,
they had to go to their mother, she couldn't go to them. And of course,
often they don't. They don't know they need one so they don't get it.

I also felt in some ways deprived myself...because of looking after her
I couldn't do the things which a father whose wife wasn't disabled could
do... Sunday was the only day we could be together... I couldn't play
golf, for example, and when my son wanted to play football on a Sunday,
unless Sandra was able to come with us I did not feel able to go with
him; so some other father had to go; I am sure this was part of the

estrangement between my son and me, which only came clear many years later…'

Some thought there was no difficulty but found out much later that things were not as easy for the children as they thought.

'I had a shock when I asked my daughter to be interviewed for training purposes by the counselling organisation I work for. I wanted her to talk about what it was like having a disabled mother. She's twenty-three now. We've always been very open about it and it didn't seem much problem. She said she wouldn't do it because she didn't want me hearing what she said. I had no idea she felt like that about it.'

Sometimes parents feel they can detect a good influence of the parent's health condition on their child's future, such as the child who determined to become a chemist to study how to cure MS, or the many children who enter the caring professions. Parents sometimes say that their circumstances have made their children more thoughtful and considerate and they are pleased about this, though they might even so have preferred it if the children had not had to grow up like this.

Most of the parents we have spoken with have not been born disabled or ill and they have had to cope with the change in their circumstances as well as the illness or disability itself. On the other hand, most have had the experience of being parented themselves as 'normal' children, mostly with 'normal' parents. This affects the ways people feel about themselves as parents.

Many, though not all, people born with serious disabilities or who acquired them when they were very young may have particular difficulties when it comes to being parents. Many have had to cope with repeated rejection from their family and from society in general. Their enforced dependence on others or their desire for an independent existence, their sexuality and their aggressive feelings may all have been greeted with extremely negative reactions from those around them. Their emotional needs and desires are more likely to have been systematically ignored and misunderstood and they may perhaps have had fewer opportunities than able-bodied children to find alternative sources of support or affirmation from people outside their family.

For some people the experience of growing up with a disability or illness is so socially and emotionally handicapping that they are unable without considerable help to form sufficiently close relationships to be able to become parents. For others, social and emotional life is far less crippled and parenthood becomes a possibility. The physical aspects of a disability may be less of a handicap to becoming a parent than the social and emotional consequences, which depend enormously on the character and resources of the people around.

How can I be a parent when I'm like this?

An article titled: 'How do you mother when you are disabled?' appeared in a Canadian magazine. In it Anne Belohorec described movingly her anxieties and fears about becoming disabled with MS, and the difficulties this made for her as a mother. She wrote: 'Is there any literature or someone who has taught people to parent in spite of disabilities? No one in this hospital seems to know these things. This is more frightening than being unable to walk.' Anne Belohorec felt totally de-skilled as a mother by her new disability. At the end of the article it is clear that she did learn how to continue being a mother to her children. She used both 'trial and error' and also professional help.

We have met women who despaired of being able to continue looking after their children. Some feared they would die too soon; some were very frightened, particularly when their condition worsened and they were not sure if it would improve again. Other mothers, and also the same mothers at other times, were full of confidence, sure they could overcome any difficulties with or without the help of others.

Some of the men with MS we have met seem to have felt themselves useless as fathers as a result of their condition. Others have abnegated responsibility towards their children, withdrawing and leaving their wives to struggle on alone. Some have been able with help to seek new ways of continuing to behave as a father to their children.

Being ill under normal circumstances seems often to make people feel like small children again: dependent, allowed not to worry about normal day-to-day decisions, permitted to hand over responsibilities and to be looked after and perhaps even indulged and paid special attention. This does not fit with being a parent. Temporary abrogation of adult responsibilities may not be seen by parents as a problem for children. They may think it is good for children to take more responsibility within the family for a while. We discuss this from the children's point of view in Chapters 2–4.

However, if a parent withdraws from family responsibilities for a long period the partner may suffer a serious loss. It is hard to bring up children while grieving for the loss of a partner's support and involvement, however little they did before. Added to this may be the burden of coping not only with the physical aspects of the illness or condition itself but also with the emotional reactions of the ill parent. Other sources of support may fail at times of illness, particularly if it lasts for a long period.

Friends, relatives and other people around (including professionals such as doctors and nurses) may be less than supportive and may increase the family's difficulties, if only by making their absence felt. Without support it can be very difficult and painful for parents to think about what is happening to the children, and to be forced to make extremely important decisions alone. A parent's illness does not stop other problems arising, and families generally have other things to worry about in addition to the parent's illness.

In such circumstances partners of ill parents may feel quite unsupported and desperately abandoned. Their own emotions are likely to be extremely raw. They may feel inside like small children who have lost a parent themselves and at the same time bitter, furious and totally hopeless about their own present and future. Their hopes and fantasies about their own goodness are severely threatened by the illness of their partner. They are likely to identify with the ill partner and with the bereaved children as well as with their own real losses. Their own past bereavements may be relived through the present ones.

The difficulty of coping with the anger and resentment of this situation is compounded when it is not clear if the ill parent is choosing to withdraw or cannot help it. In this state, even a healthy partner may be quite unable to offer their children firm, adult parenting. For a while he or she may even demand from the children themselves some kind of reassurance and parenting. In this way the children may lose vital aspects of both parents at the same time as being asked to behave as if they were adults. Parents are sometimes very aware of this and later make attempts to restore their own authority and to allow and encourage the child to return to a more childish role.

Where good support from family, friends or professionals is available, parents and children may retrieve or build anew a valuable and supportive parent–child relationship. Whether a particular child will remain available for such a relationship after a long period of parental withdrawal or abandonment is not, however, certain.

A disability or illness sometimes also increases the support available to people from their partner and/or from others. It sometimes makes one or both parents more available and more aware of what goes on at home or with the children. Newly-unemployed fathers and mothers may be able to play a much greater part in their children's lives than previously.

Wanting to be 'normal'

If an illness or disability becomes chronic, the sense of loss of normality may be extremely painful. Many parents with MS have told us how desperately they want to be what they consider a 'normal' parent. They want to be able to do what other parents do, or to have the same choices available to them: to have no more than 'normal problems'.

It can be enormously depressing being faced on a day to day basis with the awareness that there are many things which you cannot do which you always imagined yourself doing. Being at home with a small child growing up, facing new developmental stages and becoming able to do new things every day may make the loss of normality especially poignant. Being unable to have the choice of taking a child on their first bus ride or on a ride at a fun fair can be painful for some parents, though others would not consider this a loss at all. The fact that many other parents cannot do these things for many other reasons does not help at all; it may not actually be 'normality' which is wanted but an ideal state of motherhood or fatherhood invested with enormous longing from the past.

Any mother has to discover (generally with her first child) that she cannot be the perfect mother she wanted to be when she was small. For most mothers the disappointment will be mitigated by a knowledge that they can at least be as good as their own mother was. They know they loved her as well as feeling critical of, or angry towards, her. This helps mothers recognise that their children will go on loving them, and comforts them when those children turn against them for a while. For a mother with a chronic condition the loss of her illusions may be considerably more painful. She may have no belief that she will be loved in spite of her shortcomings. Remembering her own mother's mothering may bring no comfort: instead of being able to feel better than or equal to her mother, she may have to face feeling inferior again, as she did as a child.

Some people feel that the loss of some aspect of their health tips the balance between managing to be a good-enough parent and not managing at all. The 'all-or-nothing' approach to life is a real problem here: those parents who must have things perfect if they are not to despair may react very badly indeed to having an imperfect body. For these parents, being unable to pick their toddler up, for example, may mean to them that they cannot be a parent at all. This attitude may change over time as people discover what they actually can do for their children. However, it is astonishing how parents who have in fact brought up their children perfectly satisfactorily still see themselves as failures because they only look at what they cannot do and never see their abilities and their achievements.

Other parents are more able to see that something can be saved: that the loss of the use of their legs, or having to spend two hours every morning getting up and two hours in the evening going to bed, does make life more difficult and more frustrating but it does not totally destroy their ability to be a parent.

It is not uncommon to swing between these two positions: believing all is lost and believing that something can be saved. Any stressful situation, including any change, may bring on the despair; when things are settled or going well a more positive outlook may be maintained.

Some people feel they have to maintain a pretence of being positive when they cannot face thinking about their losses: this can be a great strain and a cause of even more guilt when it fails (as it generally does). Everyone around them may also become frightened of breaking a pretence which covers an unrealistic, exaggerated despair. Others allow themselves periods of depression

ney can think about the reality of their losses and sort
rs and fantasies attached to them. This process generally
omeone else who can bear the unbearable feelings for a
ight to take place. Families or other people, including
cilitate this process, or they may hinder or even prevent it
. The positive feelings which develop out of this are more
nts of real hope as well as awareness of painful but bearable
loss.

Loss of self-confidence

Many parents seem to have their self-confidence knocked by physical illness.
It is not only when they are ill themselves that they feel like this, but also when
it is their partner who is ill. People generally hold themselves responsible for
keeping their partner healthy, and may interpret illness as a sign of failure to
be a good partner. Women are exhorted in magazines to 'Keep your family
healthy'. The health of their wives may affect men's status as well as their secret
beliefs about the power of their love. People in same-sex relationships may take
their partner's illness as a sign that their love is not good and healing, as they
want it to be, but is bad, as 'society' says. Helping professionals too may find
their confidence shaken if a client gets more ill for any reason: in addition they
may be unrealistically blamed by a distressed client or family member.

The symbolism of disease, deformity, weakness, ill-health and lack of fitness
is very powerful and it influences peoples' attitudes to others and to themselves.
Both adults and children link beauty, goodness and abilities, on the one hand,
and deformity, badness and incompetence on the other. We talk about feeling
ill or more disabled or in more pain as 'feeling bad' or 'having a bad day', or
'my leg was bad today'.

Parents who 'feel bad' a lot of the time may find it difficult to believe they
have anything good to offer their children or their partners.

Taking over parental roles

Parents sometimes worry about the way they turn to their sons or daughters
for help with housework or for comfort, for help with lifting or doing various
jobs about the house. Some are concerned that they are putting unreasonable
demands on their children. Others feel it is right and natural that a child should
take over when its parent can no longer perform their previous functions.
Sometimes a child is worried when a parent is not, or vice versa. (See Chapter
6.)

Jane's mother was very concerned about Jane who at thirteen was living
alone with her mother, having to prepare all her mother's food and help

her get up and go to bed. She felt her daughter needed someone to talk to, in spite of Jane saying everything was fine. Jane resisted many attempts of social workers and others to take her on one side and talk about any difficulties she might be having. Her mother was afraid that Jane thought that if anyone knew she was having any difficulties at all she would be sent to live with her father and his new wife, and to a new school, when she wanted to stay where she was.

A father of two girls said he and his wife had decided never to ask them to take on anything they would not have had to do if his wife had been well. He undertook all the personal tasks of caring for his wife as she became more and more disabled over twenty years. As an adult, the younger daughter told him in a counselling session that she had some-times felt pushed out and not allowed to help; she had wanted to be included more and had wanted more information. She was very close to her mother and spent a lot of time with her. Her father said she had never asked anything but had always seemed to accept things as they were.

A young mother with MS whose partner left after her third child was born said she never worried about the children having to look after her when she was old: there were three of them so it wouldn't be too bad. The older one was already very helpful, and so he should be. Children were there for parents, not the other way round.

It can be very difficult for parents and children to come to an agreement about how much help and involvement is reasonable and how much is unfair. Parents themselves may disagree: some tell the children what to do; others ask; some expect the children to think for themselves about what needs doing; others say they only want help when they ask for it. There can be confused messages in both directions.

Sometimes this seems to be worked out quite amicably.

'You sometimes hear of children doing everything for their parents, I think that's wrong, I feel really sorry for them. My son is very good, he does help me get up if I've tipped out of the chair, but we don't ask him to do much. The other night my husband was away and I asked him to be back early; he came in at two in the morning. I told him I did like to start going to bed by 1.30 and liked someone to be around just in case I needed some help. He said "Oh sorry, mum"; and he was, but I was really glad he's able to be self-centred like any other teenager and not feel he's got to be thinking about me all the time...'

In this issue, as in many others, it appears that a chronic illness or disability may make less difference to family life than the parents' and children's general attitudes to themselves and to others which are, to some extent, independent of the parent's health.

Uncertainty and control

Uncertainty is, in fact, part of everyone's life, but most people seem to recognise this only when something happens to disrupt assumptions which they did not know they had. Day to day decisions may be affected as well as long-term plans. Parents may be unable to say to children 'I will fetch you from school today' (or tomorrow or next week), because they do not know if their legs or eyes will work that day or not, or whether they will have been suddenly rushed into hospital. Holidays may be arranged only with the proviso 'if we can go'.

It is very difficult to maintain uncertainty: 'I don't know what will happen now I have this illness'. A common reaction is to attempt to take control. Some people react by saying 'If I can't plan, I'll do nothing'. Others insist 'NOTHING is going to happen to me because of this illness'.

> Megan's mother brought her to the counsellor partly because she was feeling she had let Megan down terribly. Her way of dealing with her illness had been to insist she would not let it affect her. She had always promised she would never walk with a stick, and now she was having to. This made her feel terribly guilty. Megan was nine, and in counselling she talked of many things, but the stick and the broken promise seemed, in fact, of very little interest to her.

There are people who are content to take things as they come, to make arrangements knowing they might be called off, and to live their lives fully in spite of the uncertainties. We have also known families and individuals who initially panicked and stopped everything (in terms of having a social life, going shopping, taking holidays, working, starting new relationships, for example) in the face of an unpredictable condition but who learnt over time, with some help, to allow themselves to live again.

We look at other ways of taking control for example, by trying to keep time standing still – in Chapter 3.

Guilt

Parents can feel guilty about being ill and about what this means to other members of the family; guilty about not being ill when their partner is; guilty about not spending enough time with the children; guilty about not doing enough for the children or their partner. They can feel guilty about resenting the restrictions made to their lives by the children or by their partner's disability or illness: guilty about being angry with each other for not understanding their point of view; guilty about making demands and guilty about being unable to make them; guilty about having married the wrong person or having got married at all; guilty about ignoring their own needs and guilty if they try to give themselves anything.

It is remarkable how difficult it seems to be to accept bad, angry, miserable or resentful feelings even when they seem perfectly normal and justifiable. Some people have been taught not to admit to such feelings and may teach their children this in turn. Some find it hard eventually to feel anything much except guilt for failing to feel the 'right' feelings.

Guilt can sometimes be changed by meeting others in similar situations, and sharing guilty feelings can lessen them. Not everyone feels guilty all the time, and some have worked through their guilt and come out on the other side. They have managed to recognise and acknowledge the contribution they make, and the right they have to feel the way they do and be the way they are. These people may sometimes be able to influence those who are still in the grip of excessive guilt.

Some guilty feelings can be changed by counselling. Those related to quite unrealistic beliefs or fantasies may alter when they are discussed openly. One mother felt terribly guilty because she did not 'wish her daughter's MS on herself', as she felt a 'proper mother' would do. Another felt guilty because she was very resentful towards her twin sister, who never had any illness. She felt her sister's health was 'paid for' by her own many illnesses and that this was quite unfair. Several people felt they had brought their illness on themselves by 'willing' it.

Some of the consequences of such guilt can be challenged: for example, where a partner is allowed to bully or behave in other socially unacceptable ways 'because they have so much to cope with' and the victim feels so terribly guilty for objecting even secretly. In sympathetic discussion such behaviour can sometimes be recognised for what it is, and the 'victim' helped to stand up for themselves.

> A woman said she was feeling very guilty that she went to work when her husband wanted her at home. Looking at this with the counsellor it became clear that she knew that neither she nor her husband nor the children would benefit if she stopped working entirely. She needed help to allow herself to have opportunities her husband had lost, and help to enable both herself and her husband to tolerate his jealousy and his wish to spoil her life like his had been spoiled. Her guilt seemed to cover some considerable anger, but she felt that anger towards a husband who suffered so much already was quite unacceptable.

Guilt sometimes arises because people cannot bear to acknowledge that they do not have control either over their own feelings or over the situation. Admitting to helplessness and exploring the limits of their control can some-

guilt and transform it into an anger which might have more
uences. Fear of the extent and power of this hidden anger may
ple prefer to stay feeling guilty.

are missing out'

'I want us to have a good holiday this year: we haven't had one for several years now.'

'I can't play football with him like other fathers can.'

'I could never bath them when they were small; my hands wouldn't work. I think it's different for children when their mother can't do things like that. It did make them closer to their father.'

'It really hurts that I can't get upstairs to kiss them goodnight but have to say goodnight downstairs before they go up. It's not the same.'

'Children need a father, but he never takes any notice of them now except to shout at them; most of the time he sleeps or watches TV. Mind you, he didn't take much notice before he got like he is now. If he hadn't got ill I sometimes think I'd have divorced him by now.'

'I wish Martin could leave boarding school and come and live at home, but I can't cope with his mother like she is. She can't look after herself, let alone him, and I can't look after her properly and keep my business. I'm going to lose it if I'm not careful and then I don't know what we'll do. He's better off where he is, he's got some security, but I don't like it.'

All of these examples in fact illustrate not only the children but also *the parent* missing out on some aspect of parenting they very much wanted. They wanted to be the kind of parent who went on holiday with the family, played football with their sons, took the children to the park, and tucked them up in bed; they wanted to be the one who was always there to collect the children from school or the kind of mother who shared the care of the children with a strong father.

Some feel this is what their own parents did for them and that this is what parents should do. Their sadness and grief may be enormously painful but they may have a sense of being supported by loving parents in their suffering even if these parents are physically unavailable.

Others feel this is what parents should do and what they hoped to do, knowing that their own parents had failed. The pain is different if there is a strong sense of having been neglected as a child. There may be an enormous longing to make up to their own children for the lack they felt in their own childhood. At the same time they may have terrible conflicts if some part of them finds it almost unbearable to see their children having love or attention they never had themselves. There is a real temptation to make one of their children suffer as they suffered themselves, and so to share and remove the burden of the unbearable feelings. This is likely to be entirely unconscious but very powerful. The despair and suffering of such parents on behalf of their children is compounded by despair and suffering on behalf of the child they once were themselves. Their need to make it better for their children and their hopelessness about making anything better may be equally strong.

Where parents do not have a sense of being loved and supported by their own parents in the past, grief may feel unbearable and may be 'cut off' so that the parent stops being aware of feeling anything except numbness or perhaps a sense of duty or dull resignation.

Children have different ideas about what they want and what they are missing from parents; we look at this in Chapters 2–4.

'Making it up to the children'

Some parents react to their own guilt and their sense of the children missing out by trying to make it up to them. It is tempting to let children do things they want to do but that the parents know should really be forbidden or controlled, partly because it is the line of least resistance, partly because the parents feel the children have enough to suffer without yet another 'no'.

Some parents become more tolerant and less demanding than they feel they would otherwise have been. They make excuses for the children's behaviour when they feel they would take a firmer line if it were not for the illness or disability. It is difficult to decide how best to handle children who are being wild or difficult. Are they looking for someone to notice them, to say no firmly, to give them a firm adult framework to their lives? Are they best ignored in the hope that their attention-seeking will stop? We look further at these issues in Chapter 7.

Parents who want to 'make it up to the children' may benefit from thinking about what they feel their children are missing and letting the child know how they feel about it. For children to know that their parents think about them can be very important in itself: acknowledging the children's loss may be an opportunity either for the children to feel less alone with their grief, or for the parents to find out that the children see things quite differently. Some parents are 'making it up to the children' when the children do not feel they are missing out.

There are ill or disabled parents who do not think their children are missing anything that matters. Others think that their children are missing some important things, but know they have other advantages and that life can be good without being just as they would like it to be.

Will I lose my child?

Parents who become ill or disabled often worry about whether their children will be taken away.

> One mother said she was terrified to mention the difficulties she was having because she had had a 'nervous breakdown' before her daughter was born and she was afraid someone – 'they' – would take her child away if she admitted to any problems looking after her. Since she had been diagnosed with a chronic illness she had been even more afraid of this. Counselling seemed to leave her reassured: it was the first time she had told anyone of this fear and it seemed less likely once she had talked about it.

Other mothers have feared losing their children to other people: to grandmothers, to paid helpers, or to the other parent.

There are some situations where an illness can lead to a child being taken away.

> A single mother who was becoming increasingly unable to look after herself or her five-year old son was afraid social workers would take him away from her. She desperately wanted to hold out until he was old enough to look after both of them. She was not only physically deteriorating but also mentally becoming less able to remember, to think and to speak. Those who knew the child were very worried about him. His mother could not control him and neither could her helpers, who were changed frequently by the mother so that the child did not become attached to them.

> After the child had threatened to throw himself off a bridge on two occasions a case conference was called. There was talk of sending the boy to boarding school. After several years and a court case he was eventually sent to live with his grandmother who took him to visit his mother regularly.

In these circumstances the child's interests and the parent's may ultimately conflict. Parents themselves may eventually feel that it might be better for the child to be taken care of elsewhere. This is a very painful situation. It can be very upsetting and worrying to know that your child is being taken care of by someone else who you do not know you can trust. It may not be better for children to leave home if there is nowhere better for them to go.

With the Children Act of 1991 parental rights and responsibilities are not taken away if children do have to live elsewhere. Social workers now have a statutory duty to work with parents in such situations and to maintain as much contact as possible between the children and their parent(s). This may not be much comfort but it does mean that severely ill or disabled single parents have a better chance of retaining more of their parental relationship with their children than under the old system.

Residential care

Help for adults & child carers

When a parent chooses or is taken into residential care, there is some loss of contact with their children, whatever age they are. This may be a relief for one or both parents, although there may also be some guilt at feeling this relief, particularly if one partner is not happy about the arrangement. There may also be considerable guilt and distress of other kinds. It is hard to visit and to know what to say to a demented husband or wife, where home care would mean caring could be expressed in non-verbal, physical ways. Either partner can feel jealous of the other who they believe is having a better time without them.

Temporary 'respite' care can be followed by difficult periods of adjustment in which tempers are extremely frayed on both sides, as the sense of being abandoned is suffered by both partners. (This often happens with couples when a partner frequently has to travel for work purposes. The periods together may be spoilt by bickering, and relations just be returning to normal when it is time for a further separation.) Recognition and tolerance of the feelings involved may improve the situation to some extent.

Hospital stays do not figure largely in most parents' discussion of their children. We wonder if this is one area where children are generally more concerned than their parents. The time of the separation seems so much longer to a child, and the consequences may be extremely disruptive to the child's normal life. For the adult it may feel more like having a good rest, and there be some relief in not having to do all the normal daily tasks of parenting.

However, for some parents time in hospital is traumatic and causes lasting difficulty.

> Jody's mother was taken into hospital when Jody was a few weeks old. She had collapsed and was feeling extremely ill. Her husband and sister looked after Jody, bringing her in every day. Jody's mother remembered many of the events and feelings with guilt and bitterness. She felt her whole relationship with Jody had been spoiled by this stay in hospital. She had had to stop breast-feeding and three years later she still felt extremely guilty because at the time she had wanted Jody to be taken away and looked after by someone else. She felt this was inexcusable in a mother; it was totally opposed to the picture she had had of how it would be when she had a child.

> Mike, father of three children, had enormous pressure put upon him to let his wife, Marion, stay in hospital 'for her sake' and 'for the sake of

the children'. Marion said little about it except that she wanted to be at home; she left all decisions to Mike. It was not in fact clear that either the children or the parents would have been better off with Marion in hospital. It took some considerable effort to get Marion home against medical advice. Eventually she was brought home in the expectation that she would die: whereupon her health improved enormously. Mike felt bitter that none of the medical team who had opposed the move home ever admitted that he was taking better care of Marion than they had.

Finances Money

Having a disability or illness can be expensive. Not only may it be harder for one or two parents to hold down a job, but the expenses of daily life may be considerably increased. This may indirectly or directly affect the children. Attitudes also play a part.

> 'We used to be comfortable, not well off but comfortable; now we're struggling and I hate having to say to the children, no, you can't have a pair of £90 trainers, we can't afford it. It reminds me of my father when I was small, he was always saying things like that.'

> One couple living on disability allowances felt they had more to spend than their own parents had.

> Another woman said she could never have children because with her husband's disability they could not earn enough money to send the children to private school; the state schools were totally unacceptable to her.

Sometimes understandable resentment against the changes in life brought on by a sudden onset of a disabling condition can make the financial burdens seem worse. Some of these attitudes change over time.

> Margaret came for counselling to help her live with her husband's deteriorating mental condition. When she first came she talked a lot about finances. She was angry and upset at having to take over financial management of the family which previously had been her husband's responsibility. She also worried that she would disable him further by taking away an important aspect of his role in the family; admitting that he was no longer mentally capable of doing it was very difficult. Two years later she still found it hard making ends meet, but she no longer minded doing it.

It seems that not only the reality but also the symbolism of money is very important in many families. For some it signifies love they did not have as children and want to give their own children. For some, money in a savings account 'for a rainy day' seems to mean having some life saved up and still to live. For some having enough money means 'not having to feel guilty all the time about spending money which should be spent on someone else'. For others it seems to mean self-respect and the respect of society. The ability to provide for the family financially may also symbolise 'being a man' and providing sexually for a partner. Male sexual impotence may then give rise to arguments about money and financial inadequacy.

A disability or illness also has symbolic meanings as well as practical ones. It may threaten to shorten life considerably; it may threaten loss of love or loss of respect or the end of sexual relations, for example. The threat may be real and unavoidable, or imagined or avoidable. Often the worst fears about these issues cannot be spoken aloud within the family. Sometimes anxieties about the condition may be expressed in anxieties about money.

Conclusion

In this chapter we have discussed some of the issues raised with us by parents who have illnesses or disabilities. Our sample is by no means random and we do not wish to suggest that all parents have any or all of these concerns. Some parents worry about their children, others do not. Many did not want to talk with us about their children. The issues which seem important to parents may not, however, be those which seem important to children, and it is the children's concerns that we examine next.

CHAPTER 2

Some Children

Introduction

What does it mean to a child, to have a parent who is ill or who has a disability? Clearly this question has as many answers as there are parents, children, disabilities and illnesses. By relating some of the observations we have made we hope to make it easier for the reader to make their own individual assessment of the situation which concerns them.

Nearly all of the children in this chapter have a parent who has MS, and their backgrounds are nearly all white British (although very varied within that category). We are not able to say what happens 'all the time' or even 'most of the time' to children with parents who have disabilities or illnesses of any kind, from all possible different backgrounds and different circumstances. We can only show what we have noticed in these particular circumstances.

The concerns of these children seem to us perfectly 'normal' in the sense that any child might well react in the way they do, and indeed many of the issues which came up were repeated by more than one child.

We trust to readers to use the information to help them to look more closely at the circumstances which interest them. Generalisations may *prevent* observation, since they give a sense of 'I know what there is to know' which may be totally unjustified. We prefer the specific example which claims to be no more than that. Our experience also gives us no choice.

Parents' versus childrens' views

There are many issues which preoccupy parents but do not seem to concern the children we have met in the same way. 'My dad cannot...' or 'My mum cannot...' are phrases seldom used by these children in counselling. Their parents may be conscious of the things they want to do and cannot do; the children seem more concerned about issues of life and death: 'Will mum get worse?'; 'Is it my fault?' 'Is he/she being looked after properly?', and 'Is he/she going to die?'. They raise the questions of who is getting more love in the family: 'It's not fair; my brother/sister/father gets more than me/does less work than me'; or whether a parent is behaving correctly, according to the child's criteria, on issues such as clothes, how a mother carries her handbag, or whether she is concerned about her children or only about herself.

When children do mention things their parents can and cannot do, they speak more in terms of what they will or will not do, as if it were a matter of choice. It seems that the assumption that adults have total control over everything, including their own bodies, is more powerful than the realisation that they are impotent in some situations. So a daughter may be more likely to be angry with her mother because she *will not* walk better or do more housework herself, or make her son or husband do it, than to admit the possibility that she perhaps *cannot* do these things.

In Chapters 11–13 we look at some of the issues involved in listening to children and in trying to find out how they see the world. We hope that the discussion will be made clearer by the examples in these two chapters.

William

William was an attractive nine-year-old boy who gave the impression of being a thinker. He had always been very close to his father who had been diagnosed MS seven years earlier. At the time we met William his father had been unable to use his legs for several months; recently he had been very ill and needed a lot of nursing care. Mentally William's father seemed to be withdrawing from the family even more than he always did, although on and off he took a fleeting interest in his children, particularly William.

The family was concerned that William's father might die soon. William said he wanted to buy his father a sports car for Christmas 'when he got better': you didn't need your legs to work to drive a sports car, he said; you could use hand controls. It would make his father feel better. The counsellor gently said that it seemed very difficult for William to see that his father wasn't going to get better enough to drive again. William looked stricken and frightened. The counsellor said she wondered if he was afraid that if it was said, it would become true and that as long as nobody said it, it would not. William was silent.

Later, William made it clear that he felt that his mother was not taking care of his father properly. He thought she should be at home more, and should not get cross with his father when he did things slowly. He felt that if he were his mother, he would look after his father better, but he didn't like thinking this. He said he just tried to help his father whenever he could and was polite towards his mother most of the time. (Several of the children felt like this about the relationship between their parents, and we discuss it further in Chapters 4 and 5.)

William found it easier to express some of his feelings through drawing. He drew careful, accurate pictures of objects he could see. He talked of his father's ability to draw, which he had inherited, and the way he and his father used to make things together. While his mother talked, saying that she didn't think anything worried William much, he began drawing cartoons of very distorted, ugly heads. The counsellor wondered aloud at the contrast between his sensible appearance and the very frightening pictures. She wondered if he kept the more frightened or frightening side of himself hidden.

Later, when his parents were not there, it emerged that this side of William contained a lot of anger and explosiveness. He drew a picture of his family. When the counsellor commented on how his father seemed to be holding the rest of the family together, he started drawing pictures of the family exploding if his father was not there. He experimented with moving different members of the family into the gap his father left, but ended with isolated fragments of the family going off in all directions. The counsellor felt – and shared with him – the possibility that he was showing her not only what he felt about *the family* in the absence of his father, but also what he felt would happen to *him* in that situation. He would try to fill the gap, but failing that, he too would explode into pieces, scattered by anger.

The counsellor saw his mother later and heard that after the counselling session he had cried for a long time with her, and she had allowed him to cry. He had not done this before and she felt it was overdue. His mother was grateful to the counsellor for enabling her to get back in touch with William and offer him comfort in a way she had not been able to do for some time.

Matthew

Matthew, seven, was William's younger brother. He did not take much part in talking during the times he and his brother came to the counsellor. On one occasion when their mother was out of the room Matthew was moving about, apparently taking no notice while William talked to the counsellor. William spoke about his father not getting better, which they had discussed earlier, and how he thought Matthew might feel. Matthew put on his Walkman headphones and leant over his chair with his back to the room. There was a silence. The counsellor said perhaps Matthew did not want to think about things like that. Matthew nodded in time with the music and turned round. There was another silence. Then the counsellor said 'Sometimes children worry about what will happen to them if both their parents die. Do you Matthew?' rather doubtfully. Matthew suddenly turned on her and said scornfully 'Of course I do'. Taken aback the counsellor asked what he thought would happen to him and he said 'I don't know'. The counsellor took this up with the children and then with their mother when she returned.

Their mother said she and her husband had thought about this, and a friend had always said she would have them. Matthew's immediate response was 'Frances? But she couldn't cope with me'. The counsellor said it sounded as if he was afraid he was too much for anyone to cope with, and she wondered if Matthew thought he might be too much for his mother and father too. Perhaps he thought he might have made them ill by being too much for them. His mother broke in and said 'no, of course I can cope with him'. Matthew was silent.

Once when his father was extremely ill in hospital Matthew whispered to his brother that he was afraid his father had died and nobody had told him.

Rachel

Rachel was ten and she and her parents decided she should talk to the counsellor on her own. She had no difficulty talking.

Rachel's mother had had MS since before Rachel was born. The first thing Rachel said was that she thought it was her fault her mother couldn't walk, because she knew she could walk before Rachel was born and she could not now. No-one had said this to her, she had worked it out for herself. She did not seem to know that MS usually gets worse as part of the natural course of the disease: she thought deterioration had to be caused by something someone had done.

She said she didn't think the MS had made any difference to her, but she also said she thought she didn't have any brothers or sisters because her mother couldn't have more children because having Rachel had given her MS. The counsellor said she should talk about this with her mother because there were other reasons why people only had one child. Women *can* have children when they have MS and it doesn't seem to make them worse in the long term, but not all doctors or parents know this.

Rachel said her grandmother had told her not to worry her mother because it would make her MS worse. Asked for an example she said she no longer told her if she fell out with friends at school, though she used to and her mother was easy to talk to. She just didn't want to upset her. One night recently she had stayed the night with a friend and she had cried a bit because she had been homesick. She hadn't told her mother, because it might worry her.

In fact, when her mother becomes angry or upset she does shake; this lasts a few minutes or hours, and then it stops. This is not a sign of more nerve damage being done, but of existing damage showing up. The ability to compensate for nerve damage is affected by emotional reactions, as well as by heat and tiredness. Rachel, like many other children did not know this until the counsellor told her. Both she and her parents found it difficult to believe that these reactions did not mean the MS was getting worse.

When the counsellor asked if she ever worried about her mother, Rachel said that she sometimes worried about what she would do if anything happened to her father. She was not sure she could cope on her own with her mother. The counsellor asked if she would be alone with her mother; were there no relatives? Rachel's face cleared as she said that several members of her father's and mother's families lived close by, and that they would not abandon her and her mother if they should need them. She had not thought of them.

Rachel talked of the good things about her parents. She said she was glad they loved each other: parents of a friend of hers had just got divorced and she could talk about this with her parents; she wasn't afraid they would ever separate. She also appreciated her mother always being at home when she came in from school.

Megan

Megan was nine. She spent some time complaining to her mother and the counsellor that she had to do things which her brother did not have to do, and that her mother did things for her little brother which she said she could not do for Megan. She was sure her mother played football with her brother but then said she could not walk to school to collect Megan. She felt this was terribly unfair and that her mother didn't want to do things for her.

With the counsellor, Megan and her mother talked about how much her mother's MS allowed her to do and how much it stopped her doing, how unpredictable it was, and the fact that it upset her mother that she could not do everything she wanted to do for Megan or for her brother. This idea seemed new to Megan.

A friend of Megan's had been very frightened some time ago when they had been playing a game with her mother and her mother's arm suddenly began to shake. The friend had run out of the house in terror. The counsellor said it must have been frightening for Megan and her mother too, the first time it happened, and her mother agreed. Megan looked surprised at this.

Asked if she was ever afraid she could make her mother worse, Megan told the counsellor in a whisper that she thought her mother had had to go into hospital two years previously because she and her brother were playing tig and their mother was 'home'. She was standing by the fireguard and they had hit her. She was afraid it was this which had made her so ill that she had to go into hospital. Megan's mother and the counsellor were temporarily speechless with the thought of this, and found it difficult even to say that it could not be true.

Talking about this event, which had happened when she was seven, Megan said she was still cross with her mother for not ringing the school to tell her she had been kept in the hospital, but for sending her grandmother to fetch her at home-time and telling her then. Her mother was astonished and explained that she had not known until it was too late, but she had thought Megan would have much preferred not to be told by a teacher in front of all the other children. They argued about it, and sorted out the facts and the real alternatives.

Megan did not think her schoolwork had been affected by her mother's illness, but she said that when her mother was in hospital she used to cry in the cloakrooms, where she could hide. She pushed friends away and would not let them comfort her. She remembered her work was not good at this time, and was still very angry with a teacher who wrote 'You can do better: this is not your best work' on her book.

Her mother had been to the school after this and had given the teachers a booklet about MS. Megan said it was all right at school now.

At the end of the session Megan's mother said she felt bad about how little she had known of Megan's thoughts about her MS. The counsellor said that it was generally like that: children did not say many things directly unless there was someone else there. Megan had responded to a considerable amount of prompting and guesswork by the counsellor. Her mother had known she was troubled, and she knew from previous experience that it did not work to keep distressing facts hidden from children. That was why she had brought Megan to the counsellor. Megan said she was glad they had come and would be happy to come back next year.

Edward

Edward was twelve. His father had recently had to give up working because of his MS. He had thrown himself into voluntary work and was often out. When he was home he was always extremely tired and sometimes irritable.

Edward thought his father was an idiot. He told the counsellor 'He can't do anything. He's a weed.' Edward's mother sat looking at him affectionately while saying he should not say such things. She was very close to Edward, but she worried because he was difficult to handle and was very rude to his father. Edward was highly indignant that his father did not do as much housework as he did. He thought it was not fair that he should have to do more. He felt his father should be helping his mother, not just telling him to do it.

Edward thought his father's MS was his own fault, for being a 'weed'. When the counsellor asked if he ever worried about getting MS himself, he said he would never 'catch' it. The counsellor said you couldn't 'catch' MS and Edward quickly said he knew that. He thought his father got it by potholing; perhaps some minerals got into him down a pothole. They don't go potholing any more. When the counsellor said she hadn't heard that idea before Edward pointed out that if they didn't know what caused it they didn't know it couldn't be that did they?

The counsellor helped the whole family to look seriously at the idea that Edward's father was 'useless' and to sort out what he was doing and what he was not doing for the family. She tried to help them think realistically about what had been lost and what had been gained as a result of the MS. She also helped Edward to look at his own worry that he was 'useless' himself because he wasn't able to make his father well or look after his mother like a man himself.

The counsellor told Edward and his mother that she wondered if Edward was trying to be the man of the house, and that it was perhaps not a good idea to encourage this. He needed to be reminded by both parents that he was still a child and that his father had an adult place in the household, especially in relation to his mother. Edward could not take over his father's role at the age of twelve, however much he wanted to in some ways, and it might be making him very anxious to think he had to or was expected to. His mother said this made sense and she wrote later to say that the sessions had helped; Edward was much better behaved.

Amy

Amy was nineteen and had recently left home to study in a distant city. She was finding it hard because, she said, she did not feel her age and did not feel old enough to leave home. She felt much younger than she was. Exploring this it turned out that she felt about fifteen, which was the age at which her father had been diagnosed with MS. The counsellor suggested she might be trying to make time stand still in order to stop the changes she feared for her father, and this seemed to make sense to her.

Amy said she wanted to get away from home but didn't feel able to cope with independence. At the same time she prided herself on being independent, and she did not try to make friends partly to show she did not need anyone and could manage on her own. She spent as much of her time at home as possible in her own room and avoided being involved in the family.

She talked about relations within her family, saying that she felt terribly disloyal discussing them like this, but at the same time discovering many strong feelings she had about the way she and her parents related to each other. She was both surprised and guilty about these feelings, but by the end had clearly been able to sort out some of the unrealistic and contradictory beliefs she had had about the family and about her role in it.

Amy was rather surprised in the counselling session to hear herself say these things. She had not realised how she felt, and in particular, how she was restricting her own life so much as a result of rather confused ideas. At the end she said she thought that perhaps she did not need to be so tied to her room and could get out more.

Sharon

Sharon was nineteen and worked in a department store. She did not have much social life. Her mother had MS, diagnosed four years previously, which made her tire to the point of exhaustion easily and made her hands clumsy, but otherwise did not affect her much. Her mother also had a heart condition; heart attacks ran in the family.

Sharon was a quiet, rather withdrawn girl, a contrast to her attractive, dynamic mother. Her mother said she was like her father, a man of few words. Her mother worried about Sharon and she wanted the counsellor to see why she was not 'normal' – 'When I was her age I was going out all the time, she never goes out, I don't know what is the matter with her,' she said.

Sharon made it clear that she was very worried that her mother was about to drop dead from her heart condition. It was this that stopped her going out in the evenings; she was always afraid she would come back and find her mother dead. She did not feel old enough to manage without her, and she felt she would have to look after her father, who was quite incapable of looking after himself. She also felt she was rather boring and unattractive, and thought she could never find a boyfriend, though she admitted that some boys had occasionally shown an interest in her. She had never responded and knew she did not have much self-confidence.

At the end of the session Sharon said, in a rather surprised tone, that perhaps she would be able to go out more now.

Esther

Esther at seventeen did not want to have children herself because she could not bear them feeling like she felt towards her mother. She had thought of killing herself sometimes. She felt her mother was totally self-centred. She was always trying to make Esther do things she did not want to do, just for the sake of demonstrating her own power over Esther. She was convinced that her mother was 'trading' on her MS: she was limping for a long time before, but since the diagnosis she had suddenly got a lot worse. Esther was absolutely certain her mother was using the MS as an excuse to control her even more and make her do things she did not need to do. She did not tell the other girls at work about her mother, because they would be sympathetic towards her just because of the MS, and Esther felt this was unfair, they didn't know how awful she was.

She *knew* her mother could do more around the house if she really tried, and that the exercise would be good for her. The counsellor wondered aloud at how sure Esther was about this. Esther said she did not to want to think about the possibility that her mother was not pretending.

As soon as she could, Esther left home, after which her relations with her parents improved considerably.

Alice

Alice was fourteen. She came to see the counsellor because she was not getting on with her father. His MS had affected his mental capacities and his balance, and made him enormously fatigued, but otherwise, when he was not in a relapse and totally paralysed, there was no sign of his condition.

Asked by the counsellor how MS affected her father Alice said 'It makes him bad tempered.' She described how he made her do housework while he refused to help her mother, and how he shouted at her to do things when he came home from work. He had never explained to her that he suffered from MS tiredness, and that it is quite different from ordinary tiredness; she said, 'I thought he was just getting at me'. She could understand that perhaps he did not want to admit to something he might consider a weakness, and thought she might do the same if it were her.

He also complained all the time about lights being left on and kettles being filled too full of water: Alice thought he was just being mean and getting at her. The counsellor had to agree that he might be, but she also wondered if he was also seriously worried about his ability to earn enough money. Alice knew his MS had made him lose his highly paid and high-status job, and then lose several very low-paid, low-status jobs, but she had not thought that this might mean he could be afraid of losing the ability to work at all. She knew, once she thought about it, that that would seem a terrible thing to him.

Alice seemed to know very little about her father's MS. Her father never told her anything about it. After the session she said she was glad she had come, there was so much she hadn't known. Her mother had tried to tell her but Alice said she never took any notice of what her mother said because she thought her mother was just defending her father and not wanting to admit how much he hated and despised her. She was no longer so sure about this. The counsellor had tried to make it clear she was not saying that Alice had to excuse her father: it might be important for Alice and her father to fight at times, but Alice did need to know some of the unfairness her father had to cope with as well to recognise the reality of her own sense of unfairness.

Sally

Sally was twenty-five when she came to see the counsellor, but she looked eighteen. She had a brother and sister who were much older and felt very much the baby of the family. Sally's mother had been diagnosed with MS just after

Sally's birth. The family had expected her to die for the past five years but Sally had never thought about this until her father was suddenly taken ill. Sally had never asked anything about her mother's condition, but had always accepted it. She had not even connected its onset with the time of her own birth until she came for counselling.

The family lived in the Midlands: the older brother had moved to Scotland after a stormy adolescence but the two girls lived close to their parents and kept in close contact both with their parents and with each other. Sally's sister was married with two children and Sally had a boyfriend she had been dating steadily for three years, who depended on her financially.

Sally felt a great deal of affection towards her family. Her parents loved each other very much and Sally felt herself to be a favourite of her mother. This made her feel both happy and guilty: she felt her older brother and sister deserved more from her mother than they got, and that her mother's life and happiness were her responsibility entirely. She spent her adolescent years watching soap operas with her mother 'to keep her company'. She felt she was allowed to get away with things at school 'because her mother is ill, poor dear'. The many signs she gave of having difficulties never resulted in real help being obtained, though she was aware that she did not respond easily to any kind of pressure. She seemed very ready to take the blame for all the shortcomings in her education and childhood, and it was hard for her to recognise that her parents held responsibility in any way. In spite of obvious intelligence (and unlike her brother and sister who did well at school) she had never passed any exams.

She said one day that she had only just realised that if her father died, her mother would die, but that if she herself died, her mother would go on as before. She was very upset and angry about this before she eventually settled into a more realistic assessment of her own place in the family.

She found it very difficult to accept help for herself, and tended to react to difficulties by not thinking, or by going away. She seemed quite sure that her own needs should take second place to those of her mother, and seemed never to have questioned this. She was terrified of crying or getting upset with her mother, feeling that if she once started she would never stop and that this would be dangerous for her mother's health. She did sometimes cry on her own.

Rosemary

Rosemary was twenty-one when she came for therapy. She was generally unhappy but had no idea why. She was afraid she was likely to have a nervous breakdown, as several of her close friends had. She had done very well at school and university and had a steady boyfriend, and she could not understand why she should feel so insecure.

During her therapy she said that her father had had a nervous breakdown when she was two years old. She was afraid she was like him in many ways, and was therefore vulnerable like he was. She had been aware of being fascinated by friends who were 'a bit crazy', but had actually settled down with a boyfriend who seemed remarkably stable. She said she had felt safe with him, that he would not 'crack up', unlike several of her previous boyfriends, but she was still afraid she might do something to destroy her own happiness with him.

She remembered vividly being unhappy and feeling guilty for much of her childhood. Her mother had suffered from a back injury for a period of two years when she was about ten and she did not remember feeling much worse than normal at the time, but two years later had been given tranquilisers because she had mysterious stomach aches. It became clear during the therapy that her stomach aches were almost invariably a reaction to anxieties she did not recognise. As she learnt to recognise them, the stomach aches lessened.

Her fears for her mother's health were a constant source of anxiety throughout her childhood. She was afraid her anger would seriously damage her mother if ever she let it out. She was still afraid her younger brothers would make her mother ill by their bad behaviour several years after her mother had recovered. She was despairing at her inability to be close to them, which she was aware was partly a result of always trying to control their behaviour. She had left home convinced that she was the main source of family quarrels and that they would all get on much better without her.

Work with some of these anxieties gradually allowed her to feel less tense, anxious and guilty. By no means all of her difficulties stemmed from her parents' illnesses, but it seemed that she had been affected by them in ways which nobody, least of all herself, had recognised at the time.

✠   ✠   ✠   ✠

These sketches give only a brief idea of the wide variety of lives and preoccupations children have brought to us. In the next chapter we look in more detail at a brief piece of work a family did when the mother was suddenly taken ill.

CHAPTER 3

Martin
Working with Loss and Change

Martin's father burst into the building struggling loudly and angrily with his wife's wheelchair. He was telling her off for saying she could manage without it, shouting at her that they were late. She was protesting more quietly and Martin was following silently. As they came into the room the argument continued, uninterrupted by the greetings of the counsellor, the offering of chairs and the process of sitting down.

Martin was twelve and at boarding school. He sat quietly while his father poured out how impossible his wife was; how she had fallen yet again because she would not wait for him to come and help her; it wasn't necessary for her to get up at just that moment… He talked on and on in great distress, very angry and totally exasperated with his wife. He seemed to have forgotten that he had brought Martin to the counsellor today to see if she could help Martin.

The counsellor listened sympathetically. Until three months ago Martin's mother had been a busy, lively woman, running the household for herself, her own mother, her husband and her son, and helping in the family business. Now her mother had died and she had suddenly lost both the use of her legs and her good sense.

Martin's mother was ineffectually arguing back at her husband, embarrassed herself, but seeming not quite aware why he was so angry and upset. 'I only wanted to get up to answer the door' she said, 'and I knew I could, I just caught my foot…' and her husband shouted 'But you knew I would get there, they wouldn't go away! I've told you so many times! She never listens to me, I don't know what I'm going to do, I can't leave her alone any more, but I'm going to lose the business if I can't go out…' They argued back and forth for a while and eventually Martin's father finished talking with his head in his hands, a picture of despair, while his wife smiled in a rather foolish way at the counsellor and at him.

The counsellor, who had not even been introduced to Martin, saw that he had pushed his chair back as far as it would go, away from everyone else in the room. He seemed to be turning away from his father's outburst and was looking at the counsellor and then away from her, extremely uncomfortable. She said to him, 'It must be uncomfortable for you when your parents get at each other like this... What do you do? Try and keep out of it?' He smiled and relaxed and moved forward slightly in his chair.

After a pause the counsellor said to Martin's father that it must be very difficult with all this going on, and it must be especially difficult to think of Martin having to sit and watch his parents struggling to cope. The father sat up and looked at Martin directly. With a total change of voice he said 'I do worry very much about Martin'.

Some of the important issues facing children in a house where a parent is ill are demonstrated here. Martin had been brought to the counsellor for himself, but his father was quite incapable at first of remembering this. He had temporarily totally lost his father's attention, his father's care and concern for him. His father was taken over by his own troubles and frustrations. Listening, Martin might feel his father had lost his own mind, his ability to cope and his love for his wife. All of these must, if only temporarily, have shaken Martin's sense of security. The structure of his world must have seemed under threat; his father was a businessman who liked things well-ordered: here he was falling apart.

None of this would have been been put into words as such by Martin; he was simply feeling embarrassed and uncomfortable and probably extremely anxious. This kind of argument was a common event in the household, and Martin had to endure the shame of knowing a stranger was watching it.

The counsellor was feeling embarrassed and uncomfortable too at this time; worried about Martin as well as about his parents; angry with Martin's father for being so self-centred and for ignoring his son, but also aware of his terror of the whole situation. It was difficult to think through the outburst. She allowed herself a pause to feel the different threads of anxiety in the room. She could see Martin's mother looking like a small child who has been told off and is not quite sure if it will be all right or not, and she felt the huge loss to both her and the family of her role as a reassuring, competent supportive partner and mother who was able to keep the family going.

Martin's reaction to the counsellor suggested she had guessed his feelings accurately, and that the tone in which she put them into words had enabled him to feel understood and less under threat. His father at this point was prepared to allow her to look after his son for him and did not react. Her next remark, to Martin's father, acknowledged his situation and also drew him back to the purpose of the meeting. He was able to regain his adult, fathering role without feeling that his own despair was ignored.

The counsellor was attempting to 'hold' some of the distress of Martin and his father both by her non-verbal attitude and by putting words to the feelings she could sense. The mother's distress was not at that moment picked up verbally. It was more difficult to recognise and acknowledge what was going on for her. Martin's mother was smiling through adversity. Over a period of time it became clear that she felt she had no right whatever to be angry with anyone; she was a devout Christian and had to be nice to people, whatever she felt. She in fact seemed to find it very difficult to recognise her own feelings at all: when later on the counsellor commented on her anger towards some of the neighbours who were very patronising towards her, she was extremely shocked to hear her own words repeated back to her.

During the conversation the counsellor asked Martin how old he was – 'eleven', he said, and his mother said quickly, 'you mean twelve!' It is perhaps unusual for a boy of this age not to remember his own age. But when people are faced with a change that frightens them very much, such as a diagnosis of a serious illness, or a shocking death in the family, they sometimes seem to go into a 'time warp', where they try to keep things as they were. Martin perhaps was trying to keep things as they were when he was eleven, rather than be forced to know about those changes which had happened since his birthday.

> Martin talked about the fact that he hated being away at boarding school while his mother was at home. He repeated what his father had said about his mother always getting out of her chair and falling over; he said he wanted to tie her down sometimes. The counsellor said 'You'd feel safer if you could tie her down, would you?' He nodded, smiling, and his father nodded vigorously too. His mother said sadly, 'Perhaps I should let you tie me down, then I couldn't get up.'

Here Martin and his parents are expressing something about the desire to control events; to prevent the terrible disasters from happening. The only way they can think of is to tie his mother down to her chair; to prevent her physically from moving.

> Over the next hour and during a further session a week later, the family talked about the way Martin's mother still cared very much for Martin. She kept him constantly in mind; she discussed his progress at school with teachers and other parents and she was available for him to talk to about friends and life in general whenever he was home. But she did not take care of herself. Martin's father was extremely exasperated with his wife and his anger with her when she fell was taken by Martin to mean he did not care for her. This had left Martin feeling he was the only

person who cared about his mother. He felt very strongly that he wanted
to be allowed to leave boarding school and come home to look after her.

The counsellor pointed out that Martin had not lost his mother; he still
had a mother who cared for him, but he did seem to have lost 'a mother
who looked after herself'. He seemed to be feeling that he had to *be* that
mother, concerned about her rather than about himself.

When a loved person dies, it is very common for those left behind to identify
with some aspect of them. Bereaved people behave and feel in some way as if
they were the person they had lost. In children this identification commonly
appears as pseudo-maturity; children behave as if they were much older than
they really are. Some people value it in their children, calling it 'being good',
but it can have a sad or uncomfortable quality about it. There seems to be a
distance about these children: a sense of 'do not touch me', which may be
convenient and admirable from a distance, but does not make for a free and
easy relationship. Martin had not lost his mother but he had lost an important
aspect of her, and this he was trying to replace.

A further problem with this strong identification with a lost parent is that
the children may view the lost parent as quite unrealistically accusing and
intolerant. In general, the younger the children, the more intolerant and
accusing they may believe their parents to be. This may make children very
hard on themselves.

Children's beliefs about punishment and blame are not the same as their
parents'. The most tolerant parents may be surprised sometimes to find that
their small child expects to be punished, for example, for dropping a bottle of
milk, which the parent would never consider reason for punishment. The
children would feel angry and full of revenge if someone broke one of their
toys or took away an icecream they wanted, and they assume their parents
would feel the same. It is only with the children's increasing ability to tolerate
such frustrations that they see the parents as able to tolerate them too. The result
is that children who have lost a parent very early in life may have a very different
set of ideas about parents from those held by children who have grown up with
both parents, or who have lost them later.

Martin's self-accusation and intolerance was clear. It was also clear that he
expected adults to feel as accusing and angry about his bad behaviour as he
did.

After his desperate wish to stay home and look after his mother had been
acknowledged, Martin admitted to feeling very guilty about having failed
to look after her on one occasion when he was home and could have
done. He blamed himself for not going to help his mother sooner when
she had fallen and pulled over a bookcase, and his father had been out.
The counsellor drew out of him, with several guesses, that he had heard

his mother calling but was in the garden and had thought she wanted him to do something, so he had pretended not to hear. It was only when she called the third time, after a long pause, that he eventually went in and found her lying on the floor, unable to get up, with the bookcase on top of her. He had been very frightened. He had had to ask a neighbour to help get her up.

Talking this over, the counsellor and Martin's parents were able to share Martin's fear and acknowledge how guilty he felt. They were also able to say how unfair they felt it was that he could not simply ignore his mother's calling like most boys of his age could and would. His father said he used to do that himself when he was a teenager. By Martin's reaction to this it was obvious that he had assumed that the adults in the room would consider it as terrible a sin as he thought it was. Hearing his father talk like this was a great relief to Martin.

This discussion further helped Martin to undo the very black and white view he had about people caring. He was able to see that his own caring was not entirely unselfish and ideal all the time, and neither was his father's uncaring attitude total.

Martin was learning a very important lesson about life, which the loss of his mother's mental functioning might have threatened. It was so important for him to get the caring right because his mother's life was, he believed, at stake. In this situation there is no room for mistakes. Without this discussion he could have gone on for a long time believing that his actions were likely to threaten his mother's life. Eventually his own spontaneity as well as his relations with other children and adults could have been severely threatened if he continued trying too hard to be good. Alternatively, he could have turned to some kind of delinquency or to saying 'I don't care' as the agony of caring and having to acknowledge his own huge guilt and failure became too much.

It is easy to see that if his mother had died, Martin would have held himself responsible at the same time, probably, as believing it was entirely his father's fault.

In the session Martin's father was able to say how unhappy he was about Martin taking over the work of worrying about his mother. He very much wanted Martin to stay at school and have a reasonably 'normal' life, able to be a child and to enjoy it. He did not want him to have to grow up too quickly. He was also anxious that if his son was at home he would be worried about both his son and his wife.

He and Martin then explored thoroughly all the different ways Martin had been thinking he could stay home and help. Ultimately it was Martin's father who made the decision, that Martin should stay at boarding school, but he and Martin both felt the other understood better. It seemed that it was seldom that the two of them were able to sit and talk to each other reasonably about important decisions, because Martin's father was so busy and so frantic most of the time.

At this point Martin had regained a parent.

Talking to each other, patiently exploring a child's view of life, sorting out its inconsistencies and false assumptions is something which some children and parents value enormously. In some families it happens; in others it does not. In some families conversations like this cannot take place because words are not used kindly or realistically but hypocritically or to attack. Sometimes grand-parents talk to children while the parents do not. Illness can affect how and when people talk to each other, as well as the content of conversations.

Discussions between children and adults teach children about the realities of life and, as in this case, correct many misunderstandings. They allow children to feel valued and respected and to feel they have some kind of influence, or that their opinions have been taken into consideration. Where the child is simply handed a decision they may not learn how to think through different consequences, or that their opinions matter. As adults they may have difficulty deciding for themselves what it is they should eat, who they should marry, where they should work.

This interview with Martin's family shows the difficulty a partner of an ill parent can have in finding space in their mind to give a child the time and consideration necessary for this kind of conversation. Looking after his wife and his business, without the help he had always had from her, Martin's father needed the counsellor there to enable him to regain the adult, fathering part of himself that he could offer Martin.

The alliance between Martin and his father which developed in this session seemed fairly new. Previously Martin had seemed to see his father as an enemy hindering his own attempts to look after his mother. He was able to say that he did enjoy being at school in the evenings, playing table tennis, and hear the counsellor and both his parents say that this was how it should be: that his father really could and did look after his mother and that Martin was not neglecting her by not thinking of her every minute of the day.

Loss of any kind seems always to bring to the surface many unrealistic beliefs. In normal life some of these are there but cause no trouble and are not noticed. For example, children's beliefs that they are entirely responsible for their parents' well-being may cause no trouble as long as those parents are well and happy. These beliefs only become noticeable and cause problems if something serious happens to the parents: this may be in the context of a loss. Symbolism is involved here too; sometimes the more life-threatening beliefs are symbolised by more ordinary events.

Martin had said that when his mother fell over he *did not know if she was all right or not*. The counsellor asked if he was afraid she might be dying and he nodded, mutely. One of his unrealistic beliefs was that if his mother fell over, this meant she was going to die.

There are probably many strands to this belief, which we have found in several children. One is the sense that *it is not right* that parents should fall over. An adult falling over means that the world is not behaving as it should; the fundamental order of things is being shaken, and life can no longer be trusted to follow the rules. This is extremely frightening for anyone, but particularly for children when it is their mother who falls. She is the person who holds the boundaries of their world; she mediates communication between the children and the outside world; she gives them language and helps them develop their own language. Her collapse may for a time mean to the children the collapse of all they know and trust including all their ability to draw on the strength and help of others.

For Martin, the counsellor was able to mitigate the sense of despair in several ways. By listening to him she was able to help him to remain in contact with his own real beliefs and fears. But she was also able to talk with him about how soon his mother was likely to die; she said that many adults with MS do fall over, but they usually fall remarkably safely. At worst his mother might break a bone. The counsellor discussed with Martin what the consequences of this could be: a time in hospital, more difficulty walking. Martin's fears about the damage his mother might do to herself if she fell were probably also expressing his existing fears about her deteriorating condition, and this needed to be explored. What were the consequences Martin was noticing already? Increased friction between his parents was one. It may have been his father's anger, which his mother would incur if she broke a bone, that he feared as much as any other consequences.

Estrangement between close people following a bereavement is very common. Husbands and wives can find their relationship seriously strained when one of them loses a parent, or when a child is taken seriously ill or dies. Martin showed no sign of hating his mother, but children can hate parents for being ill and failing to fulfil their proper role. It is possible that it was Martin's own deeply hidden hatred of his ill mother which he feared in his father. This fear that '*someone* hates mummy for being ill' with 'not me' attached firmly to it, may have contributed to Martin's fear that his father would not look after his mother and love her sufficiently. It perhaps contributed to his feeling that his father was an enemy instead of an ally.

Grief can be shared; if it is not, the danger is that the previously-loved person is seen not simply as a neutral or caring individual, but as an enemy. It seems that unless we know that the other people we love also grieve themselves as well as care about our loss, we may feel not only do they not care for us, but they are positively against us.

A sense of abandonment and isolation accompanies grief. The fear that one or both parents might die and a sense of other loved family members becoming enemies rather than allies are closely connected aspects of the threatened loss of a parent by illness. Exploring the child's beliefs can change this situation and allow the child to feel supported rather than alone.

Changing unrealistic beliefs

The process of mourning and grief involves a gradual changing of the unrealistic beliefs brought to the surface by the loss. This process is long and slow and very painful. We have many assumptions and expectations about the world, which we use to carry on our daily lives. These can be quite seriously challenged by a loss.

> Martin's normal assumptions about his mother included, quite reason-ably, the belief that she would be able to walk upstairs. When this was challenged he went through a long struggle to prevent himself having to believe it. This process was complicated by the fact that both his parents were going through a similar struggle, at different rates.

> Martin and his parents discussed a forthcoming holiday. They wanted to stay in a hotel they had used before and liked very much. Unfortunately all the bedrooms were upstairs and there was no lift. Martin's mother was sure she could get upstairs if she had some help. His father said this was out of the question: the stairs were narrow and twisting, there was no way he could carry her, even with help. The counsellor helped them go through the argument; Martin saying 'if I was in front and you were behind...', or 'I'm sure you could do it', or 'we could both...' and his father explaining why none of these solutions would work; his mother saying over and over again 'once I was upstairs I would be all right...' and refusing to consider the difficulty of getting up the first two steps.

The unreality of Martin's mother's view of her abilities was a problem for all of them. Martin's view at first was closer to hers: 'Of course she can do it, if we both help her'. He was eventually convinced by his father's arguments; his mother simply refused to consider them. The counsellor had to pick up the extreme pain for both Martin and his mother in recognising what she could no longer do. Not being able to walk up the stairs meant the premature end of family holidays as they had always been – and much more.

Martin seemed to know with one part of himself what his mother actually could and could not do this week – which was different from last week – but with another part of himself he totally disbelieved the evidence of his own eyes. In this part of his mind his mother was still as she was last time he came home from school, and still as she was one or two years ago, or perhaps as she would have been then if she had twisted her ankle. His need for an ally in his mother, against the father he believed did not care, may have increased his desire to believe her and his own memory, rather than the present evidence of his eyes.

Martin's mother's reaction to the loss of the use of her legs illustrated one of the possible ways in which Martin could have reacted to his loss too. She was refusing to acknowledge it and refusing to think; she seemed to have lost the part of her mind which thought logically. In her case this could have been either an unconscious decision to cut off her ability to think logically, or it could have been a result of brain damage caused by her neurological condition. In Martin's case it could have been a natural desire to reject the evidence of his logical senses in favour of a more palatable memory, and/or an identification with a mother who had lost her ability to think logically in this area.

By thinking this through with Martin, his father enabled Martin to see that it was bearable to face a very persecuting, sad and disturbing reality. He also gave Martin the chance to identify with a father who had not lost his ability to think straight and had not given up thinking because it was too painful.

The counsellor helped Martin's father to do this mainly by preventing his impatience from winning, and by making him recognise that his desire to help Martin was important and could be carried through in spite of his being under enormous pressure.

Martin and his father, as well as his mother, were struggling particularly hard because the changes had been so quick. It was less than three months since his mother had been functioning relatively normally. They all found it ex- tremely difficult to believe how much her mind had been affected. The father was forced to face it on a daily basis, and his view had changed, putting him into a state close to despair. He did not yet know if life as he had known it was going to be possible at all with his wife in this condition. Martin had not seen the changes so close at hand and was more able to maintain a belief that his mother's condition was not serious, particularly as she was still functioning towards him in much the same way she had before: slightly over-concerned, very interested and caring; he had always found her easy to talk to and still did.

John Bowlby, writing in the 1950s, drew attention to the fact that separation from a mother could sometimes affect children intellectually as well as emo- tionally and in their behaviour. Perhaps Martin's predicament gives us some insight into the ways children's thought processes may be affected by loss of mothering. Children who cannot bear to see the changes in reality brought about by the sudden loss of their mother may, in some circumstances, turn against their ability to see reality at all or to think. If they do not find anyone else to attach themselves to they may also turn against their ability to feel affection or to make attachments of any kind to people. However, it does seem possible to help some children in these circumstances.

Outcomes of grieving

Martin's family was facing a serious loss and was quite clearly suffering for it. His father was afraid of cracking under the strain, but there were many strengths in the family and it is helpful to note some of these. Martin's future was not desolate. With all his troubles, like many of the children we have met he seemed to have a good chance of growing up well. His parents' abilities and his parents' decisions, their behaviour and their reactions gave him possibilities for growth and for good development. Parents (and life in general) not only set children problems; they can also provide the means for dealing with them.

Let us look at some of the gains Martin has made as a result of the way his father handled his mother's condition.

Martin's father was both prepared and able to ask for help and to take what he was offered. This can be extremely difficult for some parents, who cannot tolerate the idea that they cannot function well entirely on their own, independently. Martin's father had sufficient maturity and humility to know that he needed help. Having asked for it for himself and for Martin he initially found it hard to allow Martin to have any of the attention he knew he needed. However, once the counsellor had acknowledged his distress and reminded him of his concern for Martin, he was able to put his own anxieties on one side and to pay full attention to Martin.

Not all parents can do this, but many can. Parents can be overwhelmed by their own troubles; they do at times forget their children's needs. Some, however, seek help for themselves; some, like Martin's father, use such help to get back in touch with the adult, parenting part of their personalities. Others simply reject any attempt at support for themselves, either as people in their own right or in their role as parents. Some may avoid seeking any kind of help for fear of being accused and made to feel even more guilty than they do already. Some seem to convert their painful and negative feelings into physical symptoms, and remain unaware of their or their children's emotional distress and the need and possibility of obtaining help. Some idealise 'coping alone' and feel any attempt to seek help would be an admission of failure. Some use their children to carry despairing feelings of rejection and failure, helplessness and hopelessness, and attempt to 'solve' their own problem by passing it on to their children, knowingly or unknowingly.

Martin's father had had good experiences in the past of being helped by others, including his wife, and was able to use this to seek help in the new situation. As a result, both Martin and his father found a new relationship.

Previously, his father had left Martin very much to his mother's care and had been tied up in his business. His wife's illness forced Martin's father to take more notice of Martin. He was not only capable of doing this, but he was also prepared to take the time to do it.

Martin's father's new behaviour could help Martin in two ways. The listening and caring he received was in itself valuable to Martin in helping him to develop insight and to work out ways of looking at the problems in family life. The new recognition of his father's affection for him will have been very important to Martin in helping him to feel less abandoned and isolated as a result of his mother's condition. In addition, Martin will have learnt from his father's model that there are ways of being a father which do not involve simply earning money and leaving a wife to take care of all the emotional events in the family. For both Martin and his father this was probably a discovery. It may well help Martin to become a good father himself when he grows up.

Martin was shown something about his own reactions through the counselling sessions as well as through his experiences. He had the opportunity to see that people do not always react in the ways they would like to, and that his own bad behaviour and feelings were not intolerable and unforgivable. He was also faced with the limits of children's responsibility for their parents.

This kind of insight could help Martin towards developing a real maturity, different from the pseudo-maturity of children who are simply identifying with their image of a parent. It involves being 'sadder but wiser'; aware of some of the sorrows of life as well as the hopes; and the limitations of parents as well as their strengths. It involves developing a less idealised and more realistic view of parents and the self: a development which normally happens throughout childhood and into adulthood, but which is particularly evident in the struggles of adolescence. An increased tolerance towards his own failings could make Martin more tolerant not only towards his father, but also towards others at school and in the rest of his life.

Martin may have learnt from his father not only how to become a better father himself, but also how to be a good husband who takes the trouble to listen as well as to earn money. He may have understood that anger and an appearance of not caring do not mean the end of a relationship. He will have learnt that help can be sought and used. He may also have learnt the value and possibility of taking others and himself seriously when unhappy, rather than running away from or dismissing distress or conflict. These are lessons that not all adults have learnt, but which can facilitate the handling of relationships throughout life, and not simply at times of crisis.

On a practical level too, Martin will have learnt from his father. Martin's father was gradually taking over all the household tasks as his wife became more incapable. Growing up in a household where the father does these tasks can help a boy to become a husband who expects to share the housework with his partner. His future partner may well have cause to be grateful to Martin's parents for teaching him that men can cook, shop and clean as well as women. Martin himself may also learn to do these things at an earlier age than most young men; this is not simply a loss of freedom but (in the context of a firm father–son relationship where the father maintains his authority) may also be a development of skills and of a sense of responsibility that need not overload a young man.

Martin will have learnt much from watching his parents. Some of what he saw was frightening, but the outcome was not a total disaster. His father's anger and upset did not lead to total collapse nor to a break-up of the marriage but to a real attempt to live with the difficulties. Martin's mother will continue to deteriorate physically, but Martin will grow up and make new relationships as well as developing his relationship with his father. He will know that he has his parents' blessing in this, and that he need not restrict his own life out of a sense of guilt or self-punishment or identification with troubled parents. He will have learnt that crises do not last forever and that chaos and confusion can be followed not only by painful loss but also by a new life.

At the time of a loss, of a cause for grief or sorrow, there is no sense of being 'ennobled by grief' or having a 'growth experience'. If it is possible to feel at all, it may simply feel like hell of one kind or another, with real possibility of ending in disaster. Anger, despair, abandonment, resentment, accusation, guilt as well as sorrow, pining for a lost happiness, longing for a lost person or a lost innocent self – these words are not meaningless but have a full and sometimes horrific meaning in these situations. It is only afterwards, or from the relative painlessness of being outside the immediate, relevant situation that such a list can be compiled. It is only much later that any good or development may be seen to come out of the situation. From this vantage point there may then be a denial of the meaning of these words, or a temptation to soften the perception of their meaning in some way which may feel like a cruel rejection or insult to the person actually suffering.

Mourning involves probably at least two years of living with a loss in such a way that periods of denial gradually reduce and periods of tolerating the acknowledgment of reality gradually increase. It is probably only after this time that the changes brought about can possibly begin to feel as if they might have involved some benefit. But it is still a benefit tinged with sorrow. We did not *want* to be improved if *that* was the price. We do not *want* Martin to become more understanding and tolerant of others if the price is his loss of his mother. We want him not to have lost her, to learn these things any other way, or even to remain innocently intolerant and lacking in understanding, like most other boys of his age and many adults too.

It is only when we have no choice that we may be forced to seek the ways of dealing with grief that are least damaging and may, in the process, make discoveries or form relationships which give us something worth having. We cannot, as outsiders or as parents, compensate children for the loss of some aspect of parenting. We can only give children something of ourselves which acknowledges their loss and so enables them to live with it without also losing parts of their own mind and personality.

CHAPTER 4

How Children See It...

What can we learn from these children and others we have met?

We look first at the ways children interpret the world around them. Their understanding of behaviour, motives, symptoms, disabilities and illnesses can be very different from their parents' understanding: adults have been astonished to discover the misinterpretations of even intelligent children. Parents thought their children would be worried about things which did not concern the children at all; children actually worried about things which their parents did not realise could possibly be worries. Many of these anxieties were based on simple misunderstandings that parents could easily clear up.

Children's understanding is based not only on their own very limited experience but also on their hopes, fears and anxieties. These in turn depend on their age, their past and their family's way of seeing things. Understanding also varies from day to day and even minute to minute: under the influence of one set of feelings a child might have one set of beliefs: under another, the beliefs can be totally different.

Children's views of the world

Children, like adults, interpret anything new in terms of something they know already. If they know about broken legs they may interpret a parent's difficulty walking as if it were a broken leg. They know about being tired, so they understand neurological fatigue – which is actually quite different – as if it were ordinary tiredness. They have ideas about people being 'stupid' or 'mental' so they may use these words to understand a parent's brain damage. They may be afraid of being 'feeble' or 'a weed' and they may 'recognise' these characteristics in a parent, particularly if they have no other concept to put in its place.

> Nicky, nine, was very upset when another boy at his school called his father 'mental': he had no concept of brain damage which was not an

52

insult and all he could do was deny that anything was wrong with his father's mind.

Behaviour, as well as symptoms, is interpreted in this way. Children's interpretation of their own motives when they refuse to help with housework, for example, will affect the way they see their parents' refusal to wash up. A parent being unable to do something may be understood as 'not wanting to', 'being lazy', 'not trying hard enough' or 'just making me do it to get at me'. The idea that the parent really is helpless or *cannot* do something seems to be outside children's natural belief system. They have to be taught this and it is frightening; it means that their own sense of being looked after and protected from the world outside by all-powerful parents is threatened.

The age of the child

Children at a certain age have a certain kind of understanding of the world, which affects their interpretation of everything that happens. Beliefs appropriate to a very much younger age group are found in older children and adults. It seems that under stress of any kind we are likely to revert to a less sophisticated level of understanding. Many ideas 'get stuck'. Ideas that are too frightening may not be brought out into the open and discussed or thought about. This means that they remain as they were when they were formed. An older child may have beliefs formed at a much younger age which coexist with later beliefs and totally conflict with them, but are simply never tested against them. It is important to remember that a six-year-old will not have the beliefs of an adult, but an adult may well have the beliefs of a six-year-old.

> Andrew, twenty-nine, and his brother Steve, twenty-five, came to see a counsellor about a younger brother who was causing problems in the family. In the course of the session they talked about their father being diagnosed with cancer when Andrew was a teenager. Andrew remembered being very worried that the younger boys would make their father ill and he would die.
>
> The counsellor asked if he still thought that was possible: *could* his brother upset his father so much it would kill him?
>
> ANDREW: 'No.'
>
> STEVE: 'I wouldn't let him – I'd throw him out first!'
>
> ANDREW: 'Oh you mustn't do that, that wouldn't help.'

The counsellor was left with a distinct impression that both did still believe that children could kill a father who had cancer by upsetting him.

Many adults are confused about whether people can die of 'getting upset' or not. This is a belief which belongs as much to adults as to children.

The younger a child is, the more it is likely to imagine that whatever happens was directed at the child and controlled by the child in some way. An older child or teenager may be more able to understand (sometimes) that events can be independent of the child's own wishes and behaviour. Adults may believe, simultaneously, that an event was their fault entirely; it was caused by their mother/father/husband/wife; God willed it and that is why it happened; it was fate – nobody could help it. Older children may share any or all of these beliefs.

Children's beliefs that they caused their parents' illness or death can sometimes be reinforced by adults. We have come across more than one parent who threatened their teenage children that the children's behaviour would kill their parents. 'You'll be the death of your father', or 'You'll make your mother ill if you go on like that' are phrases that may easily be used by very angry parents in an attempt to control straying teenagers. Teenagers, in our experience, believe this kind of threat at the same time as rejecting it. Teenagers anyway are likely to see themselves at times as extremely powerful and dangerous (partly as a defence against seeing their own impotence); this kind of threat adds fuel to such beliefs.

For many children and adults the belief that 'It's all because of me' may be maintained because the alternative: 'it all happened in spite of anything I could do' seems so disturbing. The ability to recognise one's own real lack of importance in the world and lack of influence upon events seems to come only slowly with maturity, if at all.

As well as feeling that everything is directed at them, very young children have anxieties around being abandoned. Parents, particularly mothers, seem to hold a child together: making the world a safe, secure, and predictable place in which life is possible. Fathers can also be experienced in this way; as William's picture of his family exploding apart if his father died illustrates.

Changes in a mother which take her mind or attention off her child may be experienced as very threatening; the younger the baby, the more threatening and frightening this is. It happens of course to an older child when a new baby is born, and is also part of growing up. Parents usually develop their own ways of reassuring their children at times when they realise a child is jealous of care being given to another member of the family or is feeling neglected. It may be harder, but still possible, to recognise this when one or both parents are suffering themselves.

Separation of a baby or child under two or three from the mother (for example, as a result of an accident or hospital stay) affects the child's sense of security and safety. The child may feel it is not held safely and is falling apart or exploding, perhaps, into different, unconnected bits. Again, the younger the child, the more global the experience will be. An older child has more of a sense of continuity which can be maintained without the parents; a small baby will panic much more quickly. Even a baby of a few weeks will scream if it wakes and a parent or known person is not there. Children under three may quite clearly 'hold themselves together' in their mother's absence, left with people they do not know, and then collapse in tears of relief as soon as she returns.

Where the baby or child stays with someone they know and who knows them well, loves them and understands their language, their routines, their needs, likes and dislikes, the experience is very different from that of children who are suddenly put among strangers. These children feel literally held; someone else's recognition of them as an individual with known attributes and familiar experiences helps them to remember they are still the same person they were. It is unfortunate that in our society there is often no other adult who knows the baby as well as the mother does: the child's sense of security is thus enormously dependent upon one person.

Children or babies generally turn away from the parent when she or he returns after an absence which was too long for the child, and may take some time to reestablish friendly relations. They may make the parent feel rejected, abandoned, unloved, unacceptable and perhaps 'not the person I was before' – feelings the baby or child had themselves when the person they loved and depended on left them.

A parent who can bear these feelings and show the child that they recognise what the child is doing may help even a small baby to bear them too. Play is a very good way of helping a child to master such feelings; many parent–child games involve play with the idea of going away and coming back. The 'peep-boo' game is the earliest of these and probably helps the baby to learn that absence is not for ever and does not mean loss of everything.

Many adults feel their world would fall apart if their mother or father died. Children from the age of about eighteen months may have the kind of fears pictured in fairy tales or horror films. Death may be seen as 'a black knife in the heart'; corpses or uncontrollable limbs as having a terrifying life of their own, 'coming to get you'; illnesses 'catching' even if the child has been told they are not. Their 'nice mummy' may turn in their minds into a terrible witch if she goes away or starts to shake or suffers some kinds of physical change.

On the other hand, children relate so strongly to the mother in their minds that they may be apparently quite undisturbed by some changes in their mother which do not fit into the 'witchlike' category.

> Daniel was fourteen and his mother had just been diagnosed MS. She had recovered from a relapse and was left with no visible effect, though she could no longer do many of the things she did before. She said to

Daniel that she felt very guilty towards him, she was no longer the mother she was and nobody would like her now.

'Would you want to marry someone with MS yourself?' she asked him.

Daniel was angry with her and said 'Don't be silly, you haven't changed, you're still you.'

From the age of two or three, loss of a limb, for example, may be seen as an act of revenge on the part of someone, and all events be understood as caused deliberately by someone or something. The 'punishment' may be imagined to fit the 'crime'. Blindness may be seen as a punishment for looking, for curiosity, for wanting to know about anything at all; loss of hearing as a punishment for listening wrongly, or in some guilty way.

At this stage too, however, children may have equally strong beliefs that love and faith can keep people alive and make them better. Several children thought that if they or their mothers loved their fathers enough the fathers would not die of their illness. Adults also believe their love could keep their partners alive, if only it were strong enough; many feel very guilty at failing to love enough.

A more primitive version of the belief 'My love will keep you alive' is the belief 'I will keep you alive inside me'. This has many versions. Children can identify part of their body or their 'insides' with a parent, and look after this part carefully. They may have a sense of the parent being separate and different from themselves, but feel the parent is inside and can be cared for there. The child is 'saying' to itself: 'I will keep you alive and safe inside me'. The children who wanted to stay home and be with their ill parent may have been identifying with their parent inside them in this way, and trying to keep them home and safe.

Peter, a child of seven, kept swinging his legs. He may have been trying not only to stop his own legs from seizing up like his father's had, but also perhaps to make his father's legs work. The idea of 'sympathetic magic' may depend on this kind of process.

Children who thought a lot about their ill parents sometimes seemed to believe this thinking would keep them alive or as they were, unchanged. We wondered if the children who tried to keep time still (by not growing up) were trying to keep their parents inside them from changing, where time and change meant their parent getting worse physically and perhaps mentally. A more drastic version of this, with roots much earlier on in the child's life, is 'I will keep you alive by being you'; 'you and I are one, there is no separation, no difference between us.'

Some children may lose their own identity entirely and feel they become their parent or part of their parent. However, identification with parents is also part of the normal process of growing up and we look in more detail at it in the next chapter.

Some children develop their parents' symptoms. This can be very frightening, as neither the child nor the parents nor the doctor may know whether the child is developing the condition or not.

> Eighteen months after his mother was diagnosed MS, Daniel, aged sixteen, began to feel weakness and pins and needles in his arm. The doctor sent him for tests.

> Shortly after a Clinical Research Unit for *Action and Research for Multiple Sclerosis* was opened, one by one all the staff found they were getting various symptoms of MS. These disappeared after a while and did not return.

> When Jody at three complained of pains in her legs her mother was sometimes unsure if she really had them or if she was simply playing at being her mother.

Children often seem to use play identification as way of finding out what it is like to be someone else. Here the process is far more conscious. The child may be quite clear about 'pretending' but they may slide from knowing they are pretending to believing that what they are doing is real.

> The same child at two sometimes copied her mother's walk, grasping furniture and pulling herself round. Sometimes she said 'I'm just going to sit down now, I'm tired' in her mother's voice.

Jody's identification was probably partly play, partly serious. She was trying out what it was like being her mother; this would give her some information for understanding her mother. It would of course be misleading information, since she did not have the condition which made her mother walk in this way. This is always a problem when children try to understand their ill or disabled parents: they cannot know what it is like from the inside. They make their guesses based on what it looks like from the outside and how it would be for them if they looked like that.

Making parents better

Children did not ask if they could do anything to make their mother or father get better, but they often assumed they could. Several children from Christian backgrounds seemed to believe that if they were good their mother or father might have a chance of getting better. Another child wanted to be a scientist when he grew up, to find a cure for MS. William, nine, and Nancy, ten, prayed to God to make their fathers better; when she was younger Nancy had wished for it.

Both Toby, twelve, and Joanne, ten, had understood from their parents that if they could help their mother with housework she might get better or stay well; and if they didn't she would get worse. Several other children seemed to believe this.

This is a difficult problem for a family, since a mother may well feel better and less tired if the children are helpful; but however helpful they are, they cannot make her MS or other illness or disability go away. It can be very difficult to make sure the children understand the distinction. If they do not, they may become disillusioned when their mother does not get better, however good they are.

Children may feel betrayed and cheated or manipulated by their parents or by God, if God is supposed to make mummy better as a reward for their virtue. They may also despair about ever being good enough. Children who despair can become extremely difficult and destructive, both of themselves and of others. They can hate seeing happiness or peace if they feel that they do not deserve it themselves. If they succeed in destroying other people's enjoyment of life they then feel even more that they deserve nothing good; this can maintain a vicious circle of destructiveness.

Children who say they do not want to help their parents

Edward said very clearly that he did not feel any responsibility for his father's condition, and he seemed to have no interest in his father getting better. Esther felt the same about her mother. The impression both gave was that they thought they would be a lot happier if their ill parent were totally out of the way. We can take this at face value and say that some children appear not to be concerned about their parent's health.

We can also ask if this was really the whole story: was Edward, for example, simply a little Oedipus who wanted to replace his father, apparently guilt-free? Or was he perhaps hiding another side to him which needed his father to be strong? Was he, like Lady Macbeth, 'protesting too much' for fear that he had actually succeeded in killing off his father's strength, perhaps out of envy? Boys do have fantasies of defeating their fathers in battle, usually heavily disguised but clearly showing this kind of intent. If a father actually does become weak this may convince the boy that his fantasy was reality.

The consequences of this are multiple and complex. It may leave the boy convinced of the power of his fantasies; he can believe that by thinking the battle he caused the weakness. It may leave him afraid that he is stronger and better in every way than his father; this means he no longer has a father, only a 'weed'. The triumph of beating his father was clear in the way Edward spoke, but this bravado had a hollow ring to it. A boy with a weak father is weakened himself. In normal fantasies a boy not only defeats his father, but also calls on his father's strength (if only symbolically: 'the Power of Greyskull' in one cartoon) to help him defeat other enemies. If this is lost, the boy is left extremely vulnerable, particularly in regard to his mother.

Fathers help children to disentangle themselves from their mothers and so to grow up independent and separate. Edward was in danger of being left too close to his mother and unable to grow away from home. If he could not identify with a good sexual father he might also have difficulty with his sexual identity. In this family the situation changed after the mother saw what was happening. Her recognition that loss of the use of his legs did not make a father useless was important.

Esther's argument that housework was good for her mother seemed to depend on a mix of motives. She had difficulty in believing that her mother was really ill and thought it was all a pretence, perhaps at least partly because she so wished it was. She was angry at being made to do so much housework herself and at her mother for never appreciating it. She did not show any desire to make things easier for her mother, which fitted with her view that the whole thing was simply aimed at making her own life more difficult.

Probably Esther really did want her mother to take care of herself and get better, if only because she resented having to think about her mother and her health. As an adolescent, she needed time to think about herself, her own appearance, her own social behaviour, and about developing her own life. Her mother's illness seemed quite unfairly to take all the attention, particularly from her father. She could not fight her mother as other teenagers could, for fear of drastic consequences. Perhaps this too gave a spiteful edge to her demand that her mother do the housework 'for the sake of her own health'.

For some of the teenagers we met it sometimes seemed as if a battle was being fought to the death between parent and child, as if only one could survive at the expense of the other. In this situation there may seem to be no possibility of either sharing or caring. This kind of family atmosphere is more likely to be around in the most stressful times: attitudes may shift to being less persecutory when life is more settled. Grieving is part of the changeover from the one way of seeing the world to the other.

'Will I make mum/dad worse?'

Seemingly more powerful than the children's hopes for making their parents better were their fears of making them worse. It seems to be easier to believe in our power to do harm than in our power to do good. Many of the children believed they had to protect their parents in one way or another.

Children had different beliefs about their power to damage their parents. Some, like Megan, were afraid of directly causing damage by hitting their parent, even though they could not do any real harm in this way.

Some children really can damage their parents physically, and will almost certainly have difficulty with feelings about having to be in control. Where the need to be in control becomes too powerful, it may lead to extremely self-destructive behaviour, as the only way to control very dangerous parts of the self may seem to be to kill them off. The creative and spontaneous parts of the child's personality may be threatened by this. An older child may turn to drugs as a means of control. In extreme cases a child may try to take its own life. A child may be helped with such excessive need for control if the problem is recognised. Professional help may be needed.

More remarkable was the number of children who were frightened of the power of their worries to harm their parents. We have given several examples of this. We suspect that children generally feel that anything that troubles them would be just as troubling to their parents or to someone else who loved them. Adults seemed often to collude in these beliefs.

> A father advised his daughter not to ask her mother about periods because her mother was disabled and he thought it would distress her to talk about things like that. Many years later he was sorry: he thought perhaps he had prevented his wife from having a closer relationship with her daughter.

It is less surprising that 'naughtiness' was seen as a danger. Children (and parents) did not seem to realise that their 'naughtiness' could make their parents cross without causing lasting damage.

Adult children in particular may translate their childhood worries about 'not being naughty' or 'not worrying mummy' into 'stress must be avoided at all costs'. Some of them tried with varying degrees of success to prevent their parents from 'parenting' them in some way as a result of this. Some treated their parents as children, and some parents seemed to go along with this, all in the name of 'needing to avoid stress'. The guilt and fear attached to any risk of disturbing the parent's (generally illusory) equanimity was for some children enormous. It meant that they felt they had lost their parent, perhaps years before the parent would die.

Some children were freely resentful of or angry towards their parents. However, many obviously considered they were being too naughty or bad when they had thoughts or feelings about their parents which were critical, angry or accusatory in any way. This made it hard for them to be realistic about such feelings: the guilt was so strong that the ideas could not be seriously considered, and certainly not with the parents themselves. While hidden in this way, accusations remain quite excessive and children do not have the chance to test them.

When children feared that any accusation of neglect or expression of resentment, anger or bitterness towards their parents was positively dangerous, they could not test it out. Protectiveness towards the parents by even quite small children deprived both parents and children of the chance to sort out difficulties and misunderstandings that came between them and kept them apart.

Who looks after whom?

Who looks after mum/dad?

> Jody at two would say to her mother 'Don't worry mummy, you go and lie down, I'll look after you' whenever her mother got upset or angry for any reason.

Many of the children we met believed at times that they looked after their parents, rather than the other way round. Alex was claiming that he did all the housework when he was six; his mother went along with the fantasy. Sharon, Martin, William and Sally all felt at some time that they were their ill parents' sole support and carried all the responsibility. Rosemary defended her mother vigorously (and quite unnecessarily) from the normal quarrelling of her small brothers.

The children also seemed to have a sense of whether each parent was looking after the other or not. As in Martin's case, this was not always realistic. The children interpreted friction between parents as total failure to care, and ignored the ordinary daily caring that was taking place. In six out of seventeen two-parent families where one parent had MS seen at the ARMS Clinical Research Unit, one child in the family made it clear that they saw themselves as needing to be the main support for the parent with MS *because the child believed the other parent did not care sufficiently*. In some of the families the parents themselves shared these beliefs. Sometimes the idea that love could actually cure the illness or condition concerned seemed to underlie this kind of belief, with the continued illness or deterioration being understood as 'proof' that there was not enough caring.

All of these children at other times were painfully aware that they could not and did not succeed in their wishes to look after their ill parent better. At times they admitted they could not do it. Emma, fourteen, was very insistent that her mother was looked after by her father, and that she had little to do or to worry about.

Children with only one parent seemed to carry a much greater burden of worry. Darren, fourteen, who lived alone with his mother, became so worried about her that he could not leave her to go to school.

The children with two parents did have someone else to fall back on when they realised they could not look after their mother or father single-handedly. More than one mentioned how much they needed the other parent. Sharon worried about looking after her father if anything happened to her mother: her

ot ill but simply gave the impression of being unable to look after
eral children seemed to feel that all help should really be provided
ily and that asking friends or neighbours would mean the family
in some way.

It seems then, that some of these children believed on one level that they
looked after their ill or disabled parents, rather than the other way round. In
more rational moments those with two parents acknowledged that one parent
also looked after the other. Relatives and friends were consistently ignored:
often brothers and sisters too, even if they lived nearby. This meant, however,
that many children believed it was their sole responsibility if a parent had to
go into hospital, became ill or got better.

This area was one in which the children differed perhaps most from their
parents. Most of the parents we have spoken to said they really wanted their
children to leave home and make lives of their own in the normal way. They
wanted to manage the illness themselves without being a burden to their
children. This is not what most of the children thought should happen: their
definitions of being good children involved very clear ideas about caring for
their parents. In addition, some of the adolescents who left or refused to help
gave the impression of denying a huge sense of guilt rather than feeling
comfortable about living their own lives. The idea that parents want them to
stay close may sometimes be the children's own idea which it 'hears' from the
'parents in their head', rather than from their actual parents.

Who looks after me?

Most children seemed to take it for granted that, however ill they were, their
parents would look after them while they were alive. However, they did think
and worry about what would happen to them and their other parent if one
parent died. Several boys talked of looking after ill parents, but not of being
looked after. There was a hint that Matthew thought he was too much to cope
with, but this was in the context of both his parents dying.

However, at least five girls out of sixteen with ill mothers had complaints
that their mothers were not paying them enough attention. This was in the
context of rivalry with brothers or sisters or fathers who seemed by the child
to be favoured by the mother. Whether this division between the sexes is
significant or not we do not know.

Conclusion

In this chapter we have looked at children's concerns in connection with ill
parents. We have found that these concerns are very different from their parents',
and that parents often had no idea how their children were interpreting events.
Both children and parents were often trying to protect each other from what

they saw as a unbearable realities: as a result neither could learn that their fears were not reality at all.

We have come to the conclusion that children protecting their parents too much and parents protecting their children too much may be two of the most damaging aspects of a parent's illness or disability. They are also ones that may be changed.

CHAPTER 5

Who Am I?
Dependence, Separation, and Independence

In this chapter we consider the effect of a parent's illness or disability on a child's long-term development. It is well known that children identify with their parents as they grow up, and that the processes of identification and separation are important in their development. These processes seem to be affected by parental illness.

Children's identity develops in the context of parental care or lack of it. Children we met were sometimes unsure about their role as children or as substitutes for a disabled, ill or absent parent. Fundamental questions were raised about the children's right to live their own lives, or whether they had to give up everything for their parents. Family rivalries were sometimes clearly affected by illness or onset of disability in a parent. Parents had to deal with their children feeling jealous and being left out, or angry, hurt and perhaps frightened of their own power too, in connection with the way the illness affected them. Anxieties about being 'a good child' or 'a bad child', 'dependent' or 'independent' were affected by the parents' health, though many other factors also played a part.

We described some of the identification processes in the last chapter in terms of children's attempts to keep their parents alive and well by 'being them' in some way. But identification is also to do with children's developing sense of themselves.

Children identify with their parents in different ways depending on their age. They may speak with their parent's voice; behave like them; or develop the same symptoms as a parent, alive or dead. They may follow their parents' careers, want the same number of children or choose a partner like the one their mother or father chose. When one parent is not there they identify with an imaginary one.

If they are basically happy about their parents, this identification allows them to build up their pride in being a valuable and worthwhile person, with a sense of being well supported by good parents. If they are unhappy about being like a parent they may go through periods when they suppress any part of their personality which reminds them of that parent. This can happen, for example, if one parent always refers to the other one in a totally negative way. If the child continues into adulthood hating or rejecting that part of itself, it can be crippling; only a part of its personality can be used and considerable energy goes into keeping other (potentially useful) aspects at bay.

> Edna, fifty-five, said she had never had children because her mother was dying of cancer throughout her teenage years; when she knew she was ill herself, she determined she could never put a child through what she had gone through at that time.

> Roy, forty, had always hated his father and could not bear to be like him in any way. This seemed to contribute to difficulties he had finding a partner.

Illness or disability itself may be a reason for older children to fear becoming like one of their parents when they grow up. It may be important to talk with children from the age of two onwards about how they will be when they grow up. Up to the age of three, four or even five boys can think they will 'have babies in their tummies' when they grow up; they can easily think they will grow up to have legs which do not work, or eyes that cannot see, for example, if this is how their parents are.

However, what the small child sees of their parent's condition may not be what the parents see. A wheelchair may seem an object of envy to a child whose own legs get tired walking. A urine bag may seem like a real solution to the problem of wet pants for a three-year-old. The idea of not being like parents may also in itself be upsetting: a small boy may not like the idea that he will have to go out to work, for example, if he sees his father staying home in the centre of the family. There may be a sense that a disability (such as blindness or deafness) makes someone 'special' and gives them special privileges: the child may not want to be 'ordinary'.

In some families the condition is seen as separate from the person who has it; in others it is not.

> After a time Sally, twenty-six, began to talk of what her mother would have been like if she had not had MS for the past twenty-six years. For Sally these were new thoughts and they gave her a new set of ideas about the woman she could become.

When a baby is born it seeks the nipple and is comforted by the mother's holding. The baby has a very primitive sense of needing something outside itself. With the milk, it can feel it takes in the mother, and for the baby, mother and baby seem at times merged into one, with unclear boundaries.

The mother at first may have a strong sense of the strangeness and separateness of the baby, but after a few days she may fall in with a merging of identities. Mothers interpret their babies' wants and needs partially by identifying with them. This is partly why the scream of a newborn baby is so painful to adults; they identify with the baby and know how they would feel if they screamed like that.

As it grows the baby learns to talk like the mother, make faces like her and copy her in many ways. Gradually, the child becomes able to bear awareness of the separateness between itself and its mother. 'I am like my mother', replaces a much more primitive, non-verbal sense of 'My mother and I are one; neither of us exists or can survive without the other'. Traces of the merged relationship remain alongside a sense of being different from the parent.

The separation process is always to some extent a struggle. It involves many conflicts and takes place under pressure. It does not happen unless there is good reason for it. The presence of a rival for the mother's affection is one such reason, which is probably why children may seem to grow up more quickly when a younger brother or sister is born.

In losing some closeness with the mother who does things for them, children find they can do things without her. They gain access to part of themselves that is like her. At first this may seem very much 'her', and they may, for example, talk themselves through tying their shoelace as their mother talked them through it. Gradually this becomes part of themselves that is not felt to be their mother's personality but their own. They learn to think for themselves where previously she thought for them; they learn to look after and take responsibility for themselves and their own lives.

The sense of the holding and feeding mother 'taken inside' does not disappear. If the child was reasonably comfortable with the dependent relationship with the mother the separation process builds up a sense of having a good mother who is not totally identified with the baby *inside* as well as outside. This mother does not go away and can be relied upon throughout the rest of the child's life. When the actual mother dies, at whatever age the child, this internal mother may for a time seem to be lost, but through the process of mourning gradually return in a more secure way.

The presence of a partner for the mother is another factor that both forces and enables the child to separate from her. The child can identify with the partner and so can the mother, who is reminded of her more adult self by her adult relationships. A mother with good adult relationships may find it easier to encourage her child to have good relationships with other adults, and so to separate from her.

The separation process is closely involved with rivalry and jealousy: rivalry for the love of the mother and for the love of other people both play a part. Living through such rivalry is important for the child's later relationships as well as for the development of the child's sense of identity.

Gradually children usually learn to allow their mothers to have a life of their own, and can tolerate her relationships with other people knowing they will continue to be loved themselves, though no longer exclusively.

> Alex's mother was not only ill and disabled but she also rejected all relationships with anyone except Alex, who was six. She and Alex seemed to be in a state where their closeness was virtually a merging. The boundaries between them did not seem very solid; they slept in the same bed; they constantly spoke for each other, and watched and interfered in whatever the other was doing. At meetings of people with disabilities, which his mother sometimes attended, Alex was a model 'carer', looking after all the women in wheelchairs and speaking in a very charming and mature-sounding way. However, at school he dirtied himself and could scarcely function at all. On his own he conveyed to the counsellor a strong and frightening feeling of his insides falling out.

Part of Alex's difficulty was that he did not seem to have developed an identity for himself: he only functioned as a part of his mother. He had become his mother's 'arms'; her memory; her 'legs': he drew different parts of the body disconnected from each other and faces without boundaries. His sense of not being held together, of having no boundaries and not being able to hold his insides in seemed also related to his mother's state of mind. Her father had been very intrusive both emotionally and physically until she broke off all relations with him; as a result she too had a sense of being unsafe and unprotected in her own body. In addition, her brain was affected by her illness.

If the child feels its mother is 'held' by other people and her own mind, the child is able to feel more held by her itself. The child does not have to be the carer and the boundaries between parent and child can be firmer.

Children who decide to mother themselves and completely identify with an internal 'bigger than me' mother not only fail to develop their own child identity but also lose their sense of being contained and held by someone who is bigger than themselves and in more control. This sense of not being safely held affects relations with other adults; with organisations and institutions such as hospitals, even with food, cars and houses as well as with partners and lovers. Such children and adults may have to be 'independent' for fear of being nothing. They may pretend they are in control but in fact know this is a pretence and may live in fear that it will be shown up as such. As children they may reject adult care and concern, because this is felt to be too painful, reminding them of their own unbearable ignorance and dependence. As a result, help is neither asked for nor expected, and these children may live in a sealed world of their own. What adults do offer and provide is taken only on condition that the children can pretend it came from themselves. They may appear mature and sensible, like Alex did when his mother was there, but this maturity cannot hold.

As children separate from their mothers they gain a sense that each can exist independently. Surprisingly, it seems to be hard for all children to believe their parents can look after themselves, and if a parent is ill or unsupported, it is even harder. Sally was by no means the only child who held on tightly to her mother, devoting her whole life to her in an attempt to keep her alive. It was as if her mother's life were more important than her own, but both were at risk. It seemed that separation would mean loss of everything, including her whole reason for existence. It may be that parents are often identified with the needy, dependent part of the child, as a defensive reversal of the real situation.

Other children had more of a sense of themselves and were able to resist the temptation to give up their own lives to their mothers or their fathers. Sometimes this meant battles within the family; we know of many daughters who handled this conflict by leaving the country, working in the caring professions abroad. The older the children were when their parents became ill or disabled, the better seemed their chance of holding on to their own existence and believing that their parents would survive without them. Some children who had difficulty separating from their ill mothers achieved this eventually through therapy and/or with the help of a strong partner. Others had younger brothers or sisters who looked after the parent, allowing the older one to separate, perhaps with a fight, and to leave.

In good circumstances children do not have to reject their childishness and can continue to make use of it, not only in play but also in certain kinds of risk-taking. They can allow themselves to grow up in fits and starts, reverting to being more childish at times of stress.

Where a mother is ill, children may not dare to allow themselves to be childish and dependent. They may avoid any situation they cannot control or in which they do not feel totally secure. They may deprive themselves of many childish pleasures in this way, finding them no pleasure at all. Loss of mothering means loss of childhood for these children. If adults are aware of this they can help to prevent it by providing real alternative mothering and holding for the children and the parent: very often adults are not aware of children's need for a parent.

> Frank, at forty dependent on a devoted wife, described how as a three-year-old he was very independent and had to look after his mother while his father was away at sea. He found it difficult to see that his ideas about independence and 'looking after himself' (at three and still as an

adult) were illusions that enabled him to deny the role of his mother and his wife in looking after him.

A social worker struggled hard to persuade children in a family where the mother was ill to go out to a youth club. After considerable resistance the children went; saying that it was 'childish'. After a few visits they began to enjoy it.

Children sometimes decide to mother themselves for other reasons.

Theresa, thirty-six, told how she had always looked after herself. She said this was because her mother was not as clever as she was, and her father preferred her to her mother. When her father died she did not know what to do with herself; her whole life had been directed at him and she had never developed relationships with other men.

The kind of adult or child who talks as if they run the world, as if they can do anything, regardless of reality, may have 'inflated their ego' by identifying with a child's view of an all-powerful imaginary parent figure as a compensation for feeling 'unmothered' and having 'useless' parents. The loss of reality-sense is sometimes painfully and pitifully obvious; so too may be the 'little boy lost' who is clearly visible behind the blustering front. Identifying with a powerful imaginary parent in this way is unstable for two reasons. In the first place there is always a risk of recognising that the self is the helpless, vulnerable child without good parents: in the second, there is the risk of feeling like the 'useless', devalued and supposedly contemptible parents.

As adults these people may behave and feel in very infantile ways at times, particularly towards their partners. At work they may be perfectly competent and adult; but at home or in love relationships they may be quite different. They may be extremely dependent upon their partners but refuse to admit it. The superior attitude to their mother or father, developed as a defence against the pain of losing that parent's care or attention, may simply transfer to a very superior attitude to the partner who looks after them as an adult. Having poured scorn on their mother's care when they were small they may as adults pour scorn on anyone else's attempts to care.

It is clear from our work with adults that a child or adolescent who has been forced to parent themselves in some way may still be able to develop gratifying and satisfactory relationships as adults. A good partnership can allow the partners to develop and mature. Some of these relationships will break down, forcing a replay of the traumas of a deeply hurtful separation in which infantile anxieties about abandonment and cruelty are re-experienced. However, reliving these as an adult is different from living through them as a child. Adult abilities may eventually re-emerge strengthened by the experience.

The anxieties about falling apart which we described in Chapter 4 are probably strongly influenced by the way children feel themselves merged and identified with their ill mothers. The fears of losing themselves if a parent dies may be partly a result of fears of *having already lost both their parents and themselves* in a merging identification.

For Sally and Sharon as well as for Darren and Alex, their need to keep close to their mothers seemed to be adding to their difficulties in developing a normal independent life. Their schooling and social life was affected so that they seemed more likely to be facing adult life without the education or social support network that would have made it easier to cope without a mother. Perhaps they would be able to compensate later for the years they had been unable to concentrate on their work and their own lives; perhaps they would not.

It seemed that a mother's illness tended to pull the child back into a much closer, merged relationship with her or sometimes to prevent normal separation and growing up processes taking place. Some children resisted this and some did not. The tragedy seemed to be that the 'nicer' children were most at risk in this way, and the children who tried to salvage their own lives appeared as aggressive, angry and rejecting, and censured both by themselves and by others. Which fare better in the long term we do not know.

We have a tentative conclusion from the work we have done: children often need help to sort out the extent and limits of their responsibility for their ill parent and their responsibility for their own lives. Both 'good' children and angry, aggressive and unhelpful children may benefit from this.

It may not always be possible to give children this help. Children's behaviour (and their parents') is often very resistant to change. It may not be easy to persuade children who are trying too hard to keep their parents alive that they do not need to sacrifice themselves. Equally, it may not be easy for parents to encourage and support their children's separation from themselves if they feel that their children's help, affection or closeness could save their own lives.

CHAPTER 6

Housework

'There ought to be a law against children doing housework.' – *girl aged ten whose mother was seriously disabled*

'I don't think it hurts the children to do something around the house. I had to, and it means I can do everything…but my wife won't make them, she thinks she has to do it all herself…and now she's ill she can't so she just wears herself out and won't let me do anything about it.' – *Father whose wife recently became ill*

'I can't bear it when my illness affects them. But I get so cross and I know it's because I'm trying to do too much, that can't be good for them.'

Housework is commonly spoken of apologetically by adults as a 'trivial' issue, and yet it is far from being trivial. In a study by Philip Abrams (1972) of the causes of communes breaking up, difficulties over housework was one of the most common issues cited. Issues of who is in control of the family, of the house, of life in general may be involved in conflicts about housework.

It is not really surprising that people feel strongly about the level of cleanliness, dirt, mess, or comfort they and their children live in, or about anything to do with the provision of food. These are issues that have attached to them feelings belonging to our earliest relations with our parents, particularly our mothers, often including strong moral overtones. They may encapsulate anxieties about being loved and lovable as well as being clean or dirty, in a mess or in good order, hungry and deserted or fed and comforted in all their symbolic as well as practical meanings. It is therefore not surprising that people do not easily accommodate to others' standards and others' priorities.

Housework may be an area where a new disability or illness shows up the cracks in family relationships and where changes involving power, authority and control within the family or between the individual and the outside world are seen to be made. A parent's illness or disability may have a significant effect not only upon the number of people available to do housework, but also on the amount of work to be done. It is also possible that some of the feelings about a parent's illness or disability which cannot be expressed otherwise are sometimes expressed through the 'normal' conflicts about whose turn it is to do the washing up.

We pointed out in Chapter 4 that children interpret an adult's refusal to do the washing up, for example, in terms of their own motives for refusing and may find it impossible to comprehend the difference. An illness may make the parent really seem wilfully 'bad' to the child as a result of conflicts over housework.

Handing over housework

Handing over housework may be something that an illness or disability forces on a parent of either sex. For some people this is a relief and a pleasure: they are happy never to clean another saucepan or wash another floor. For others, it is a serious loss and a cause of great anxiety. Some women do not want to give up housework, feeling it means they have failed as a woman, a wife or a mother. There are also men who do not want to give it up. Either may feel that no-one else can be trusted to do it 'properly', to their own standards. This can be quite a serious difficulty for a family and it may need to be taken seriously.

Many mothers who were ill seemed to want to do all the housework and not allow their children to do any. Others were proud of the fact that their children could and did provide real help around the house. Some wanted their children to do more or less than they actually did. Many had all these feelings at different times and in different contexts.

Fathers on the whole seemed more keen that the children should help around the house. There sometimes seemed to be a rivalry between fathers and children as to who was to do more. Some managed to coordinate a joint effort between themselves and the children: others took over all household tasks and left the children, in their opinion, 'free'.

> 'My wife and I agreed early on that I would take on the housework that she used to do, that we wouldn't ask the children to do it. It was bad enough for them without that as well.'

> 'I'm better at making the children help around the house, they don't seem to make so much fuss when I ask them to clean their rooms as they do when their mother asks them. Now we've all agreed we should do this it works fine.'

In the second example the father believed the children could and should help; his wife had previously felt that all housework and the happiness of her children should be entirely her responsibility. With some difficulty she learnt to allow her children and her husband to take more responsibility themselves. She later said that her illness had forced the family to make changes they should have made years ago.

A few fathers who were seriously disabled or ill seemed to take to an 'invalid' role when they could, in fact, have contributed more to the household.

> A father who had always gone out to work and earned money, leaving all the household tasks to his wife was suddenly disabled. He sat around and expected to be waited on all day in spite of being quite capable of doing more. Neither he nor the family expected him to take on any of the household tasks which he could do. He never showed any concern for his wife's situation but shouted at her or the children if they were slow or late doing something for him.

For adults as well as adolescents, feelings about cleaning and housework are sometimes connected with feelings about sex. There is an obvious connection when sex or sexual thoughts are seen as 'dirty', but it also seems that a good sexual relationship can spill over into good ways of working together to keep mess contained and the house in good order without persecuting people by obsessive cleanliness. We examine some of the symbolic aspects of housework later: here it is important simply to register that difficulties about housework in families are as common as difficulties within sexual relationships, and that change is not likely to be easy.

How Much Housework Are The Children Doing?

It is very difficult to assess how much housework any individual is doing. Cleaning or even food preparation is something which is likely to be noticed only when it is not done and taken for granted when it is. This means that in extreme cases each member of the household may be convinced that they do all the work that is done and nobody else does anything – or only very little. In the happiest of households it is very easy to have the impression that you do far more than anyone one else. The amount of time spent cleaning, preparing food, or doing any other household tasks may also be very difficult to estimate accurately; and the impression people have about it may not match up to the reality when they are asked to count it. They may be surprised how little or how much time is spent in this way.

Some of the children we saw were perhaps doing a little more housework as a result of their mother's or father's illness. Some were probably doing less, where their mothers' illness meant she was at home rather than out at work, or where she was trying to compensate them for what she saw as the terrible burden her illness inflicted upon them. Our impressions are to do more with the feelings expressed by children and parents rather than the reality of the housework undertaken.

Some of the children were living with very disabled parents, and it was difficult to get any idea of how much a child actually did.

> Alex at six was reported by his mother to be able to get a meal and vacuum the flat, and to be angry because she would not let him go to the launderette on his own. In different contexts he was reported as 'doing everything' and 'really' being well looked after by his mother. 'He only puts a pie and oven chips in the microwave…he likes to come shopping with me but I tell him what to get; he tells me what he likes and he goes and gets things to put in the basket. Sometimes he gets things and I have to put them back, he's naughty like that, aren't you?' This was said with a fond smile at Alex; it seemed a game mother and child played, in which Alex tested to see whether he could get his own way or not and his mother made it clear that she was actually in control.

> Emma insisted that she did little, when her mother said she did a lot. Jane's mother fluctuated between saying that Jane did far too much and saying that she only did what was entirely reasonable for a girl of her age.

Some children made no complaint about the amount of housework they were asked to do. Others complained of being made to do too much; others such as Martin (see Chapter 3) of not being allowed to do more. We came to see housework conflicts as expressing many different aspects of relations within the family.

Fairness and Related Issues

> Sharon (described in Chapter 2) was angry at having to do so much housework when her brother did not. He went out all the time and shouted at his mother to do things for him, and her mother doted on him. She did all the right things, never shouted and never went out and her mother still didn't love her as much as she loved her brother. She did not dare shout at her mother about how much housework she had to do because she was afraid it would give her mother a heart attack. When she worked out with the counsellor exactly how much time she did spend on housework, she was surprised how little it was.

> Esther (also described in Chapter 2) talked about housework. She spoke bitterly about her mother using her illness to get more attention from her father, leaving Esther feeling he was no longer 'on her side' as he used to be in her arguments with her mother.

>> She described how one Saturday she and her younger brother spent several hours cleaning the house. When her mother came

home she simply said 'Why can't you always be like this?' Esther was furious and determined never to do it again.

Talking about housework Esther was quite explicit that 'Mothers are there to do housework for children, not the other way round.' She was certain that her school friends did not have to do any housework at all.

Even though their parents might have felt it was 'unfair' that the children should have to cope with an ill or disabled parent, none of the children we saw expressed this feeling. The children's ideas about fairness seemed always to be expressed in terms of housework, in comparisons between the amount of housework done by different members of the family: 'It isn't fair that I should have to do more than my brother/sister/father/mother'. Esther, at seventeen, was the only child openly to compare her family with other families, and this was specifically over the issue of housework. It seemed that many of the children were using housework as a means of judging who was most favoured, generally by the mother. This, of course, is common to families without an ill parent.

Fairness was not the only issue which was discussed in terms of housework.

Megan (nine) said (hesitantly, and only with encouragement from the counsellor) that she did not like having to make tea for her mother: she was afraid of scalding herself, which she had done once. Her mother was very surprised: she hadn't known about the scalding and hadn't thought Megan minded making tea. Megan said quickly that the scalding had been a long time ago but she was still frightened of it. Her mother wondered aloud if she was asking Megan to grow up too quickly.

Megan's mother's insight could well be applied to other children's complaints about housework, particularly where a parent has been ill for some time and the child has reacted (like Martin) by trying not to grow up. In such a situation children might well be saying that they do not want to be treated as if they were their actual age, and they may use housework as a means of representing this. Megan was saying throughout the session that she did not want to be treated like a 'big girl' and she envied her little brother the extra care he was given which she no longer received.

Megan, in common with many of the other children, had not understood that her mother was also sorry that she could no longer look after Megan as she used to. Her mother had hesitated to tell her this, feeling it was better to 'encourage her' by dwelling on the positive aspects of her 'grown-up-ness' than to talk about the way she might be missing out. Megan was left alone with her sense of something missing, with no means of checking her view of what it was. As a result her interpretation of the situation was quite different from her mother's.

Edward was also described in Chapter 2. His father was disabled by MS (mainly with fatigue) and his mother did all the housework. His feelings about his father were strongly expressed in his attitude to housework.

> 'It's not fair, he expects me to lay the table while he just sits there doing nothing. It would be all right if he did something, but he doesn't so I don't see why I should.'

It was clear from the way he spoke about housework that Edward saw himself as a successful rival to his father and completely discounted his father's authority within the family. His mother was allowing this to happen for her own reasons, though she stopped it when she realised what it was doing to Edward as well as to her husband and herself.

Looking after mother

With many of the children the atmosphere of the interview or counselling session was not particularly difficult or heavy. The children were happy to talk and even if they had complaints or worries these seemed bearable and could be modified within the session.

However, some of the children and young adults conveyed to the counsellor an entirely different sense of heaviness and despair. With these children the counsellor had the impression of an enormous and hopeless task to be undertaken; a task which both she and the child were quite incapable of even starting, it was so huge. This task seemed clearly related to their mothers' mental and physical condition. It happened with two children who felt themselves (probably realistically) to be their mother's sole support, and with two young adults who feared for the life of both their parents. None of these children complained about housework and, if anything, would probably have done more without complaint; their anxieties seemed to be more to do with their own existence and their mother's life or death.

We wonder if the children from other families who did complain about housework were in fact expressing something about a more manageable but related task. The children who did complain all knew they had a second parent who both could and did support the children's mother in some way.

For Alice and Edward (and other children with ill fathers too) it seemed that their main concern was for their mothers; as far as they were concerned their father's job was *to help them to look after their mother*, regardless of who was ill. For these children, their father's illness seemed to mean that he was not able to do this task properly. Their complaints about housework may have been complaints that this task, of 'looking after mother', was to fall on them. Martin too was very concerned about who should look after his mother. This 'looking after' was spoken of in terms of housework but also in terms of 'keeping an eye on' her: a task which seemed to have much more emotional significance than basis in reality.

Leaving home

It is normal for teenagers to have mixed feelings about growing up and leaving home. When a parent is ill the conflicts involved may be stronger. For example, the desire to stay and not grow up may be stronger; so too may the desire to grow up quickly and to leave home. Fantasies of keeping a parent alive by 'keeping an eye on them', or ideas of being with them for as long as possible when faced with fears of losing them prematurely, may keep some children close to home.

Where children are actually keeping their parent alive by single-handedly feeding them, taking them to the toilet, putting them to bed or whatever, the children will also clearly have difficulty leaving home, and may feel they have to give up their own education, career and even social life to keep their parent from institutional care. These children do not have the same choice that others have.

Resentment at having to do housework may be part of the normal conflict of adolescents wanting to separate from their parents. It is the parent's house which is being cared for, not the children's own; the parents' rules that are being obeyed, for the parents' sake. The adolescents' desire to have their own place and their own rules may perhaps be stronger if they are sure their mother is well looked after by someone else; a father, another partner or a sibling.

One girl left home because she said she could not bear to see her mother suffering: she was unable to help her because of her own illness. Rosemary wanted to leave because she was afraid of causing more suffering to her mother (and herself) by her own unruly emotions. An adolescent's fear of being trapped into staying out of pity or guilt may also be increased by a parent's illness and expressed in a refusal to be any more involved in the household than they must. More than one older teenager seemed to be staying at home out of a kind of paralysing, hopeless despair, neither helping in the house nor seeking their own place to go.

Symbolism of housework

Housework has strong symbolism. Houses themselves, as 'home' or the more old-fashioned 'hearth' (a word connected with 'heart') have deeply resonant meaning to do with mother-love, comfort, and security, as in 'going home to mother'. Pictures of idealised houses, particularly drawn by children, often resemble faces or bodies or both. The psychoanalyst Melanie Klein found that houses and spaces of all kinds signified a holding, containing aspect of their mother to children, and many of the fears she found in children were to do with their fears about their mother's ability to hold, contain and love them. In other words, some of the children's deepest fears, really about their mothers, could be played out in terms of their relationship to the rooms and houses they lived in or used in their play.

Adults do not lose this sense of houses being personified in a particularly female way. The building society advertisements exploit this; and if someone is burgled (which burglars in some places call 'screwing') they may well say they feel as if they have been raped. Children's bodies and those of their mothers are not clearly separated in children's fantasy life and, for adults, home may also represent a kind of 'second skin' just as their mother did when they were young; the walls protecting them from the dangerous outside world, the doors representing ways they control entrance into their private worlds; and windows like eyes a means of looking out or looking in. If this is the case, it is not at all surprising that people should have strong feelings about clearing up, cleaning, decorating and repairing their own living spaces and that of their parents.

In counselling as well as in psychoanalysis it becomes clear that it is not simply for practical or rational reasons that some people cannot feel comfortable in a dirty or untidy house; or that others feel comfortable only if there is the right amount of untidiness or even dirt. How warm or how cold the living space is may also have important meaning in terms of comfort, love and loneliness, as well as having practical meaning for someone with a neurological condition who cannot function in extremes of temperature.

The ways people feel about their living space often seems to mirror the way they feel about themselves. Individuals who are seriously depressed may live in a house 'like a pig-sty' not only because they cannot be bothered to clean up, but also because on some level they want their internal 'mess' to be evident to the outside world. Many people recognise a feeling of 'having a mess inside' (in themselves or in their heads); the mess in their rooms may fluctuate with this feeling, not simply for the obvious practical reasons. Cleaning up the mess in a house or a room may also give a sense of clearing up the 'mess inside'.

Melanie Klein thought that one of the main tasks people set themselves as children and then symbolically as adults is to repair damage they did to their mother's body in unconscious phantasy. In their minds young children at times attack their mothers with all the weapons at their disposal – their nails, excreta, voices, eyes – out of all kinds of feelings, including hatred (for giving them any pains they had) and envy (of her bounty and creativity and ownership of everything they wanted) as well as the more obvious frustration when they wanted her to feed them or give them something and she was slow or did not do as they required for any reason. The unconscious fantasies created in children then, of a damaged mother in need of repair, live on as they grow up. These fantasies may well make up part of the idea of a mess inside themselves which needs to be put right but they fear they cannot. Klein thought that when children (or adults) are in a state to want to make things better in a realistic way rather than simply by magic, they feel they need a strong father to help repair their mother or her body (his strength is seen as much greater than theirs).

Such fantasies may well be symbolised in a child's feelings about their mother's house. They may find it very difficult to admit that they have made a mess because they are afraid of this more elemental, primitive mess they made of her body in their minds. Any attempt to make them clear up may be understood at this level as a requirement that they acknowledge that they damaged her and made a mess of her. Some children are hopeful about their own ability to make things better and may not mind too much; others cannot bear to know what they have done for fear that they will see a total disaster that cannot be repaired. It may be something of this symbolism which makes it so hard for some children to clean up their parent's house or flat; a house or flat of their own would have a slightly less guilty and persecuting meaning for them and might therefore be easier to clean.

Children often seem to keep their own rooms in a mess, which may have many different meanings. For some it is seen as a deliberate act to show their parents they are in control – or are choosing to be less in control than their parents are. For others the mess seems to be less a matter of choice and more clearly an expression of some kind of hopelessness. Some say they just feel more comfortable that way and cannot explain why. They may insist on the room being left untidy, or they may allow a parent to help them clear it up. This may give messages to their parents about their level of independence, their acceptance or rejection of their parents' standards, and their acknowledgement or rejection of any hidden longings to be 'mothered'.

The desire for privacy and a separate existence from their parents too may be expressed in children's control over who comes into their room. Parents may respect this or may sometimes insist on entering and cleaning or helping the child to clean. Some of the symbolism may be almost conscious: the parent may be establishing that they are not going to allow the child to reject all mothering yet; that they are going to insist on their own right to do what they want in their own house and that the child will have to abide by their rules while they live there. Depending on children's state of mind and circumstances this may be experienced secretly as a welcome relief or as a cruel unjustifiable intrusion, for example.

All of these feelings may be influenced by a parent's illness or disability, and parents may read the signs of their children's state of mind by their attitude to their room. This is difficult since the parent's feelings about mess or tidiness may be different from those of their children. Sometimes parents probably understand very well what the child is trying to express: this itself may annoy a teenager who *wants* to feel misunderstood in order to justify his or her own angry feelings towards the parents.

Admitting that one hates one's parents out of envy or jealousy is not something a teenager is likely to do; they are more likely to be busy devaluing them and saying there is nothing to envy except the teenager's own life and youth. But this leaves them with no reason for their angry feelings towards their parents and they may create some reason in order to relieve the fury in some way. Refusing to do housework or leaving a mess in the bedroom may be a way of externalising many different internal conflicts. In a practical way it may be a means of attacking parents, in particular a mother and her role (in the child's inner world as well as in reality) as a container and cleaner of dirt and rubbish and anything else the child wants to get rid of.

Equally, doing housework may be a way of relieving conflicts or expressing hope, particularly concerning the desire to make things better, repair the damage, mend and love an ill parent. When children can help in the house or clean their own room, they may feel their own constructive impulses have won – they are capable of making things all right again – and for a while they may feel good. This can be a great comfort and reassurance, particularly if the mother is ill and the children feel bad a lot of the time.

Parents and children often conflict with each other about housework; it is probably far more common for couples to have different standards and opinions about housework than for them to coincide; children may exploit such differences as well as bringing in their own ideas from friends outside. This makes it very difficult if illness causes some change in areas of responsibility around the house. Living to someone else's standards of cleanliness or tidiness may be learnt, but it takes time and can be painful.

CHAPTER 7

Aggression and Control

The linked questions of aggression and control, like those concerning house-work, arise for both parents and children. Each member of the family has to deal with his or her own aggressive feelings, anger, frustration and irritation: each has to find ways of controlling his or her behaviour in the face of these feelings. In addition, parents have to control their children and help them learn to control themselves.

Disabilities and illnesses can make all of these issues more difficult. An illness or disability can make people more aggressive and increase their need or wish to control those around them. It can also make them more vulnerable to the aggressive or controlling behaviour of other members of the family. The uncontrollability of the illness may increase everyone's desire to control others: Martin wanted to tie his mother down and Rosemary wanted to control her small brothers; both children were hoping in this way to prevent 'something terrible' happening to their mothers.

An ill parent may need to make requests and demands, and be helpless if children refuse to obey. If their body is uncontrolled or weak or in pain parents may be unable to enforce compliance with their wishes. They may also be unable to take the initiative in hugging or comforting children physically, and this may make discipline harder to enforce. They may feel as if they are falling apart and convey this non-verbally to the children and to their partner.

Children also have thoughts and feelings about their parent's condition which may influence the way they respond to parental authority. Children with disabled parents may not have the same freedom to refuse to help their parents that children with more able-bodied parents have. When or if they do pluck up the courage to disobey they may feel they are very bad indeed and (like Martin) feel very dissatisfied with themselves.

A parent's weakness, stiffness, vulnerability, irritability or changeability, for example, any of which might result from a disability or illness, may be experienced and given meaning by children not only on a physical, practical level but also on an emotional or metaphorical level. Edward's statement that his father was a 'weed', and William having to deal with friends saying his father was 'mental', are examples of this which had quite clear implications for discipline. Other children seemed to be too anxious to be able to challenge their ill parent in a normal way: they were so convinced their parent was weak and feeble that they alternated between feeling too powerful themselves and fearing that they were as weak as their parent. This too made it harder for them and their parents to handle discipline.

In this chapter we look at these issues from the point of view of both parents and children.

Children

A parent's illness or disability can affect the kind of beliefs children develop about their own aggression as well as their actual behaviour.

Children normally behave well not just because their parents force them to, but also partly because they are afraid of what will happen if they do not behave within certain limits. They can be afraid for themselves or for their parents or other people they love. They do not fear only punishment; they also, and more important, fear the power of their own destructive feelings towards those they love, being afraid that these feelings will destroy those around them and leave them unloved and abandoned through their own fault.

Children may believe that their anger, bad behaviour or bad temper has directly caused damage to their parents, making them ill or making them worse. This may make them well-behaved or may have the opposite effect. It seems that some children can and do control their aggressive impulses to a considerable extent in such circumstances. It may, however, cost them.

In certain circumstances they may be so afraid of what they would do if they let themselves go that they never let themselves go. Their angry and 'bad' feelings may build up inside, never tested against reality, and seem far more frightening and dangerous than they ever could be in reality. These feelings may be mixed with terrible shame, guilt and fear of retribution, and may erupt in various disguised ways: one 'very good' child fell out of bed almost every night; Alex at seven and eight dirtied his pants in school; Toby at twelve wanted the naughty boys at school to be expelled. Sharon had great difficulty standing up to her mother partly because she was afraid of what this would do to her mother. As a result she had very unrealistic ideas about her grievances towards her.

One of the 'very good' children had a terrible fear of fires which she knew was irrational. She said she had to say magic words to an imaginary friend in order to ensure that the house did not burn down. It is possible that her aggression was so frightening to her that she denied it belonged to her at all and felt it coming at her from the outside, as a threat to her life. She had to split off another part of her mind (the imaginary friend) to save herself from this.

Some physical symptoms – for example eczema, allergies or asthma – may, in a complex way, be related to feelings children cannot bear to have. Excessive guilt about bad, angry feelings may be unbearable and may be expressed as an exacerbation of a physical symptom rather than be allowed into thought.

> On several occasions Linda suddenly had an attack of cystitis after speaking to her sister on the telephone. In therapy she realised that her sister had aroused very angry feelings in her, which she did not like to admit. Once she became aware of these feelings the phone calls were no longer followed by cystitis.

Children who are reacting in this way are likely to deny any sense of guilt or responsibility for their parents' condition, not because they do not have any, but because they cannot bear to feel it. They may become quite destructive towards the source of their guilt (perhaps the ill parent; perhaps the other parent, who, they may feel, is damaged even more by their own failure). They may prevent themselves thinking in various ways. Having a symptom instead of a thought is one way. Others include being overactive and rushing around or fidgeting excessively instead of sitting still, and obsessive reading or playing computer games. All of these activities may have other causes or may be perfectly all right in themselves but they can also be used as defences against thought when they could be used as ways of contributing to it. Reducing the sense of guilt and responsibility these children have may enable them to feel it and to attempt to make things better, but this may be difficult when the child does not admit to having such feelings.

Fear of the consequences of aggression may also prevent ordinary parent–child banter. Wrestling or punching or even teasing may stop if a parent's illness becomes worse, and may not resume when they recover. The fact that children learn from experience, and may learn lessons that are not true, is one of the reasons why life does not return to the previous state after a parent's illness. A parent going to hospital for any reason may mean to children that their bad thoughts are as dangerous as they feared. This lesson is not cancelled out by their parent's coming back from hospital, though the return will give hope that their love has some power. Small children in particular have no way of knowing that aggressive thoughts and feelings do not have enormous power; except when their parents do survive and are not damaged. We say 'if looks could kill…', and as children we did not know they could not.

Children who are afraid of their own aggression may also react by becoming very violent or abusive, swearing and being disruptive, partly as a way of attempting to test the reality of their fears and the adults' strength to withstand them. They may in this way try to confirm their ability to destroy the adults' capacity to contain the child and keep the child safe. This may give them a sense of control over the situation which they would not have if they simply waited for their aggression to arise as a response to something someone else did.

Physical and verbal fights with friends and siblings, at home or at school, can help children develop a reasonably realistic view of the extent and limits of their own power. They can learn how much damage they can do and how much they want to do. They can learn about hurting people emotionally and making up again. These fights may help the children to test or challenge their frightening beliefs about their own power to damage or even kill their parents. Such fights may be very important for children with ill parents for this reason, and a child who does not fight in this way may be in more difficulty than one who does.

Fights or battles of wills with parents or teachers also give children some sense of the power of people in authority; their cruelty or generosity; how they can behave reasonably and how they can respond in an arbitrary or foolish way. Children learn from this and later are themselves likely to behave as those in authority did to them.

Where children have an ill parent who appears very weak, testing the reality of aggressive and hateful impulses with the parent may be harder than usual or impossible. They may not dare test their real fury with a parent who they believe is unable to stand up to attack or to prevent them causing real damage to another child. Physical or verbal attacks on their parents may have distressing consequences, far greater than they would with healthy parents.

Where children do not dare test their aggression with a parent, they may test it in a context where they hope or feel the adults around can be trusted to keep control. School or other activities may provide such other adults. Generally, some kind of attachment may need to be felt for the child to be able to use such situations in this way. Adults who can tolerate some bad behaviour in such situations without losing control or either over-reacting or failing to react at all may be of great help to the child. Letting the child know that some adults are strong but not unkind or cruel can be very important if the child is trying to prove the opposite.

Parents

Parents may put considerable effort into influencing those aspects of their child's personality which are to do with control of aggression. Sometimes they are aware of having difficulty in controlling their own temper and want their children to be different. Sometimes they want their children to have the same kind of control as they have themselves. Sometimes they are more tolerant of their children's behaviour and feelings than they are of their own: they feel it is 'all right' for children to shout and make a fuss but it is not 'all right' for them to do so themselves. Sometimes they enjoy their children's defiance of authority and may even subtly encourage it.

> Rosemary had always been afraid to upset her mother because she knew her mother was often in pain. When her small son challenged her mother she was scared but also pleased that he had done something she had never dared to do.

Expressing feelings through children

Parents sometimes seem to use their children to express for them feelings that they cannot express directly themselves. This is a mechanism used in families with or without disabilities.

> A very disabled father used to laugh whenever his wife told their son off. This made his son rude to his mother, who became furious. Talking about it, first the father said he could not help it: the doctor had told him that his illness made him laugh and cry without reason. His wife knew this, but also felt that it was quite deliberate and he did have some control. The counsellor suggested it might be worth also thinking about any reason he might have to actually want to do this. He then said how much he hated being unable to discipline the children himself.

> The counsellor said she wondered if he might get some satisfaction out of seeing his wife just as unable to discipline them as he was. He might feel she then knew what he was going through. This was a difficult idea because neither of them liked to think he could be feeling this. However, after this conversation he became more supportive of his wife's disciplining and his son behaved better.

In this situation, the son was being provoked by his father to undermine and attack his wife in a way the father could not allow himself to do openly. His more mature and loving self did not want this, but his more childish, revengeful, angry self did. The idea that he might want to undermine her and make her life worse was almost unthinkable to him. It was only when he was able to see this as a means of communication with his wife that he was able to admit responsibility and control it.

Parents who are not ill can also do this. For example, a mother who wants to run away from a difficult home life may consider this unacceptable for herself, but may encourage a teenage daughter to go. If the mother knows that this is what she is doing she may be able to help the child to leave in a way which enables the girl to feel still loved, loving and supported. If the mother is quite unaware of encouraging her daughter to leave, though this is happening, the girl may leave with a sense of fury, shame, guilt and abandonment, which are exacerbated by being shared but not acknowledged by her mother.

Parents' control through discipline

Discipline is a real problem for some parents with certain disabilities. There are the practical issues; for example being unable to pick up a screaming toddler and remove it from a situation. There are the social issues; for example, having to restrain helpful passers-by from intervening in a parent–child dispute or from taking over and doing something a parent wants to do for their child, however slowly or however difficult it may be. A strong voice, strong arms, working legs and good eyesight are all extremely valuable when it comes to controlling children, particularly when they are small. So too is self-confidence. Yet parents who are blind, deaf, weak, in wheelchairs or lacking in self-confidence do manage to bring up children.

Parents who cannot lift their toddler away from trouble may have to use words they would rather not use. Parents who cannot see what their children are doing have to use different means of finding out if they are getting into trouble or of preventing it. The balance of power between child and adult may be affected by a health condition, though this will depend on the character of the parent as well as his or her bodily condition.

Parents can also foster self-discipline in their children.

> A two-year-old always ran down the street whenever the front door was opened. His mother was frightened; she would chase him and bring him back. When he was three she hid her fear and said 'Now you are old enough to go out, I'm not going to chase you.' He never ran out again.

A very disabled parent may be able to encourage self-discipline in this way more effectively than a physically healthy but very anxious parent. However, parents' actual ability to control their children physically can affect (as well as be affected by) the parents' self-confidence and the children's confidence in them. These may need to be reinforced in other ways if a parent does not have physical strength. Partners can be very important here.

Sometimes people in a good relationship can work with an able-bodied partner so that the child feels the efforts of the disabled parent to be strongly backed up by the support of the able-bodied one even when the able-bodied one is not present. Other parents undermine each other over issues of discipline. Support offered by outside helpers may also enable a mother to control her child effectively. However, there is no guarantee of this.

> Jonathan aged four was very aggressive towards his severely-disabled mother at times, and would not obey her. His mother felt his behaviour was related to the difficulties of having three paid helpers, all of whom

had different views on bringing up small boys, and all of whom were new, the previous ones having recently left. His mother was exhausted and resentful at having to persuade three new women that her own way of running the household was workable. What she wanted most of all was to be left alone to bring up her son herself. Unfortunately, this was impossible.

The emotional state of parents is important. Age and experience make a considerable difference here, as does timing of the onset of an illness or disability. A mother who is shaky on her legs can use various means to ensure her baby feels secure when carried, but if she is feeling emotionally very shaky herself she may find this hard to organise. Practical and emotional help when she is feeling insecure may be of great importance in helping her to be firm enough with her child from a position of strength, and may help discipline later. The age of the child also affects discipline issues. A child who learns early on that its parent is strong may continue to respond to the memory of strength even if the parent later becomes weak. To a child an adult is enormous and even a weak adult has reserves of strength to call upon which to a small child may seem boundless. Love itself is a powerful disciplining factor, of course, but even in the best of circumstances children's confused, angry and destructive feelings towards their parents sometimes override their feelings of love and affection.

Discipline is also affected by parents' mental state in other ways. Parents who are in great pain may not have the attention and patience they would like to give their children, making their discipline harsher than they would like. Attention, patience and tolerance may also be lowered in a parent who is having to give a lot of time to an ill or disabled partner, particularly if either is bad-tempered about the situation. Some situations would really try the patience of a saint, and few parents are saints.

Parents who have lost the support of their partner for any reason may well feel unable to insist on standards from the children without some other kind of support for themselves, from close friends, relatives or a counsellor, perhaps. They may be afraid of losing the affection of the child too – but at the same time be afraid that if they are too soft the children will end up running the household and/or running amok, and neither loving nor respecting their exhausted, resentful parent.

For parents who have had time to come to know and manage a long-term disability, discipline may be less of a problem than might be expected. To some extent, it seems that the children learn what they can and cannot do safely from an early age. They tend to stay close to a wheelchair even though their mother cannot physically keep them there. The children of blind and deaf parents may learn not to take advantage of their parent's disability very early on. They may learn to treat a parent's crutches or stick with great respect, when they could cause the parent to fall or be unable to get up if they took them away. Children do seem to know which issues are of real importance for their own and their parents' safety and dignity.

> The daughter of a blind woman said she learnt very early on never to leave anything lying around but always to put things back where they belonged, for fear her mother would fall over them or be unable to find them. She knew what was important for her mother and her family life, and it did not seem to her that she missed very much by having to learn this so young.

Some of the discipline issues become resolved differently. A mother may learn to use approval and disapproval where she would otherwise have used physical restraint. The children of someone in a wheelchair or of a blind or deaf parent may learn to respond to different cues from the ones they would use if the parents had the use of their legs, eyes or ears. For example, their fear of losing or hurting their parent may stop them running off, or prevent them from attacking their parent or from being disobedient in a way the parent cannot detect. A mother who cannot speak may be able to control her children in non-verbal ways. Deaf mothers and their children communicate with each other in their own ways. Sign languages have a richness of their own, particularly when they have been used and developed between mothers and their babies.

For some families the style of discipline does not seem affected by a disability or chronic illness; for others it does.

> A mother who had always disciplined the children continued to do so when her husband developed a chronic deteriorating condition. The onset of the father's disability upset them all and made them all more bad-tempered, and she found it difficult having her husband at home interfering with discipline, but her methods of trying to make the children behave remained the same.

> Jody's mother was determined not to use what she called 'moral black-mail' on Jody as her own mother had on her. She wanted to be the kind of mother who removes her children from situations rather than relying on words. For her, loss of strength in her arms and legs was very upsetting: it meant she felt she had no choice but to behave in the way her mother had. Eventually, with a counsellor, she found other means of controlling the child without resorting to moral blackmail.

Children seem to respond to the cues their parents give them, and issues of discipline are particularly well suited to express the internal conflicts of parents. However, they also express the internal conflicts of children, and parents may at times feel unable to exert any influence on their child. Both parents and children contribute to maintaining the situation, whether it is a basically comfortable one or an uncomfortable, or even threatening one.

Social workers are more likely to meet families where issues of discipline are more troublesome and where children or adults may actually be a danger to each other. Destructive and self-destructive behaviour always poses multiple problems for professionals, particularly when children are involved. In addition, fear of being accused of being unreasonably opposed to a parent's custody of a child *because of the parent's disability* may make it very much harder for professionals to decide what is an acceptable risk for children and their parents.

Parents as role models

Parents provide their children with a role model when they deal with irritations, frustrations and serious setbacks, sorrow or sadness. This model can work in a positive or negative way.

Children may behave in the way their parents do, whether they like what they see or not. If they and their parents are happy with the way the parents deal with anger and frustration, this is the easiest option. Children or their parents may, however, not be happy with the parents' model of behaviour, particularly when it comes to aggression and control. Children may be afraid they are behaving like one parent and try very hard to react differently. There may be pressure on them from the other parent to do this as well. This can be very difficult, as a whole part of the personality may be suppressed and children may develop a persona that comes across as false and strained. It is also unlikely to work in the long term; and violence may erupt on occasion when control fails. Both of these situations exist in families with illnesses or disabilities just as in other families.

Managing aggression in the wider society

For a boy, loss of a father or loss of his attention sometimes results in challenging behaviour, particularly towards men, but also towards strong or authoritative women. This may provoke a firm or aggressive response, particularly from male figures. In some cases such children may seek trouble with the police. The difficulty is that such children may provoke a response from men which fits with their fantasy of a father. Small children have exaggerated fantasies of fathers and men, made up not only of their experiences of their own father if they had one, or men in general, but also of their own feelings. If they have no real father to correct their fantasies they may grow up seeing men as cartoon figures with exaggerated characteristics: enormously powerful, dangerous, and perhaps even violent; or as the depriving, punitive and mercilessly 'fair' policeman father of their conscience. In particular, they may separate their loving and caring feelings from their aggressive ones, attributing the caring ones to mothers or themselves, for example, and their angry and violent feelings to fathers, or vice versa. Children with this kind of fantasy may go out of their way to seek men in the real world who represent these stereotype images; and they may find them.

We have already referred to Alex and his mother, who had difficulties socially, emotionally, physically and intellectually. Alex said he never got angry with his mother. He drew pictures of a house without a base line, a face without boundaries, a disconnected body with limbs in the wrong places and a man he said was a father, with big strong legs. He was bullied at school, and it is possible that the bullies represented for Alex some kind of combination of his fantasies about an absent father and also his own disowned aggression. Bullies deal with their own weakness and fear by proving that they are big and strong and that *someone else* is weak and frightened. Faced with a child like Alex they could 'feed' their own strength from his expectations of them. The bullying thus would enable the bully to feel stronger partly because Alex saw them as unrealistically strong and himself as unsupported, not held together properly and without a strong base.

The armed forces, the police force and the prisons are institutions in which aggression is managed in different ways by society. A young person who has difficulty with their own aggressive feelings may become involved with one of these institutions. The institutions themselves provide a particular kind of parental care and authority, and many of those who join them, whether as law enforcers or lawbreakers, may relate to them as to a kind of family. In good circumstances the firm, 'fatherly' discipline within tight rules provided by these institutions may offer the kind of containment young people need for their aggression, which can then be channelled into a form which is used for the benefit of society. A good affectionate relationship with a father-figure in such an institution may enable a boy to mature into someone capable of affectionate fatherly relationships.

In less happy circumstances the aggression and violence of young people within these institutions is channelled into much more destructive behaviour, either condoned by society, as in a war, or not condoned, as in criminal behaviour or abuse of various kinds. Abuse by those in authority in these organisations will leave young people liable to become abusers themselves.

The child's comic-book stereotypes may be an important part of the social belief system of these institutions, reflecting the way in which people relate power, authority, aggression and masculinity.

Anger

Parental anger and irritation help children to recognise when they have gone too far. Knowing there are limits to the parents' tolerance may make the whole family feel safer and more in control. Excessive tolerance by parents may make children more frightened of their own aggression. It is not necessarily bad for children if parents are sometimes pushed by an illness or disability into showing anger, bad temper or irritability that they think they would not have shown if it were not for the illness. Children also have to learn to cope with the moods of adults and to recognise when they have provoked those moods and when they have not. Tolerance of such moods in their own future partners and in themselves may be learnt in this way.

Both adults and children may use various methods to make others angry when they feel angry themselves but do not want to know it. This can be one of the reactions to an illness or disability.

> Angela's mother, who was ill, was always very obliging. She never complained and always agreed to everything her husband said. Angela's father would get very impatient and totally exasperated with her, and Angela saw him becoming more and more angry. Angela herself some-times became obliging and 'accepting' like this with her husband. Her husband one day said that when she was like this it felt he was wading through treacle, that nothing he said was getting through. It seemed this happened when Angela was really angry but did not want to say anything about it. Angela realised that she had always thought her mother was the innocent party and her father guilty, but she could now see that her mother's behaviour was, in fact, making her father feel impotent and furious.

Adults or children who have observed violently angry behaviour in their parents may be very frightened of their own anger. They sometimes control their own behaviour and temper very tightly under normal circumstances, but break out violently at times. During these outbreaks they may feel out of control. They may at the same time also be trying to take control of very frightening experiences from their past. They may behave like bullying or frightening parents towards younger children, or later, to their own children or partners. Later too, they may use drink, tobacco or drugs in an attempt to get rid of their destructive feelings. Doing it in this way perhaps enables them at the same time to identify with a parent who seemed to want to damage or perhaps kill them.

Some parents seem to be frightened of their children's anger and resentment towards them and may constantly try to placate them. This may be exacerbated if a parent is furious about their own ill health and imagines the children are feeling the same. They may also try to placate a child out of a sense of guilt. In response the children may express something of the parent's insecurity, becoming very demanding, for example, or attacking the parents, voicing the parents' worst beliefs about themselves and making them feel even more guilty.

Children who have reason to be angry with their parents are sometimes given or allowed something 'to make up for it': in other words, to prevent the children being angry with the 'nice' parents. This may be very confusing for the children; it can make them feel guilty for being angry or worried that their parents are not strong enough to withstand their anger. It is important to remember that a gift or a treat does not compensate for a real loss. Presents and treats of various kinds can be real demonstrations of affection or signs that the parent has thought about the child, and important to both child and adult as such. However, they may fail to satisfy if they are given instead of open acknowledgement of real cause for grief or anger or instead of honest attention or affection.

Anger is a normal reaction to many situations but it may be a reaction which is inconvenient or disallowed in a family. Children may be taught to cover it up in one way or another, or they may decide for their own reasons to try to prevent themselves feeling it. This can continue into adulthood: many adult women talk of trying to 'be a good girl' in situations where this means swallowing their anger or otherwise hiding it. Over-eating, drinking and smoking are sometimes used as means of suppressing anger with others while expressing some destructiveness against the self.

Sometimes children react angrily to a parent's illness or disability without it being entirely clear what is happening. Parents can then react very angrily to the children's behaviour, partly out of their own sense of enormous guilt and distress. It may even be that children sometimes provoke parents' outbursts out of a sense of their own guilt and failure.

> Jean asked her daughter to vacuum the room before going out. The daughter said 'I shouldn't have to do that.' Jean was furious, saying that it was perfectly reasonably that a sixteen-year-old should take a share of the housework. At the time the daughter was also making her mother supper, as her mother could not use her hands at all. Her mother also relied on her for using the washing machine.
>
> Discussing the situation Jean admitted how very bad she felt about her daughter having to prepare all her food. It was striking that the girl had complained about the vacuuming when she had never complained about all the food preparation she had to do. It was as if she were allowing her mother to put her in the wrong, and as if both were trying to ignore the real thing she 'shouldn't have to do'.

Jean said she found it almost impossible to say to her daughter how bad she felt about the things her daughter had to do as a result of her mother's illness. She wanted her daughter to come with her to the counsellor so that she could be helped to say it, but the daughter refused.

Catherine said her four-year-old daughter Susie had behaved very badly one day when they were visited by another mother and daughter. She had ended up by smacking Susie in a total fury. This was unusual and had distressed Catherine, as well as Susie, very much.

In counselling it emerged that the visiting mother was very physical with her own daughter and played aeroplanes with her, throwing her around. Susie had watched for a while and then said 'My daddy does that with me'. She had then bounced round the room and become very loud and naughty.

Catherine hated the fact that she was not physically capable of doing many things with her daughter, including playing aeroplanes. Her own upset had been both lost and expressed in her fury with Susie. Like Jean, she found it impossible to say to her daughter how upset she was at not being able to be the kind of mother both she and Susie wanted her to be. Susie's behaviour perhaps was aimed to protect and distract both herself and her mother from the enormous disappointments they suffered on a daily basis. Catherine did not know how to share her own grief with Susie. Admitting that Susie herself might have reason to feel grief made Catherine feel desperately guilty and upset: this added to her fury.

Neither Jean's nor Catherine's daughter said directly to her mother that she was angry and upset at her mother having disabilities which affected her own life. Both provoked situations where their mothers were quite reasonably angry with them. It is possible that this felt safer than acknowledging the real cause of grief, which nobody could control. Their mothers needed help to face the reality of their daughters' reaction to their real losses.

Nagging

An illness or disability may reduce the sense of control, power and authority of ill parents or their partners. Nagging may be one response to this situation. Where it never stops, but goes on and on relentlessly, perhaps over years, it wears away at affection, respect and self-control. Ultimately it may lead to violently angry feelings or even violence, even in people who previously would have considered themselves incapable of such behaviour.

Nagging occurs when someone has to ask several times that something be done. It is an expression of both anger and powerlessness on the part of the nagging person: since the request has failed the first time the need to nag (rather than simply to get angry) is a sign that their word has no authority. Neither the nagging nor the nagged person is showing respect either for their own or the other person's right to make a request or for their own or the other person's right to refuse it.

Nagging and accusations of nagging take place where there is some kind of collusion to avoid open discussion of unpalatable refusals and unjustified requests or demands. Sometimes such discussion cannot take place, for example where dementia has affected the mind to the extent that rational discussion is no longer possible. Sometimes families feel that an ill or newly disabled person cannot be challenged openly simply 'because they are ill' or 'because they have so much to cope with' and they feel they can express their own objections to demands only covertly, by agreeing and then not complying. The whole family may have conflicting ideas about their own and each other's rights and needs. The feeling that the ill person has all the rights, and the others none, may alternate with the opposite feeling, that the ill person is really undeserving of all the extra attention. Other members of the family may feel at times that they have no right to sympathy or consideration for their own pain and misery, either for minor troubles or even troubles (such as bad toothache or backache) which would normally be seen as serious. At other times they may bitterly resent this. Wherever such issues cannot be addressed, nagging may be involved as part of an uncomfortable *status quo*, which is seen as preferable to the fears of challenging *all* the rights and responsibilities, power and authority of all the family members.

Family violence

Violence within families is not uncommon and a certain level is perfectly normal. Children fight with each other when they are young and parents will often allow them to sort out the problem themselves. Adolescents may use fighting as a means of expression or communication. It is also normal that illnesses and disabilities provoke extreme feelings in the person who has them and in those around.

> Susan admitted that she sometimes got so angry with her very disabled husband that she could scream. Often when she tried to move him, he would tense up and make it harder for her. She knew it was just physical spasms and he had no control over them, but she couldn't help feeling he did it on purpose. She felt really bad because one day she had shouted

at him in frustration, he had shouted at her and she had flung him down violently. She felt she was a monster to behave like that.

Some illnesses cause violent outbreaks over which the person seems to have no control. Other people's reactions can make matters worse. The amount of patience and tolerance available may depend on many factors, including the past history, experience and character of those around. Brain damage, either through accident or illness, also affects tolerance levels and may lead to serious behaviour problems.

> Mike's father, brain damaged by an accident at work, used to beat Mike, his brother and their mother. At the age of forty-five Mike told the counsellor some of the horrific things his older brother used to do to him when their parents were out. He had never told his parents. Mike was still frightened of his own violent temper which erupted against his partner from time to time. He had not had children partly because he was afraid of what he might do to them.

Parents worry about the effect of their own or their partner's violence on their children.

> A mother who had been subjected to great cruelty from her own parents feared her violence towards her own children and needed help to prevent the cycle being repeated. Her disabling illness actually made it easier for her to obtain help: she had a social worker as a result of her condition and was able to use this contact to ask for and obtain real help.

> Ann had been sexually abused by her father while her mother was terminally ill when she was a child. When she was diagnosed with a chronic illness herself she became extremely concerned about her own daughter's safety.

When mental changes accompany an illness, feelings may run particularly high and violent behaviour may result, not only because of the frustrations involved but also because words can no longer be used to regulate the relationship in the same way as before. Where words and reason fail, many people find themselves wanting to resort to violence as 'the only language s/he understands'. This can add to the guilt and self-blame of healthy partners who already feel their own health makes them guilty and bad: their own violence (sometimes in people who have never been violent in their lives before) scares and disturbs them.

Should we do anything about the violence of others?

It can be very hard to know how to relate to discoveries of violence within families. It seems, for example, that children whose parents are violent towards them do not necessarily fare much better if they are simply removed from home. They may put such pressure on foster parents that they cannot settle, and the continuous disruption of their lives which results may not be any better for them than their original situation.

Similarly, adults of any age who are physically abused by members of their families may make it clear that they prefer to stay with those families rather than to move. Some people do seem to provoke violence. With strangers, they might get the violence without the underlying attachment. Violence can take place in institutions just as much as in homes.

It can be very distressing to learn, and difficult to accept, that families are relating to each other in a violent way. Children witnessing violence are at risk of becoming violent or victims themselves, though not all do. There are some situations where it is clear that children need to be removed from violent parents, at least temporarily; there may be situations where those around cannot stand by and know that somebody is being physically abused. But a violent family may also experience strong emotional bonds and be very muddled up with each other in their minds. This provides a kind of security as well as an addictive excitement. Couples who treat each other violently may be unable to separate, and may join together in a very threatening way against anyone who tries to intervene. They may also get back together after a separation, leaving onlookers in despair. Couple bonds in these situations may be stronger than child–parent bonds and a child victim may lose both parents if one is prosecuted.

It is important to ensure that the family doctor knows about violence taking place within the family, though it may not be easy for the doctor to decide what, if anything, to do about it.

> Joanna came to the counsellor in great distress. Her husband had been taunting her cruelly with words for months as his motor neurone disease got steadily worse. He clearly hated his dependence upon her and took it out on her at every available opportunity. Eventually she had been pushed too far. He fell over and once again swore violently at her, calling her names, accusing her of incompetence and stupidity and saying it was all her fault that he was in this state. She could not defend herself verbally, but she kicked him violently where he fell and then left the room.
>
> The counsellor tried to establish how much damage Joanna had done and could have done. She tried to help Joanna to think through the event and its consequences. This was difficult because Joanna felt so terribly guilty. However, it was worth the effort. Her husband, Joanna said, had been much better since; he had not in fact been injured and had stopped

shouting at her like that. She had gone back within five minutes to help him up. But she had not told the doctor, nor had she called the doctor to examine him.

She decided that if it did happen again she would ask the doctor to examine her husband. She had no wish to leave her husband and it did not seem he wanted to leave her. The couple obtained further help through the social work department which recommended a local organisation specialising in helping families where violence was involved.

Social workers and the NSPCC (see Useful Addresses) are the professionals with knowledge and experience in this area; they may be consulted even if the decision is made not to call them in. They may be able to help assess whether lives are at risk and whether a really better alternative exists. They have a legal duty to ensure the safety of a child but also to maintain parental responsibilities and contact. Sometimes they have to help children and parents to separate. Fear of the possibility of being separated can prevent families from asking for help, even though social workers often work enormously hard to keep children with a disabled or ill parent when this is appropriate.

Decisions in these situations are extremely difficult and fraught with anxiety and grief for the professionals as well as the clients. Professionals have to act knowing they may be strongly accused either for not taking sufficient action to protect a child or alternatively for removing a child unnecessarily. These accusations may be made by themselves as much as others. They may identify painfully with both parties in the conflict, and suffer with both parent and child if a child does have to be removed. Meanwhile they may be vilified by others involved, who perhaps do not know all the details and cannot be told for reasons of confidentiality. Self-respect and job satisfaction are likely to be under threat in these situations for the professionals involved. This reflects the situation for the clients, who are almost certainly suffering from a lack of self-respect and lack of satisfaction with their performance as a parent or child within the family.

Discipline as a cover for cruelty

Children often believe their parents are being deliberately cruel when they are not: the children have simply interpreted the parents' behaviour in the light of their own feelings. However, some people, parents included, do have very cruel impulses and may express these towards their own children. This can happen where no illness is involved. Cruelty is not the same as the exasperated fury which any parent may feel at times; the moment when new parents discover how angry and violent they can feel towards their child can be quite shocking for otherwise calm and apparently not 'bad' people.

An illness may make cruel impulses harder to control. An illness itself may feel like a cruel attack – on the body, on relationships, on life itself and everything that makes it worth living. People who feel like this may at times actually want to attack their children; to make the children suffer as they suffer themselves. At one extreme they may feel they do not care any more, do not want to bother, and they may withdraw from parental responsibilities, which itself can result in apparently unintentional cruelty, such as neglect. At the other extreme, there may a more obvious attack. Some parents attack their children on the slightest pretext. They may use the pretence of discipline as a cover for cruelty, and their punishments may become more damaging than the children's original offence. Instead of helping their children to deal with the children's own aggressive and cruel impulses the parents may be adding to them. The parents' own feelings of impotence and dependence on a fickle and cruel world, of huge guilt and unbearable responsibility for the ills of everyone around, may be evoked in the children. The parents, for the moment at least, may feel relieved of their burden.

Partners of people with disabling illnesses may also react in cruel ways at times, particularly if they have past experiences of being trapped by unloving or cruel adults. They may see the children as well as their partner as a reincarnation of the demanding and accusing adults of their past, and treat them accordingly.

When parents are cruel to children, they forget their adult, caring selves. They may momentarily really hate the children for everything they represent; life, hope, love, a future, all of which they feel has been snatched unjustly from them. Afterwards, they may experience real sorrow and enormous guilt: they may be quite shocked to discover this level of emotion and sadism in themselves. Sometimes the guilt leads to a determination not to repeat the action, and this may succeed. Sometimes it leads to attempts to find help.

Unfortunately, however, this guilt sometimes leads the adult to repeat the cruelty: parents who cannot bear their own guilt may try to destroy the evidence of it (in the children's reproachful eyes, for example, or in their own minds) and so provoke the child again until punishment and attack seem justifiable. In this way the pain of knowing that the child was unjustly and painfully made to suffer is blotted out temporarily, and a vicious circle is established.

There is a distinction between *controlling a child* and *making a child feel excessively controlled*. Children very often mistake the one for the other; adults too may have difficulty deciding which is going on. Partners may have different views on this; sometimes they can restrain each other at moments of stress and fury.

Sam said that whenever she came in her father (who was virtually unable to move) would call her to do something for him; she never had a moment to herself; he always wanted something.

Her father said he had to catch her while she was there because she disappeared out of earshot as soon as she could and then wasn't around to be asked. If he needed something he could not do for himself he might have waited several hours before she came in; he felt extremely angry, frustrated and impatient with his body, and he knew he often sounded as if he was feeling this towards his daughter.

Sam sometimes felt her father just wanted her to do something silly which could wait: she felt he just didn't want her to live her own life.

Her father said he sometimes knew he wanted something but he couldn't remember what it was: he was afraid Sam would go away again so he would ask her to do something just to keep her there while he remembered what it was he really wanted. He knew she wanted to get away; this just made him more nervous and angry and made it all harder. He would have liked to get away too: she didn't have to live with it like he did, it wasn't unreasonable to ask her to do just a few things for him, she had the rest of the time to herself, she could go out...

As we have said, adult control is important for children, and adults who are too frightened of taking control and behaving with authority may be less helpful to their children than those who are more able to react with firmness and resist children's manipulations. However, adult cruelty sometimes involves attempts to make a child feel controlled to the extent that they cannot move or live or breathe freely. Again, this may arise if the adult feels they themselves live like this; an illness may make parents feel excessively controlled either by their body or by those around. Some adults in some situations can bear such feelings without passing them on; others at other times cannot.

A more concealed kind of cruelty is involved when adults try to control or punish their child by intentionally exaggerating the effects of the children's bad behaviour on themselves.

'You'll make your mother ill/you'll kill your father if you go on like that!'

'I can feel one of my headaches coming on...'

Some parents believe or half believe that these accusations are a reflection of the truth. The intention is important here; whether the child is being made to feel bad because the parents want to make them suffer, or whether the parents are simply desperate to make them behave in a way they think is right and best for the child too. The first may be cruelty; the second not.

Children seem to be quite realistic at times in interpreting whether their parents are exaggerating or not. However, they may react with guilt and placation even where they feel they have been manipulated. Consciously, they may be sure the parent is exaggerating: unconsciously they may believe them. Even where children have learnt to ignore repeated accusations and threats, and have eventually escaped from home, they may be left with extremely guilty feelings as well as resentment and fury.

When threats are used in desperation children may recognise them as cries of extreme parental pain and know that the parents do have their interests at heart. Afterwards, parents may be sorry and very worried about the things they have said. Whatever the parents' intention, the children may go on fearing that the threats are true: that they could make their parents ill or kill them by their bad behaviour.

A physical illness can affect parents who make these threats in two ways. An illness may make it harder for the parents to believe they can influence their children in less extreme ways, and drive them to the limit of their patience sooner. It may also undermine their authority in the family, leaving the illness as the only weapon they can use to assert any control over anyone. It may even feel like the only identity the person has or is allowed by others.

Conclusion

Perhaps a primary task for a family is always how to allow love, sympathy, concern and care to flourish amongst all family members. These are always under some threat from impulses such as envy, rivalry and greed. Illness and disability may add to the threat in many ways. Discipline and control become important in this context. Both too much and too little control and discipline threaten the love and care felt and expressed by children for their parents, and by parents for their children. Fear of losing the child's sympathy and love may make a parent cruel, which then threatens the child's loving impulses, so increasing the parent's belief that control is the only way of obtaining the care needed.

Many families work out ways of dealing with these issues which encourage both feelings of love and practical expression of loving care. Others are less able to do so, and may exist in an atmosphere in which sympathy is absent and the predominant states of mind are attack and blame, despair and rivalry: in which there is no possibility of sharing anything good, but only a state of permanent warfare in which the question is 'you or me', never 'you and me'.

Where families are struggling with these issues, an outsider, such as a nurse, a Home Help or a doctor, may be drawn into the family system and experience similar feelings to those in the family. Where these feelings are predominantly loving, any form of intervention may be a good experience. Where love and care within the family have disappeared, leaving a shell of heartless care, cruel discipline and excessive control, the experience of any involved with the family may reflect this and be deeply unsatisfactory.

PART II

Offering Help

CHAPTER 8

Who Can Help?

Parents are the most obvious source of help for children. However, other people can help children. Step-parents, grandparents, teachers, doctors, parents of the children's friends, home care workers and social workers may all be faced with some very tricky questions when considering how much they should be involved and how much they should keep out of the way. We raise some of these issues here.

Anyone who wants to help a family or a child may ask themselves some of the following questions.

Does the child want me to help? Do its parents want me to help?

This issue is clouded by the interplay between verbal and non-verbal messages. Children may ask for help or offer a confidence and then avoid any further contact. Families may say 'I'll let you know if we need anything' and then say nothing. An offer of specific help may be rejected, and it may not be clear whether the refusal is for the particular offer or for help in general.

Parents often find it very hard to accept help or to think what kind of help would really be helpful. Children or adolescents may say they do not want a particular adult to care about them, and then turn up on the doorstep daily on some pretext or another. An offer of help may be made in such a way that it is rejected.

> A woman whose husband had been severely ill for several years always replied to the doctor's routine enquiry with 'Everything is fine!'. When one day the doctor said 'And how are you?' in a different tone she responded quite differently and actually told him how she really was — which left the doctor feeling extremely ashamed of his previous thoughtlessness.

Step-parents or new partners of divorced parents are in a difficult position in such situations. They may be more able to think of the children than the parents themselves, but be inhibited from interfering by concern for either parent. They may be heavily criticised for getting involved in any way, yet be unable to stand by and watch the children being ignored by their preoccupied parents. They are also likely to have their own feelings of jealousy and rivalry with the children and with the other parent which may make involvement more risky. All the issues of step-parenting, before and after marriage to the parent, may be made harder by illness or a new disability, whichever member of the extended family is the patient. On the other hand, if circumstances do permit, a good relationship between a child and step-parent or parent's new partner may be a source of considerable comfort and help to all concerned.

Am I intruding?

Deciding to 'intrude' by offering help or even enquiring seriously can be difficult even when the person knows from experience that they may be able to help and even if they have been given a clear request. Being afraid of invading a family's or child's privacy may be legitimate, or it may be a way of evading their own sense of responsibility as adults.

Can I take it?

In some relationships adults have considerable freedom to choose whether to get involved with the children in a family or not. There may be times when they feel strong and available enough to invest considerable energy in helping a particular family, and other times when they cannot. A family doctor may be in this position: so too may a nurse or home care worker.

In other relationships adults do not have a choice. A social worker who has been called in has to respond, whether the family want the response or not.

What responsibility do I have towards others in general, or this child in particular?

The answer to this will depend both on the particular relationship and on cultural beliefs. Grandparents have different responsibilities from parents; teachers from doctors. Some families and some religious or cultural groups feel strong responsibilities towards their own members but none to outsiders; others feel a sense of responsibility towards a much wider group, but may be unclear about the extent and limits of this responsibility.

Should a GP, for example, invite the children of parents with a deteriorating condition in to talk about how they feel and how the situation affects them?

Some people would be clear that a doctor should do this, and others would think not.

Teachers, too, have certain responsibilities towards helping the children in their care, but they are not counsellors or social workers and they have responsibility to whole classes as well, which may conflict with their desire to offer a more confiding relationship to certain children.

Step-parents' responsibilities generally have to be negotiated with the parents. Often new partners agree to leave all responsibility for the children to the actual parents; sometimes there is an agreement for shared responsibility in some form. An illness or new disability may require that these arrangements are re-negotiated, perhaps with considerable pain on all sides.

Am I in danger of pushing someone else out by pushing myself in?

There are people who try to help others in such a way that someone else, an adult or another child, always feels pushed out.

It is important to ensure that offers of help or attention do not undermine the child's other relationships, particularly with its parents or brothers and sisters who live at home. Even cruel or rejecting parents are very important to a child, and undermining the relationship of a child to its parents in any way should be avoided. Even in the worst situations, if the child's life is threatened by a parent, for example, it may be possible to help the child to remember and acknowledge the good and loving aspects of the relationship while not ignoring damaging aspects.

A child who is being given extra attention at school or at home often feels bad and guilty about taking it away from other children: this can be acknowledged.

'Busybodies', 'Noseyparkers' and 'Lady Bountifuls'

There are people who enter into other peoples' business primarily for their own purposes, though they may be quite unaware of this. They may want power, control, influence over events, gratitude, or acknowledgement of their superiority over others. They may make others feel inferior; or spread malicious gossip; or be using the opportunity to get their own back on others they feel have injured them. They may find it unbearable not to be the centre of attention and insist on offering help in order to be noticed.

Being 'helped' by someone like this can be a very demoralising, irritating or frustrating experience but it may be very difficult to reject the help firmly but kindly. A fear of being seen in this way may prevent some people (such as some teachers) from offering any help at all.

Support for the supporter

People who are offering help or emotional support to anyone else over a period of time should seek support themselves, from a friend, colleague or perhaps a counsellor or support group. Regular sessions planned in advance are generally more useful than 'I'll call you if I need you'. It may be when they do not realise they need help that people need it most. Some professional organisations recognise this and provide supervision; others still expect even young and new members to cope with very little support. Junior doctors and nurses, for example, may have access to support from senior nurses, but this is likely to be irregular, intermittent, and in some cases stigmatised. It may be insufficient to enable the professional to remain emotionally available to a patient under stress, or may even actively discourage empathic communication. In these circumstances the junior doctor or nurse may learn only how to cut off and to retreat from emotional demands, while idealising this response as 'remaining professionally detached'.

Good support can help either a professional or non-professional supporter to remain in touch emotionally with the patient while keeping boundaries around the relationship. They may need help to end a conversation, for example, or to say 'I have done enough, I can't do any more just now'; or 'I will offer this but not that'. They may also need help to recognise the value of their presence for the patient, whether parent or child, particularly during difficult times when it seems that nothing else can be offered. Good supervision can also help a supporter to see more clearly what are their own needs and what are the needs of the people they are helping. It can help to clarify confused thoughts. A supporter, whether professional or not, who can accept help may understand better what it is like for those being helped and may be less likely to behave in a high-handed fashion.

Who should talk with a child?

There are many people who could talk with children about any thoughts or feelings they have about a parent's illness or disability. Children who do not have ill parents might also benefit from such input: they too can have ideas, thoughts or feelings which cause them unnecessary trouble.

Parents?

Sometimes one or both parents are the best people to talk with children about serious issues. Parents often find this kind of conversation very difficult: they are afraid of saying the wrong thing, of making a fool of themselves or humiliating the children, and they are afraid of making things worse. When they do manage to raise serious questions they may be relieved to find how well the child reacted.

Mrs Jones was worried about her teenage son. He was going around the house in a morose way and no longer fooled about with his father. His father had returned a few weeks earlier from hospital after a serious relapse of his MS and was more disabled than before. Eventually Mrs Jones plucked up all her courage and asked her son if he was afraid to play-fight with his father any more. She wondered if he thought he might damage him. Her son scoffed, but his mood changed and he began to whistle around the house once more.

Jennifer was six. She would talk about 'when daddy gets better we'll...' It took a long time before her mother could bring herself to say to Jennifer 'Daddy isn't going to get better, you know.' Jennifer was quiet, and later she and her mother cried together.

Mike got on very well with his teenage daughters. When their mother began to lose her memory as well as her ability to walk he talked with them about it. When they shouted at her and then ran upstairs where she could not follow, he told them to come down and finish the argument, saying that it wasn't fair for them to leave like that when their mother couldn't come after them.

However, parents are not always the best people to talk with children about serious issues.

Some find they cannot talk to their children about the most important issues. They may not be able to bring themselves to show their feelings to their children, and feel that their own grief is only permissible in the utmost secrecy. Others talk to their children about their own feelings, but cannot bear to allow the children to say anything which does not fit in with the parent's ideas. Yet others may respond to their own losses, whether of their own health or their partner's, by manic activity which attempts to blot out all thought and feelings of loss. They may tell their children to do things 'to take their mind off their troubles', but be quite unable to listen to them.

It is not only parents who may prevent discussion between themselves and their children. Many adolescents, as well as some younger children, do not want to talk to their parents about their most painful and private thoughts. Adolescence is a time when children are separating themselves from their parents and they may fear being pulled back into a more childlike role. They may have other sources of support outside the family and prefer to turn to them.

Children of any age may have many reasons to resist telling their parents their thoughts or hearing what their parents have to say. They may, for example, be trying to protect their parents from their painful thoughts or may be punishing their parents for their parents' withdrawal by withdrawing themselves.

Sometimes it is both possible and valuable for parents, in the face of an initial reluctance, to push a child into talking, and perhaps crying, about a very disturbing situation. Sometimes parents cannot do this or do not feel it is right to try.

Other relatives or close adult friends?

Adults who can be trusted by the children to care about both their and their parents' wellbeing may be better able to talk with them than their own parents can. Close relatives or adult friends may be asked by parents to make themselves available or may be enlisted as confidantes by a child. Where parents are separated, step-parents may in some circumstances be able and willing to make themselves available to the child. Grandparents are often in a good position to help. They may be seen by children as allies against the parents; this may even be encouraged by the family as long as it does not overstep certain boundaries. Many teenagers and children, distressed or otherwise, find some kind of second home or supportive relationship with the parents of friends.

Teachers, school nurses or school counsellors?

Teachers may be able to talk with children in their classes on a one-to-one basis, or they may be able to work with the relevant issues differently. Teachers are often anxious about talking with children about emotional issues, but schools may have specially trained staff whose job it is to help children with emotional difficulties. A school counsellor or school nurse may be of help, either to a concerned teacher or directly to the child. The role of the school in general is discussed in Chapter 10.

Schoolfriends?

Schoolfriends sometimes play an important part in helping children to cope with their parents or their parents' difficulties, but adults may assume that children are getting more help from friends than they are. In our experience, children generally seem to have hidden their difficulties and worries from each other.

In addition, if a child feels unloved, unworthy or not good enough at home they may carry this into school: this may make it hard for them to find or keep close friends. In the short term friendships may survive rejections.

Megan said that when her mother was in hospital she hid in the cloakroom and pushed all her friends away: 'I told them to go away and leave me alone'. Later, she made it up with them.

In late adolescence young people who already have good relationships with others may be able to turn to friends for help and support, though they may find that their friends' patience is not inexhaustible. Sexual relationships also intertwine with confidences exchanged, which may comfort for a while, but may also add to the complications of a teenager's situation.

A further difficulty is that friends may not understand the anger, resentment, even hatred, which a teenager may feel towards a sick or newly disabled parent. They may simply be repelled by attitudes that do not fit with their ideas of right and wrong. The teenager may sense this and find themselves feeling increasingly distant and out of touch with others as he or she has to hide so much of his or her real feelings.

Relationships between younger teenagers with difficulties at home may be of the kind in which troubles are denied and temporarily left behind rather than in which confidences are safely exchanged. Groups of children who bunk off school together may support each other in despairing, negative beliefs about adult society, and bolster self-destructive or damaging behaviour by sharing the guilt while denying that it matters. They may provide temporary comfort by enabling the child to feel less alone.

Friends also provide access to other adults, such as club leaders or their own parents.

General Practitioners?

The potential for General Practitioners to help families is considerable. They may be able to offer time to listen: they may be able to drop in on a regular basis to check up and see if any help or emotional support is needed. They may take note of a 'carer' partner's state of health and feelings as well as an ill partner's.

In our experience GPs faced with a patient who has a long-term, chronic illness seldom take the initiative to enquire if help is needed with the children (or in any other way), but if they are asked openly by a patient, will often do their best. Some will take time to give information to children as well as to adults at the time of a diagnosis or accident. Some can even pick up physical complaints in children or carers as perhaps reflecting an emotional difficulty, without making the parents feel blamed and guilty. Some can listen without judging and without making the patient or their relatives feel they are wasting their time. Some are prepared to suffer the feelings of hopelessness and frustration with the family and do not leave as soon as they think there is 'nothing more they can do'.

There are also GPs who will search for useful information for a patient who is newly disabled or ill, and will take time and trouble to arrange services for them. This kind of GP may be the kind of person to whom a child can talk, or with whom a parent can discuss the needs of their children without fearing the consequences. A good doctor will be aware of some of the interactions within the family of a patient and may be very happy to be asked for time to discuss this.

Unfortunately, in our experience, such a relationship with a doctor is the exception rather than the rule. Doctors may add to families' distress by failing to give information, by refusing to discuss death or drugs or other anxieties, or by making it clear they have no time. Patients may have learnt to expect no better; very few complain even when the grievance is clear.

Some doctors do know how to 'be there' to provide basic emotional support for people grieving for a loss or in any other traumatic or difficult situation, but find reasons and excuses for putting off a visit. Sometimes barriers of class, religion or race may divide patient and doctor and increase the difficulties of communication.

Professional counsellors or psychotherapists?

There are some issues that are best discussed with someone who is specially trained and who can listen and help in thinking without the child or adult having to worry about the effect of their thoughts on the listener.

Some of the anxieties children have may seem too frightening, guilty or dangerous to be exposed in a social situation of any kind. They dare not risk their worst thoughts with anyone who has any other role in their life. An adult uncovering these thoughts may not be able to see quite why they had such power for the child; why the child found them so frightening; and once they are spoken, the child too may find them no longer disturbing. Until they are spoken, however, the child may feel they are so bad that no-one could hear them without condemning the child for ever.

There are difficulties in making the decision to take a child to a professional counsellor or psychotherapist. It requires an acknowledgement that the adults around need help. It may require some kind of an acknowledgement that there is 'a problem'. Some parents feel their condition is their own fault and they cannot bear to know the terrible damage they fear they have inflicted on their children by becoming ill or disabled.

It may be difficult to find someone whom the parents feel they can trust. This is easier if the counsellor is part of the GP practice or of a clinic which specialises in the parent's condition, and if seeing the counsellor occasionally for a 'check-up' is seen as a normal part of consulting the doctor. Some self-help organisations (see list of resources) provide counsellors who have specialist knowledge of a particular condition and who are prepared to see family members as well as the person themselves.

Older children may be able to take themselves to professional counsellors; there may be a local organisation which offers counselling for teenagers or young people free or relatively cheaply. The British Association for Counselling can advise on this. Such an organisation may also be able to help parents who need to think about talking with their teenage children.

Some adolescents may find it a relief if an adult takes the decision to send them for a consultation to see if they need help. Parents may insist that the child attend for a certain number of sessions before deciding whether or not to continue. In the long term adolescents, like adults, have to have some awareness of their need and desire for this kind of help if it is going to be any use but parents' insistence can be important in helping them make an informed decision. Even one or two sessions may be useful.

Younger children are more dependent on their parents' deciding to take or send them. Child guidance clinics or a Family Welfare Association or other organisation may provide a local service for children and parents when there is a recognisable problem. They may be prepared to help parents talk to children about a serious illness or a bereavement in the hope of preventing problems from becoming evident later. Social workers may be able to advise on the availability of such organisations locally; school headteachers may be in a position to advise on the basis of other parents' experience.

In some areas it is very difficult indeed to find anyone locally who can help. In this case, the telephone is a possible source of help (see Useful Addresses). Parents who are worried about their children may find that, if they can, it is worth travelling a long way for one session with a specialist who will discuss the problem with them. Children of any age can also benefit from just one session with a counsellor who is interested in them and will keep their anxieties confidential.

Cultural issues

When trying to help children from another family and another culture there may be many misunderstandings. Adults' assumptions about how children from their own cultural background see their parent's illnesses are in our experience generally very wide of the mark. When this ignorance is compounded by their assumptions about a child's racial, religious or class background, the chances of them guessing what may be troubling the child may be even more slim.

Even the process of talking to a child may have complications. A male teacher who wants to help a teenage girl pupil needs to think very carefully if the girl is from some cultural group where men are not supposed to talk to girls. Within the school itself some of the cultural rules may be relaxed; if he wanted to visit the girl's home or speak to her outside the gates she might be extremely embarrassed. The girl's reputation and her marriage chances might be quite seriously compromised if anyone saw her with him. It can be difficult for a man from a more liberal cultural group to grasp the reality of this, and he may try to dismiss it. However, if he assumes it is the case for everyone of the girl's culture, but this particular girl is actually from a slightly different social group, where they look down on families who segregate the sexes in this way, the girl might be offended at the implications and at what she sees as his ignorance.

We have also met more than one child whose parents did not react at all in the way other people assumed they would. These children were from cultural backgrounds which seemed much like their teachers' but in fact were not. Teachers, doctors or anyone else may assume that parents are loving and caring and that they want the best for their children, but children who are unconvinced may be right. Sometimes children want to hide things from their parents for good reason. Even letting parents know that a child has told anyone outside the family about a disability or illness within it may cause difficulties for the child which the outsider cannot begin to imagine.

It is enormously important to acknowledge our own ignorance when we try to understand how someone else, child or adult, sees the world.

Summary

In this chapter we have looked at questions about who can or should offer help to a child or family with an ill or disabled parent. Clearly each family and each individual will have his or her own opinions about these matters. Sometimes help, affection or support will be offered and taken, to the satisfaction of all concerned. Sometimes offers will be refused. Sometimes a child or family seeking help will not find what they need when they need it.

CHAPTER 9

What Can Parents Do?

In this chapter we look at ways parents can help their children. It is important that professionals are aware of the vital role parents play in their children's lives if they are to be able to support and encourage parents to think about their children and their own role in the family. In addition, any direct help professionals offer will be powerfully affected by their attitude towards the children's parents and the parents attitude towards them.

Recognising the importance of parents

Parents know they provide for their children in many practical ways: they may be less aware of the more subtle ways in which they contribute hugely to their children's lives. Particularly if the practical things become problematical, some parents see themselves as unable to provide their children with anything else worth having. Others are very aware of their importance to their children, whether they are healthy or unhealthy, different from others in some way, or consider themselves 'normal'.

Most people, if forced to think about it, know that fathers provide role models to children of both sexes. The father's personality and behaviour influences the kind of man a girl will ultimately marry, if any, and the kind of man a boy will become. Fathers (whether they are present or absent) can influence children's emotional, sexual and social development in many ways. We think that fathers often influence the kind of worker a girl will become.

Equally, few people would question the importance of the mother. She gives meaning to the children's lives, affects their sense of security and value, and influences her children's later choice of partner. Mothers affect the behaviour and feelings of both girls and boys in many obvious and more subtle ways. (Freud pointed out that we repeat with our husbands and wives the quarrels we had with our mothers.)

However, when parents are ill they may forget how important they are to children.

> A mother with inoperable cancer said she did not mind dying because it would end the extreme pain. She thought her children, aged eight and ten, were quite old enough to manage without her. Her own father had died when she was five.

> A woman who had been severely injured in an accident came out of hospital disabled and in pain, and thinking she would never be able to do anything for her children again. She felt she was completely useless to them and to everyone else; she was only a burden and they would be better off without her.

In such circumstances parents may need to be reminded of their importance to their children and of the importance to the child's future of their relationship with both their parents.

Other people may also disregard the importance of a mother for her child. Advocates of boarding school education may believe that it is better for children to be separated from their mothers for their own good from a certain age. Some grandmothers believe they can mother the children better than the mother can. A young social worker once told me his teenage client's mother could do 'nothing' when she in fact did everything except drive the car.

> A doctor was pressurising a mother to go into hospital for tests in spite of the fact that she was breast-feeding one baby and had a toddler. Only when firmly challenged did he admit that the tests were not urgent and could wait until the children were older.

Many parents, particularly mothers, who have been forced to leave their children for stays in hospital worry about the long-term as well as short-term effect on them. However, there are things parents can do to help their children both at the time and afterwards. Some of these suggestions may prevent children having disturbing reactions many months later, though they may also be used if children have not had this kind of help immediately but eventually show signs of being troubled.

If a parent is rushed into hospital children may not show outward signs of being very affected for some time. Particularly young children may only show slight signs, which can easily be overlooked. They may simply appear more tense than before; they may cry or have tantrums over trivial events; they may revert to more 'babyish' behaviour but they may never say 'I am missing mum (or dad)'. They may show they are seeking the lost parent, perhaps looking hopefully at every stranger's face, or at every new person who comes to the door; but the adults around may not notice this. They may try to attach themselves to someone around, particularly if that person shows any interest in them.

If left too long without anyone to attach themselves to they may give up seeking human contact. A very young child may sit rocking rhythmically or sucking, withdrawn and apparently uninterested in what is going on, perhaps causing no trouble. A child who withdraws like this is likely to need psychotherapeutic help either at the time or later; a child who protests, cries, and continues to seek contact is more likely to recover when the parent returns or a long-term substitute is found.

Keeping contact with parents who are in hospital, even if they are unconscious, is important for children. The children may be distressed, but they need to be allowed to be distressed. The adult who takes care of them will need to allow them to behave badly (within limits) after a disturbing visit, for example, and to talk about what they saw and what they felt. Their bad behaviour may be an important part of working with their feelings about an upsetting situation. Children who are simply quiet, show little sign of upset and continue to behave well in such circumstances may react later, or may later need professional help. What they are thinking may be quite unrealistic; they may have frozen all feelings.

Protecting children from their parents (and vice versa) creates a barrier between them and may add to the real difficulties of the illness or disability. Sometimes, however, children really have to be kept from one or both parents. The length of time involved may be crucial. Young children will be affected by a separation of a few days: older children may be better able to bear a longer parting without losing all sense of the goodness of their parents and themselves. Telephone contact may be possible if a parent really cannot be visited: this can help even young children who may be afraid their parent has gone for ever or that the adults are lying about the situation. William was afraid his father had died in hospital and no-one had told him; a daily telephone call would have reassured him enormously.

If a parent was involved in some traumatic disaster involving other people, their children may gain support from contact with others who were involved themselves or whose parents were involved. They may feel these people understand in a way others cannot, and gain considerable relief from knowing that they share some of the horrifying experiences and feelings.

Parents who behave badly

A mother may find it very hard to acknowledge her children's need for their father when the father is not only ill or recently disabled, but is also behaving in a very angry and abusive way. A father may have a similar problem with a wife who is reacting badly to illness or disability.

> Marie told how her husband had withdrawn from contact with the family since he had lost the use of his legs and just kept saying he wanted to die. Every now and then he would come out of his room, when he would shout and threaten them all. He threatened his wife with his stick saying 'I'll break your legs then you'll know how it is!' Marie wondered whether she should separate from her husband for the sake of the children.

There is a great temptation in such circumstances to get rid of the troublesome parent in the hope of restoring some peace and normality to the household. The social and emotional pressures to stand by disabled or ill parents, to excuse their bad behaviour or simply to put up with it for fear of what others would say are, however, considerable. Abusive behaviour is much less visible than an illness and a suffering wife may find it very hard to tell people, including the children, why she wants her husband out of the house, particularly if she has been able to cope in silence with his abuse before the illness aggravated the situation.

> As long as Mrs Bull was out at work during the day she could put up with her husband's abuse when she got home in the evening. Their child went to a nanny, paid for by her work. She then became ill and lost her job. Her husband's behaviour became even worse and she thought about leaving him.

Unfortunately, even fathers who behave badly at times are important for their children. Sometimes separation does seem the only alternative to parents, but it may add to the children's difficulties. Parents' and children's needs may conflict.

> Marion said that her father left when she was nine because he could not cope with her mother's illness and increasing disability; she was left to look after her mother alone.

Marion needed help to understand what her parents had done to each other and to her, and to come to terms with the effects of their actions upon her.

Being There

As we said in Chapter 1, sometimes parents who become disabled talk with enormous regret about being unable to do the things with their children that their parents did with them. Sometimes they arrange for their children to be given the opportunity to do those things with someone else. What seems to be important is to recognise that it is the *relationship* the child wants and needs, not necessarily the *activity*.

Peter (in Chapter 2) argued with his mother in a counselling session about whether he minded that his father could not play football. His mother said Peter had played with a friend's father, and Peter said no, the other boy's father had said he was too old to play, 'just give me a header'. He insisted that he did not mind that his father could not play.

> He said he was sad, however, that he could no longer make his father laugh: he said 'Even if I told him one of my best jokes now he wouldn't laugh'. He sometimes played snakes and ladders with his father but he now found that boring because he had to make all the moves: it was like playing by himself.

It seemed that what Peter wanted from his father was not the games of football which both his parents thought he wanted. He wanted to be noticed and valued and loved and appreciated by his father; a friend's father could not provide that. Acknowledging Peter's sadness at what he had lost in his father would make it easier for him to enjoy the opportunities he had with his friend's father without feeling these were supposed to make up for his loss.

There are many other aspects of parent's existence that children need and value. To children, parents, however ill, may hold their world together, providing an important 'home base' to venture out from and to return to; giving meaning to the child's life. C S Lewis's story *The Magician's Nephew* revolves around a child seeking a magic apple to restore his mother to health. All his adventures, which include witnessing the creation of a new world, are motivated by this search. Another adult may find it takes a long time to restore this sense of life having a meaning for a child, and it may not be possible. In adult life a partner may provide it, but the child who loses a parent's affection is likely to retain a yearning for it throughout its life.

Parents who are ill often seem to overlook the importance to their children of their presence. A parent's sick room can be a place of quiet in a noisy household even if the parent cannot offer attention, speech or thought. The fact that the ill or disabled parent belongs to the child and to the other parent too is important: he or she may seem to hold the family together. This parent's reaction to the child and to other members of the family will be noticed and will matter to the child, even if it is never discussed. How ill or disabled parents express or conceal anger with children, with themselves and the rest of the family, their impatience and their irritation are also important, as with any parent. In interaction with parents the children learn how to behave, including how to argue, to be angry and forceful or whining and complaining themselves. Parents also give children a sense of reality by their own awareness of it.

The authority and the responsibility parents hold for their children are also important even if they actually do little and their role is mainly symbolic. Children endow their parents with far more power and authority than they actually have, whether they are ill or healthy. Parents set and maintain boundaries in many important ways. The fact of a father's presence in the house may keep mother and child apart at times but this may be beneficial in preventing them 'suffocating' each other or merging. An adult who says 'no' about anything, or whose presence in the parental bed means the child cannot sleep there, for example, may be very important for a child's sense of security.

The child's feelings towards the parents are also very important to the child, and do not depend simply on what the parents do or say. Parents represent and 'hold' certain aspects of the child, providing a kind of testing ground where the child's beliefs and fantasies about adulthood are tested out. Parents who are unable to look after themselves, and are looked after by their family may provide a powerful lesson for children about the helpless and dependent part of themselves as well as of the parent.

Parents who fight for their lives, who stand up for their rights, who insist on being heard all give messages to their children about the strong, powerful aspects of living. Parents who keep together may help the child to integrate aspects of their own personality; those who separate may reinforce children's fears about the destructiveness of their own behaviour or feelings.

Parents with severe disabilities or illnesses provide important models for their children, just as any other parent does. Their behaviour as parents and partners, their concern and respect for themselves and for others (or their lack of it), their demands, their expectations and their authority, as well as their discipline and play, will all influence their children's assumptions about themselves and other people in the world.

Sharing grief

Parents who have been disabled or ill in a constant way for a long time may be more aware of their importance to the child 'as they are', rather than 'as they would have been'; on the other hand, they may not. When parents and children can acknowledge some of their feelings about such an illness or disability and grieve together each can feel supported and relieved. However, any such sharing must be carefully tailored to the children's needs: the adult's needs must be taken care of elsewhere. The adult has to be in control of such discussions: making children confidantes gives them too much burdensome responsibility. If a child is to be told of their parent's sadness or anger they need also to know that they are not expected to make everything better but that they can have their own feelings. Even when the parents' feelings are bad, children often know of them; speaking about them may make the knowledge easier. The adult needs to recognise the good and hopeful feelings as well, even if buried, and discuss these with the children at the same time.

We look further at sharing grief with children in Chapter 11, under the heading 'Upsetting the adult' (p.152).

Parents' care

Children are sometimes very surprised to find that anyone cares about them. They may not even realise that their own parents care, particularly if their parents are ill. Sometimes children may feel this because their parents really do not care; in some cases it seems to arise from the child's misunderstandings. Children can interpret a parent's illness as a sign that they have done something terrible; in particular, that they have failed to love and care for the parent enough. If this is an unbearable thought they may reverse the situation as a way of dealing with it; they then feel their parent does not love and care for them enough. Parents may be quite unaware of such feelings: they know that they love the children and they find it difficult to think that the children might not recognise this.

To what extent a parent with a serious illness can show care for their child will depend on many factors. Any affection or love they can show, any form of communication they can develop, in general, is worth far more to children than affection and attention from anyone else. However much another adult offers, the parent's love and affection (or refusal of it) is likely to take precedence in importance for children of any age.

Parents may believe it is part of their role to comfort and listen to their children, but their children may not realise this. They may not realise that their parents can find pleasure in caring for their children in this way. Some of the children we met actively tried to prevent themselves being 'a burden' to their parents, and so deprived both themselves and their parents of a close relationship.

We have described how many children feel either an ill or an apparently healthy parent is not being sufficiently well looked after. This troubles them. Both children and adults may need to be helped to see that even where marital relations are not good, the children, the ill parent and the healthy one are being cared for in ways that may not be recognised. Where there is a real lack of care there may be something that can be done about this, or it may simply have to be acknowledged.

It can be difficult for parents to let their children know they care for them. Parents who are not in the habit of telling their children that they love them may find it awkward to say. They may have always relied on non-verbal messages and the assumption that if they know, then the children know.

Non-verbal communication, while reading a bedtime story, or giving quiet attention when the lights go off at night, may have conveyed parents' love and concern previously. These activities may break down under pressure of illness, and the child be left feeling bereft without being able to justify demanding that they be reinstated.

More poignant is when, because of their illness or disability, parents become unable to show their children their love by, for example, carrying them or hugging them, kissing them goodnight in bed, collecting them from school or running to them when they fall or are in trouble. It may be clear to the parents that they still love the children, but children may interpret the parents' inability to do such things as a loss of desire to do them. If children feel their parents no longer care for them, they may respond by showing their parents they do not care for the parents either.

Some parents seek out new ways of conveying their love non-verbally. Activities that might seem 'babyish' may be appreciated by children who would otherwise have grown out of them. One family insisted on the children always kissing the parent on the cheek when they left the house, as French and Italian families do. In this way physical contact could be maintained throughout the children's growing up, when other opportunities for it were lost.

Play is a very important way in which children communicate with themselves and others, and adults who can play with their children can show their care in this way.

Music is another means of communicating feelings, and teenagers in particular may use music to recreate a sense of being contained and held in a world of their own. Music may touch deep feelings and help a child to work with them, as well as being used at other times to block out difficult feelings. Sharing musical experiences can create strong bonds between adults and children. The words of a song may be used to give a clear and direct message to an adult which the child cannot speak or even acknowledge openly.

Writing and drawing are other ways some children and adults can express and discover feelings and thoughts, particularly in difficult situations. These are activities that can be undertaken together or separately. Children may want to show their work or may want to keep it private, and adults should respect this: the act of getting thoughts or ideas down on paper is valuable in itself.

Children normally communicate with their parents by their behaviour. Affection, concern, indifference, anger, frustration, rebelliousness, hopelessness, despair, attempts to be a good child, fury and anxiety are all generally conveyed by behaviour or actions rather than words. The difficulty with this is that behaviour needs interpreting, and adults and children often interpret each other's actions in ways that would astonish the other.

Parents may be very good at interpreting their children's behaviour and understanding what they mean by it. However, if there is reason to be concerned about a child, it may be a good idea for adults to try to put into words how they understand the message. The child may have meant something quite different.

Talking is the most obvious means for communicating ideas between children and adults. It is the most subtle, allowing for distinctions between past and present, intention and hope, 'if' and 'when'. Feelings can be conveyed in the way something is said as well as in the content. Perhaps because talking can be so revealing, it may be very hard for a child to talk with an adult and for an adult to talk with a child. We look further at communication between adults and children in Chapters 11–13.

As children grow, they normally lose some forms of contact and communication with parents and develop others. Some of these changes may become confused with the parents' illness. Nancy, at the age of ten, for example, said she was very sad because her father could not carry her on his shoulders any longer because of his MS; she had not realised this would now have stopped anyway because she was too big.

Caring and sexuality

Sexually provocative behaviour may be one way in which distressed teenagers or children try to gain adult attention and affection. They may not be conscious of how provocatively they are behaving. Sometimes parents' loving and affectionate feelings may be swamped by a muddle between sexuality and loving or caring, particularly if, as children, they themselves were involved in a sexual relationship with an adult.

Especially where there is an ill parent, older children may revert to or retain ways of behaving more common in younger children, while at other times they may behave as if they were much older than they are. They may want to be cuddled and comforted, for example. For some parents this may be confusing. It may be a particular problem if they are feeling both a lack of comfort themselves and a mixture of angry and resentful feelings towards an ill or changed partner. Their own sexual relationship may have been spoilt by health problems: some people feel this very keenly. They may also be confusing themselves by drinking too much. A small girl may feel it is her duty to 'make daddy happy' and be quite unclear about the ways in which she can and the ways in which she cannot. If the father is also confused and unclear the child is seriously at risk.

If the adult does respond to the child with sexual attentions, however provocative the child's behaviour, the effects on the child are disastrous. There is plenty of literature on the effects of child sexual abuse. The child loses the adult as a parent and protector; as a real source of affection and care. The child loses the safety and security of knowing that an adult is in charge and can stand out against both the child's and the adult's damaging impulses. The guilt and fear of being permanently damaged inside, both of which follow any sexual activity of a 'wrong' kind, may last a lifetime and may lead the child actively to seek damaging relations in later life. Some people who have worked with adults who were sexually abused as children think that it may be even harder for the child in the long term if it did obtain some kind of enjoyment out of the sexual relationship.

Adults involved in sexual activity with young people may not be aware of what is involved. They may be sure that a girl or boy either 'asked for it' or enjoyed it. They may also be convinced that they are 'making the child feel someone loves them'. Children who have already been sexually abused by adults may be especially vulnerable to adult sexual attentions; these children may indeed 'ask for it', partly out of despair of ever having any other kind of relationship. The adult's own guilt feelings may also be reduced by a sense that the child is already damaged. Also particularly at risk are children who are not protected by their parents, for example as a result of a parent's illness or long-term absence.

Stepchildren are another group at risk. Step-parents may have to make a particular effort not to be carried away by sexual feelings towards stepchildren. If the child's own parent allows him- or herself to become aware of the potential attraction and the risk it poses he or she may be able to protect both child and step-parent, and prevent any overstepping of boundaries. However, a professional or friend who tries to draw attention to such a risk may find themselves attacked by deeply offended parents.

The difficulty for professionals of deciding what to do if sexual abuse comes to light is enormous. Both action and inaction involve threat to the child. Separation from either parent is traumatic: if the abusing person is also the carer of an ill or needy parent the issues are extremely fraught. Abused children are sometimes rejected by their mothers and may be scapegoated if their revelation involves the loss of the mother's partner even when the mother is not physically dependent on the partner. Whatever is done or not done by any parties concerned, the central fact of the abuse leaves a trail of wrong in its wake.

Most fathers do not sexually abuse their children, whatever the situation. Many families have the opposite difficulty. Fathers may stop physical contact with their daughters out of fear of their own sexual impulses, and may become quite angrily rejecting and critical for the same reason, without realising it. A father may reject his daughter if he feels he is no longer a sexual man as a result of his health. If his wife is in hospital he may particularly fear his own impulses towards his daughter making mutual comfort an impossibility. The daughter may be very hurt and anxious for her father as well as for herself. However, a certain amount of rejection from her father may be important in encouraging her to find relationships outside the family. Fathers who never push away their teenage or adult daughters may make it harder for them to find a sexual partner.

Sons may reject their mother's closeness for similar reasons. Their own sexuality may disturb them and they may fear it will be noticed by their mother and will trouble her. The only solution for the child may seem to be to withdraw from close contact with the mother. This is normal in the teenage years, and it may leave the mother frustrated because she is unable to comfort or advise her son as she would like. Where it coincides with an illness or changing disability it may be complicated by the mother's vulnerability to feeling rejected. She may interpret the rejection as implying there is something wrong with her, for example, rather than seeing it as part of the normal process of separation between mother and child. The separation process may be hindered by a parent's illness or disability in this way, if the child or the parents are too frightened of upsetting the mother: separations are upsetting and children need to allow their parents to cope with them.

Making the parent better or worse

We have already looked at ways in which children as well as adults find it very difficult to believe that what they do cannot affect the outcome of a parent's illness.

It may be important to watch to see if, for example, children are restricting their own lives or depriving themselves of some pleasure, perhaps even of food, in an attempt to bargain with God or with some other 'higher authority'. Children's accidents, reckless behaviour or giving up on school work may be attempts to punish themselves. If they recognise it, parents may be able to pick up such behaviour and deal with the underlying feelings of guilt.

Guilt that is too strong leads to a sense of being attacked and may produce an attacking response. Parents or children may attack each other out of a sense of enormous guilt; this can increase demands for apologies which cannot be given. The child or adult who attacked originally out of such guilt may be accused even further and may give up in despair. Attempts to *reduce* the guilt felt by family members may enable them to change from attacking to attempts to make things better.

The idea that stress makes illnesses worse is a real problem for those families who tend to define as 'stress' anything they do not like. It is important to recognise that stress is an important and natural part of daily life, and, in particular, of the role of being a parent. Take away stress and the person can no longer be a parent. In some families it seems that fear of stress has led to the ill parent choosing to withdraw entirely from family life and giving up every role except 'patient'. (Other ill parents withdraw for other reasons, over which they may have no control.) The stress caused not only to the children but also to the other parent is then considerable. This can also rebound on the patient. It is not enough to tell children that stress will not harm their parents: parents have to recognise this themselves and behave in ways that make it clear.

Some of the feeling that the task of caring for an ill parent is impossible may be modified if the adults give children a task that is not impossible, and recognise their contribution in doing it. For this reason, it is probably good for children to be allowed and encouraged to help in ways appropriate to their age. Making a real contribution to the household economy may give them a sense of relief even if they complain about it.

Children may be doing something to try to prevent themselves from getting the condition that their parent has, and parents can also watch for this. Peter, at six, swung his legs constantly; he may have been trying to keep his legs from becoming paralysed like his father's. Avoiding contact, emotional or physical, with the affected parent may be another way a child may attempt to keep the illness or disability at bay: if parents can notice this they may be able to discuss it.

Child carers

Some children are left to look after a very disabled parent single-handedly. It seems that social workers or district nurses (and sometimes parents, themselves) may expect children to do all kinds of tasks for their parents, particularly at weekends, when other services are not provided. Children may go along with this, becoming very responsible, mutely assuming that this is how it should be or must be and scared of being separated from the parent they love and whose presence makes sense of their lives. They are not, however, given the money or information that adults in the same situation would be given, and they do not have the inner strength of an adult who has been well mothered.

In terms of social provision, these children are nobody's responsibility except their parents'. They need the support of adults who recognise what is going on, who care for them and make it clear that they do. Their parents may be able to provide much of the support they need, but single parents in particular themselves need support, and their children feel this keenly.

Much of what these children need may not be available. There may be little alternative for them but to spend their childhood caring for their parents. They may simply have to live with the difficulties and conflicts the situation produces both in the short term and in the long term. As adults they have to cope with the results of this as best they can, seeking help where they can obtain it.

It may only be as adults that they become aware of feelings such as fury, betrayal, resentment and guilt, which these situations provoke. Recognising the origin of these feelings in a situation they could not control may be very important for such children. A powerful sense of responsibility, a knowledge of the workings of the health service and a conviction of the importance of others over themselves may also be developed in such children. They may become professional carers themselves, attempting to care for others as they were not cared for themselves. These strengths can be used to enhance their own lives, but they may need to learn how to allow themselves to be looked after and cared for by another person. They may find it difficult to imagine that they are worth caring for themselves if they are not ill. Some of this learning can take place while they are still children if people outside the family can help.

Conclusion

In this chapter we have looked at the importance of parents to their children. Parents who are ill may depend on their children for practical and emotional support to the extent that they may imagine that they can give the children nothing, and the children believe this too. In fact, whether their parents are ill or healthy, children depend on them to give meaning to their existence. Parents also teach children the difference between reality and fantasy, and enable them to establish a sense of worth and the ability to love and to trust others. In the following chapters we look further at ways parents and others can help children.

CHAPTER 10

Helping and Being Helped
by Other People

A woman of thirty-eight whose husband earned a good salary, depended for help with the children on a girl who had been eighteen when she came and was now twenty-two. This girl lived with the family during the week and went home at weekends. It seemed that the arrangement was extremely satisfactory for everyone concerned. The girl came from a rather neglectful family and depended on the older woman for motherly concern and support. She was happy to do as she was asked and grateful for the affection she was given.

A new mother, aged twenty-eight, with a disabling illness had a series of people sent by social services to help her while her baby was small. She wanted them to help her with the housework and leave her to use her limited energy to look after the baby. The helpers always seemed to prefer looking after the child. The mother was very unsure of herself and found it intolerable when her son preferred the company of the helpers to being with his mother. She felt trapped and resentful of the helpers' lack of understanding.

Claire was twenty-five and had MS, which made her very tired. She lived round the corner from her mother-in-law and went to her home every day for company and because she could not manage on her own with a small baby. She said her mother-in-law would take her son and change him, feed him, or give him toys, completely ignoring her, even when she knew Claire did not want him to have certain things. Claire found it very difficult to tell her mother-in-law how she felt. She needed her and could not afford to have a serious fight with her. She was afraid that any criticism would lead to terrible trouble, not only between her and her mother-in-law but also between her and her husband. She felt she could

128

not find alternative sources of support because 'who would be prepared to help me like she does?' Friends could not be expected to look after her in the same way.

Sharing children

Sharing children with other people is something parents may have to face as a result of an illness or disability. Parents have to cope with their own feelings about this and also to help their children to handle it. It may not be easy for the child-minders themselves. Here we consider all three points of view.

Some families in normal circumstances are fairly self-sufficient. Others find child-care arrangements convenient and/or good for the children. If a parent becomes ill, normal child-care arrangements may become stretched or parents may feel forced into making arrangements they would not choose. They may have to allow someone else to take over their child for a time while they look after themselves elsewhere (resting or attending hospital for example). To the carer this may seem much the same as looking after a child while the mother is working; to an ill mother and to the child it may be very different.

In other circumstances an ill or disabled mother may be forced to allow someone else to be present or to help while she looks after her child. Looking after a child in company can be a lot more fun than looking after a child alone; all mothers identify with their children and can feel overwhelmed by this and in need of support from an adult. However, an ill mother may not experience or recognise the benefits of this relationship if her maternal rights and wishes are not fully respected by the other person or if she believes that the 'right' way to bring up a child is 'mother alone'. It can be difficult handling the relationships in these situations, whether the third person is a close relative (including the mother's mother or husband) or a stranger.

Children may have their own reasons to dislike being cared for by someone else, with or without their mother, or they may find it difficult if their parents are not happy with the arrangement. Both parents and children may also find unexpected benefits and pleasure in the arrangements. Relationships with people other than their parents can be good for children. Any parent, however healthy, may suddenly be called away and be forced to leave the children for a while: if there is already someone else who knows them well and loves them, they will be safer. If the minder has a child of their own the children will also be able to get to know other children.

Leaving a child for a while

If the children have some continuity – for example, by being looked after in their own home – they will feel less disrupted than if they have to go to a strange place. This may not be possible, and for long-term arrangements it may be better if the children are in the place where the person looking after them feels most comfortable.

Children will be strongly affected by any person who looks after them during the temporary loss of a parent or as a long-term arrangement. Particularly young children need to develop an attachment to the person, and parents need to be sure they can encourage an attachment. If relatives are available and suitable, they have the advantage of providing long-term follow-up relationships. A father may well be the best person to take over the care of the child if the mother is ill for a while: sick-leave may be arranged for this purpose, though the father may have to cope with colleagues' envious and unhelpful attitudes (as working mothers often do). Neighbours may offer considerable help to a father in this position.

It can be very difficult to agree with someone else, whoever it is, how a child should be looked after. This is particularly difficult if two people are present at once: it may help to decide how responsibility is shared and to make this clear to the children. 'I'm "on" now, leave mum alone, I'll get your drink'; or 'No, Susan's going to bath you today, I need a rest, you can come and cuddle me afterwards...' Disagreements may be inevitable, but mutual support and clear lines of authority make a big difference. Some people can manage this: others find they work best if they look after a child separately. Children will have their own feelings about this and may force adults to make adjustments to the arrangements.

Children can learn to behave in different ways (even to speak different languages) with different adults. They do not become confused if each person has their own rules and behaviour and keeps to them. It is better for the children if parents can accept that the other person will have their own ways of doing things, which the children will get to know. Unless the other person is doing something that seems very wrong it is probably better for a parent to allow that person to make their own decisions, particularly if the other person is the other parent. It can help children if adults are explicit and matter of fact about the differences between themselves: 'You can do that with Susan/your mum, but with me you do this', for example. 'Susan/your mum gives you sweets but I don't.' No explanation is needed except that different people do different things.

Where there are strong differences of opinion, a carer is unlikely to obey a parent in their absence; and parents need to take seriously any anxieties they have about the behaviour of someone who cares for their child. Discussing these worries with someone else may help sort out whether they require action or not. Similarly, carers who worry about the behaviour of parents towards a child need to take this seriously.

Mothers are often afraid that the child will forget them and love only the minder or carer. In fact, love works the other way. Love given by and to a mother-substitute keeps the mother alive in the child's deepest memory. A child who develops a loving relationship with another woman will carry over love and affection into the relationship with the mother when she returns, whether at the end of the day or after a period of time. Love received from a mother-substitute or given to her increases the love available from the child for the mother; it does not take it from the mother or supplant her love.

This carry-over is illustrated by the fact that sometimes children call their teacher 'mum' or their mother 'miss'; when they have two caretakers they may use the wrong name for them. If they know the two like and respect each other this makes it easier for them; they do not have to think carefully each time they speak and make sure they are not causing trouble by using the wrong name. In addition, if both parent and carer can reinforce the child's affection for the other, both relationships will benefit, as well as the relationship between the parent and the carer.

Similarly, children transfer feelings such as anger and rejection backwards and forwards between their parents and other people who in some way stand for them in the child's mind. Anger caused by one parent may find an outlet in a relationship with the other parent or with a child-minder, home help or grandparent, for example.

Children sometimes say painful things comparing one mother-figure with another. 'I like Susan better than you', or 'gran cooks better than you do' may be a child's attempt to hurt its mother; it may also be an attempt for the child to see if Susan or gran and mother will turn against each other and if the child can divide and rule. The child may also be trying to deal with their own jealousy of the relationship between Susan and its mother. It may be hard for the mother (or Susan) to bear the child's jealousy without hitting back; comfort from another adult may help.

Children whose parents are disabled or ill may be trying to find ways of expressing their feelings about the disability or illness when they talk to or about a mother-substitute or mother's help.

> When Jody at three was ill, she pushed her mother away and said she wanted her nan: 'She can carry me and you can't'. Her mother felt very angry and hurt. She found it too painful to talk with Jody about her inability to walk, and like Jody she sometimes expressed her own anger and hurt by pushing people away.

> Later, when Jody was five, her mother was more able to talk about these feelings with Jody and to allow Jody to have a good relationship with her nan.

This kind of situation can be very painful indeed, especially if the mother has no previous experience to tell her she is a good mother.

Competitiveness between parent and care-giver may cause trouble. If each indulges the child in order not to become a 'baddy' the child may lose any sense of being firmly held and cared for and become quite frightened of their own power. This can make them feel insecure.

Where the responsible adults are against each other the child may find it difficult to hold a picture of him- or herself as one person rather than several contradictory personalities. Parents who try to set their children against a substitute parent for any reason are likely to be causing trouble both for themselves and for the children. Yet the temptation to do this may be very strong. Parents who feel bitterly deprived by some illness or disability may find it very difficult indeed to be supportive of their children's attachment to a substitute, particularly if that person is the new wife of the children's father, for example. All the things that person did which the parent would not have done or could not have done may be a source of real distress and anger. Support from another adult may be essential if the child is not to bear the brunt of these feelings: such pain cannot be borne alone without spilling out in unwanted places. The child too may be helped by talking about the situation with someone else who is not directly involved.

Parents may also need to resist the temptation to change the people who are caring for their children in order to prevent such carers becoming rivals for the children's affection. The danger is that the child will eventually become unmanageable for the parent too as they try to cope with the legacy of an unmanageable number of care-givers. Children faced with too many changes find it difficult to develop a sense of being one person themselves and may feel fragmented and lost. They may stop trying to make attachments to any other adult; this will disturb their relations with people in general, including the parent.

Parents often feel guilty, either for wanting their children to be taken care of elsewhere or for being unable to supply everything they need. There is no reason why parents should think they can or should provide everything for their children: children are sent to school or to the doctor or even to the shops to provide things parents cannot provide. Some parents have difficulty recognising that the children's other parent might be able to give the children something of their own, different from the things they offer themselves but valuable to the children.

WHILE THE PARENT IS AWAY...

Whoever looks after children while the parent is away will have to help them to bear the fact that their parent is missing for the time being. Trying to forget or ignore the absence can make the children feel very lonely and disoriented. Children need to be encouraged to talk about the missing parent, whatever the reason he or she are missing and even if the children only have a few words.

The name they use for their missing parent will be one of those words, and can be used. A young child may be comforted by making a song using the name for the parent; a piece of the parent's clothing may help, as well as a picture, perhaps, or a toy that the mother gave the child.

Adults standing in for an ill or absent parent need to be able to bear the fact that they cannot make up to the child for the loss of the parent. They can help the child more if they encourage the child to let them know its sad or angry feelings about this, rather than simply rejecting or being angry with a child because it wants someone who is not there.

> At the age of thirty-eight Susie remembered how as a child she travelled from one set of parents to the other at weekends, and how she could never tell either that she missed the other, for fear of upsetting them.

Carers also need to be very careful always to speak well and respectfully of the child's parents, whatever their private opinion. Finding those aspects of the parents that they do like and approve is obviously better than pretence: children see through pretences.

Children who have lost one or both parents and have suffered more than one change of carer may provoke trouble. They may try to get themselves thrown out by a carer. Firm control which repeatedly assures them that they will not be abandoned again may be necessary, but it may be difficult to ensure that the situation of loss is not repeated.

> One family made a joke of their foster-child's constant attempts to get himself thrown out. They would laugh, saying 'you're trying to get us to throw you out aren't you...' as well as discussing it seriously, and acknowledging that there were things he could do which *would* force them to throw him out; though they hoped he wouldn't. He would constantly challenge them, saying 'You're asking me to leave aren't you?' whenever they opposed him. Gradually this too became a joke.

The more losses of parent-figures or parent-substitutes children have, the harder it may be for them to believe that they are lovable. They may try hard to destroy any goodness or loving they see around them in order to get rid of the pain of knowing they do not have it themselves.

RETURNING HOME

People who look after a child while the parent is in hospital also have to be able to cope with returning the child to its parents afterwards. Saying goodbye and allowing a child of any age to 'cling' for a while can be important. The child should be allowed to say that they do not want to go home, and even to express anger with their parents if this is what they feel. It can help to let them know that whatever they feel is only one part of their feelings, that when they are back they will feel differently, and that they can come and visit, though this may not immediately comfort them. Excessive fears and exaggerated hopes about returning home may be picked up. Talking about bad feelings towards parents, if handled with respect for the parents and acknowledgement of the child's underlying love, can enable children to behave better and make them less likely to express their feelings in bad behaviour. Sometimes children temporarily turn against parent-substitutes as a way of trying to deny the pain of losing them.

When the parent returns the child should not be expected immediately to give up their relationship with the person who looked after them in the parent's absence. The children need to go back and visit; recognising that they have not been forgotten by the person who cared for them can be comforting. It may help them not to lose the sense of themselves that they developed in the parent's absence and that they need to integrate with their 'old' and 'new' self. The care-giver may need to offer comfort and 'mothering' to the mother at this time as well as welcoming the children back. Acknowledgement that the mother may have felt less well cared-for than her children during the time of separation may prevent her from making the children suffer for it. Gratitude perhaps should not be expected: if it is there, it is a bonus.

Children who have stayed some time with a substitute parent sometimes seem to react more badly to leaving this person than they did to leaving their own home or to the parting from their own parent. Our understanding of this is that the reaction to the second parting is made more painful by feelings belonging to the first but suppressed then. We think too that children may feel safer to express such feelings with their own parents there than they were with the substitute. They may also be making the parent feel the hurt they felt when the parent left them. Parents may misunderstand this reaction and be very upset, feeling that their children do not want them any more and prefer the substitute.

Even if the parent left a child only with the other parent, he or she may find themselves jealous and angry at the new relationship which has built up during their absence. For the returning parent the longing to take up where they left off may be very painful; it is enormously difficult to recognise that some aspect of the child's development has happened in the parent's absence and that this cannot be wholly retrieved, though the child may want and be able to take some 'babying'. Particularly with a baby or small child it may be important to ensure that they do not entirely lose the relationship they have built up with the other parent while one was away. However painful, it may be necessary for the father, say, to continue putting the child to bed for a while at least, even if the mother used to do it and wants to take up again where she left off. Children may make it clear that they want one parent rather than the other at certain times, and it may be important to respect this if the children are not to feel abandoned once again.

The hopes that the whole family had for the return may easily turn into disappointment and perhaps anger; young children in particular may say that it was better without the returning parent and he or she should leave again. Older children may keep such wishes to themselves and feel terribly guilty about them. Both parents may also think how much simpler it was being apart. If such guilty thoughts can be shared, or even better, discussed beforehand as thoughts which are to be expected, it may be enormously reassuring. Some families can joke about such ideas; others cannot.

With a return from hospital there is likely to be a hope that everything will be exactly as it was before. And yet it cannot be. The family will be forced to face realities they could ignore while the parent was away. Everyone will have changed and everyone is likely to feel they have been left out.

Giving support to parents

One way in which other people, professional or not, may be able to help a child is by offering support to the parents. Both practical and emotional help may make the difference between a parent being nursed at home and being left in hospital, for example. A parent caring for an ill partner and well supported by other adults may also find it much easier to facilitate good contact between the children and their ill parent.

Sometimes home helps can become an important source of mothering for the mother, enabling her to mother her own children better. Home helps may be seen as a support or a threat, critical or friendly, sometimes because they stand for a mother-figure and are not simply seen as themselves. They may also have strong feelings or opinions about the way the mother relates to her children and this can cause friction. A mother who is ill, newly disabled or unsure of herself for any reason may need assistance either *from* the home help or *against* the home help, to establish her own position as a mother.

It may be important not only to support one or both parents but also to bring this to the children's attention. Children may be jealous if they recognise an adult's relationship with their parents, but this jealousy is probably preferable in the long term to the sense of guilt and responsibility children must bear if they feel totally alone in looking after either or both of their parents. Children can behave badly with nurses, home helps or their parent's friends because they do not want their parent talking with these others and leaving them out. They can behave much worse when both parents are present than they do when only one is there; during an illness they may have to cope with this situation much more than usual. However, they are learning important lessons in such three-way relationships if they and the parents can bear it.

Parents' relationships with people outside the family particularly help the children when it is time for them to leave home. They need to know that they are not the only person in their parents' life and that when they go, the parents will survive.

As we said in the previous chapter, parents who become disabled or ill may have lost the opportunity to be the kind of parents they wanted to be to their children. They may have to grieve for this loss if they are to recognise their value to the children as they are. If, like Martin's father, they are too wrapped up in their own losses they may not be available for the children emotionally. Someone who helps the adult to grieve may help the children regain a parent.

Cheerfulness may be encouraging at times, but it may be more helpful at other times to share an understanding of depressing thoughts and feelings, and of the fact that no amount of 'positive thinking' is going to make them go away entirely. It is important to think through the reality of depressing thoughts and feelings; if they are simply pushed on one side they remain worse than reality.

> 'It's funny, I know I'm frightened, but I don't know what I'm frightened of.'

Finding out takes some of the fear away.

Where social and cultural differences are involved, it may be very difficult and complicated offering support to a family. Messages on both sides may be distorted in ways that are not obvious. Differences about polite and offensive forms of behaviour and ways of understanding offers and requests for help make the issues very confused indeed. Different expectations towards children and friends make it very difficult to sort out what is a result of cultural differences and what is a result of an illness. Issues of cultural imperialism, racism and mutual distrust add to the problems.

Giving support to children

Adults (and children) may also be able to offer more direct help to children of ill or disabled parents on an informal basis, as a friend, neighbour or relative, for example. They can provide some of the understanding, caring and loving that children need. Parents are usually the most important role models, but other adults can provide role models that are very different for children, enriching their experience and increasing their potential. If, in addition, they do things with the children or adolescents and notice their needs, particularly unspoken ones, they may be able to become an important resource to the family as a whole.

Even these informal relations may give rise to conflicts, for the children themselves, for the other adult and for the parents. Recognising that parents may envy the comfort and love their children receive from others may be very important; making sure that the parents, too, are getting attention can prevent a relationship with a child breaking down.

One of the most important things an adult can offer a child is simply being available. Adults may be able to provide a safe place to which a child can escape temporarily from a difficult situation, or in which they can be a different person with a different role. A welcoming relative, school or friend's house may be a refuge where the child can be a child with other children rather than an emotional support to a harassed father or mother.

> Darren's grandfather took Darren with him to the pub. The fact that he valued Darren's company and the unspoken acknowledgement of Darren as a young man were perhaps as important as anything for Darren. With his mother, a single parent disabled with MS, Darren had to be the provider of many things; with his grandfather he could be someone else.

Children with a parent who is severely incapacitated or ill may benefit greatly from the company of an adult of the same sex as the ill parent. This adult may, among other things, provide a role model of a man or woman who is not incapacitated like the parent. The children's loyalty to their parent needs to be respected and acknowledged if they are not to feel a sense of betrayal in the company of someone else. They may need to be reassured that it is possible to love more than one person at a time. Talking about the way they feel, perhaps that they love the parent and the other adult differently, and that the parent *cannot* be replaced by anyone else, however much anyone wants this, may help. If the parent themselves can encourage the relationship with the other adult the child may be enormously relieved.

Doing things together is one way in which children can build up a relationship with adults and other children. Playing games, watching television together, making go-carts, mending bicycles, buying clothes, going to the park, a market, a football match or a film with a child may all be ways in which adults may show their care for the child while enjoying themselves. Taking a child out may be a help to the parents as well as the child.

Children with ill parents may not want to go out because they are too anxious about how their parent will cope without them. This needs to be taken seriously. Parents do not always admit to outsiders how much help they need and children may not be able to explain their need to stay in. It may be difficult to sort out whether the children really do need to stay or really could leave. Finding someone else to stay with a parent who needs company may be a very significant kind of help: so too may helping the child to see their mother or father can look after themselves.

If an adult takes an interest in a child and offers it support, this may need to be sustained while the child grows up, perhaps through times when the child rejects the adult, otherwise the child will learn that allowing themselves to feel dependent and childish only leads to disappointment and betrayal. The child's own rejection is likely to be forgotten and the adult remembered as rejecting.

This is a serious problem for professionals who want to support children: they are unlikely to be around for the time it takes the child to grow up. One social worker is not the same as another, and children can feel very hurt and misused if they are encouraged to make a relationship with a social worker who then leaves with little warning. If this is unavoidable, the temporary and professional nature of the arrangement needs to be made clear to the child from the start, and the child prepared in good time for the ending. Teachers need also to bear this in mind, and to think about whether their involvement is for the period the child is in their class or their school, or if it is to continue, and if so, how.

When adults say or imply to children that they care about them, it is very important to ensure that they are saying no more than they can actually deliver. Very distressed children may imagine much more than they are being offered: they may imagine they can move in and live with another family, or with their teacher, for example, when this is not, in fact, a possibility. As with all dealings with children, it is extremely important to be truthful, even if it means spoiling happy dreams. Adults need to help the children bear the pain of the truth, which includes handling the limitations of relationships. Often adults avoid doing this and leave the children to suffer alone. Where a relationship has to end saying goodbye is very important.

It is clear that other adults can provide this kind of input in the long-term only if they are prepared for the development of strong bonds of affection between themselves and the child and possibly others in the family. Affection brings with it the potential for being hurt as well as potential for development (of the adult and the child) through the relationship. Jealousies and misunderstandings, accusations and guilt, disappointments and a sense of failure may be unavoidable aspects of such relationships that have to be accepted along with the rewards. Rivalry with parents is also a serious risk. The adults may be hurt, and the adults are in a position to hurt the child.

It is important even for a very demanding child that the adult has other sources of support and does not rely entirely on a particular child for his or her own satisfaction with life.

Caring and sexuality

For any man who is not the child's father, a relationship with a child may raise many difficulties, social and personal, as well as provide an opportunity for long-term rewards. This is particularly evident in the area of sexuality. Women may have difficulty here too, but generally less. Unspoken communication between father and daughter that acknowledges her attractiveness may be very important for her belief in herself. Where a father is absent or too ill to notice, the attention of other adult males may be very important to both girls and boys.

Melanie Klein's father was going senile throughout her teenage years and died when she was seventeen. In her later years she remembered with affection and gratitude an uncle who paid her attention and told her she was so beautiful she 'would marry a Rothschild'.

Unfortunately not all uncles are remembered with such affection. We discussed the serious problem of sexual relations between children and adults in the previous chapter because parents are particularly vulnerable to the temptations involved. But other adults are also at risk of allowing their sexual feelings to overcome their good sense. Confusing caring and affection with sexuality is common: we discussed this in Chapter 9. On the other hand, too much fear of the sexual issues can prevent the development of a good and valuable relationship.

Clearly, parents need to be aware that their children may be at risk from close and affectionate adult friends of the family. Children do need to be taught from early on that their bodies are their own and that they can say no to adults who want to be too close. Any reluctance on a child's part to visit or be left alone with an adult needs to be taken seriously, particularly if it is a change. There may be signs that something has been going on, but parents may be so horrified at the idea that they cannot bear to see them. A child whose parents saw an adult attempt to fondle her but said nothing felt totally betrayed by them and later said that this was the worst thing about the whole event, even though by then she knew that her parents had in fact taken steps to prevent a recurrence.

While younger children do have sexual feelings and thoughts, adolescents are more likely to be preoccupied with them. Their own developing sexuality may cause difficulty between themselves and the adults around them. Adolescents may more quickly interpret innocent concern or overtures of friendship as sexual, or as an invasion of privacy. They may be confusing their own sexual feelings with the adult's, or they may be responding to an adult's sexual feelings which the adult is hardly aware of, is trying to deny, or thinks they have under control. Physical contact in particular can be interpreted in this way, with the adolescent at times repulsing any action which seems to threaten their boundaries. Physical contact may also be feared because the adolescent is terrified of having needy, dependent feelings awakened by someone who cannot satisfy them.

Adults may need to allow adolescents in these situations to keep their distance, and to recognise that there is a limit to the kind of help they can give at this time. They also need to make it very clear to the young person that they are not at risk and that their space will not be invaded.

In some circumstances a young adolescent may ask or demand to be treated in a way that would be far more appropriate for much younger children. They may recognise an adult (for example, a foster-parent) who will and can respond to their infantile needs, which had not been met at the appropriate time. This may be difficult to handle, but may also create a satisfying and loving relationship if an adult is prepared to undertake this kind of parenting. The parent-substitute may need help later to let the child grow past this stage. A foster-father, for example, may take over more care of the young person as it grows past the stage of wanting to be mothered.

Helping children in damaging relations with their parents

Parent–child relationships can sometimes be careless, neglectful or even cruel and malicious. Parents can make sexual and emotional demands as well as practical demands that most people would consider wrong or excessive for a child of a particular age. Parents may misuse alcohol or drugs or be sadistic or mentally unstable in some other way that puts the child at great risk.

Some kinds of ill-health (physical or mental) can also change parents' characters or states of mind from being normally affectionate and interested or indifferent towards their children, to being extremely bad-tempered, withdrawn, wildly paranoid or even violent. Changes may also be of a more subtle kind.

> There was considerable concern for Alex because his mother's memory and thought processes were unreliable, but she did not seem to turn against Alex at all. There was a question amongst the professionals who knew her as to whether her unrealistic state of mind was itself damaging to Alex.

In these situations it is important to notice not only the potential or actual damage being inflicted, whether it is physical or emotional and how serious it is, but also the benefit to the child of being with the parent. Children seldom want to be separated from their parents in the long term even if those parents have hurt or damaged them.

The decision to take children away from home or to separate them from a parent, however ill or bad, is an extremely difficult one to make. It is difficult to be sure that what is offered is really better. The importance to children of continuity of care should not be underestimated, yet children who lose a parent may in addition provoke other adults into leaving them. Maintaining contact with parents when children are removed from their care is now part of the brief of social workers, which may help some families. However, finding a new home for a child does sometimes seem to be best or the only thing to do.

Whether or not children are still living with neglectful or otherwise damaging parents, they need help in seeing and bearing the reality of their situation. Ignoring these issues does not help the children. It is very painful indeed for children to recognise that their mother does not want them, for example, or that she allowed or caused them to become HIV positive. They may resist such knowledge strongly. They may prefer to feel their situation is entirely their fault, that there is or was something wrong with them, even if they were rejected or infected at or before birth. They often blame themselves for being born and consequently ruining their parent's lives. Without considerable help, children in this situation are liable to convince themselves that they are unfit for any human relationships.

Young children often also seem to feel that their own life is less important than their parents'. This may make it very hard for them to understand if they have to be removed from an unsafe situation: they may prefer to take any risks, even of illness, abuse and death, rather than be separated from a parent. If the parent is not actively abusing them, it may be even harder for the children to grasp why they cannot stay with them.

It is very important to help children to tease out and hold onto the good aspects of their relationship with their parents. If their parents failed them in any way, whether through personality or through illness, it is also important to help them gradually to acknowledge that the responsibility for the parents' actions was their parents' rather than their own. This may be particularly hard if the parent is a drug abuser with AIDS, for example. The child has to live with their own identification with their parents as well as with the consequences of their parents' actions.

People who care for children of a parent who is 'bad' in some way may fear that the children will follow their parent's footsteps. Denigrating the parent may make this more, rather than less, likely. Children may feel their own badness means they cannot live up to the high standards required, and they may choose to follow the 'bad' parent out of despair or defiance, or during the process of separating from the other parent or foster-parent during adolescence. They may defend themselves from the pain of hearing a parent denigrated by idealising them – 'I know better' – particularly if they cannot meet them often or discuss their good points as well as their bad ones.

Adults who become very involved in trying to help teenagers or children from difficult home backgrounds are likely to find themselves at times being the victims of attacks that mirror the treatment the children either actually have experienced or imagine they have experienced. Step-parents and foster-parents in particular are vulnerable to this treatment. They may for a time represent to teenagers their own rejected 'bad' self, or the 'bad' and rejecting parent they feel they had, and be treated as such. Adults may be pushed extremely hard to repeat some act of failure in caring which the children have previously experienced, including sexual abuse, cruelty and rejection. If this succeeds, the child has 'proved' to itself that all care is hypocrisy and that the lost love was nothing.

In this situation it is very hard to insist on normal discipline for fear of becoming even more of a baddie and losing the child's affection. It seems that the opposite may, in fact, be true: a certain amount of sensible restrictions and firmness may reassure the child and increase their respect for the adult in the long term, and their affection and gratitude. Children do need adults to say 'no' kindly and firmly, and the short-term difficulty for the adult is worth tolerating. The adult is likely to need firm support from at least one other adult who knows the situation and should not attempt to cope with disturbed children without such support.

The role of the school

A school has an important role to play in the life of children who have an ill parent. One important aspect of this role is to maintain an atmosphere of normality for the children and their family if possible. However, a child with an ill or disabled parent is not in a normal situation, and it may be important at times to acknowledge this. A teacher may be too hesitant about encroaching on a child's privacy and may ignore hints that the child would appreciate some expression of concern and perhaps intervention.

Parents can help teachers to help their children by giving them accurate information about their illness and about the children's situation. This may have to be repeated with each new teacher as teachers do not always pass information on. A parent who shows sympathy for the teacher's difficulties may help a teacher who feels under pressure themselves to be more sympathetic towards children who may add to those difficulties.

A school may not seem very supportive if there is no way a parent in a wheelchair can attend school functions, or if deaf or blind parents' needs are ignored. A school can increase the disability and handicap experienced by a family by failing to take their practical needs into account. Enabling disabled parents to do the usual things that parents do helps maintain normality and may reduce a parent's and child's frustration.

Missing one meeting with the staff may not seem much, but where no other contact with the school is possible, and where many other outings are being missed by the parent because of lack of access or by the children because of lack of money caused by a disability, the annual parent–teacher meeting may be very important. It may be one of very few opportunities for the children to feel that their needs and achievements are being considered by the parents. Providing ramps for wheelchairs and an accessible toilet and making arrangements for deaf or blind parents may be socially cost-effective. Where parents and teachers with disabilities can be active in school, general awareness and respect for people who are 'different' can be encouraged. Such experiences will also help those children who will have to cope with disability or chronic illness later in life.

Some schools allow or encourage the development of close, concerned relations between children, parents and staff.

> 'When I was diagnosed I told the boys, they were ten and twelve, and I answered all their questions and it seemed all right. But I rang the teacher in case something came out at school which they couldn't say to me. The teacher rang back the next day and said I'd obviously done a good job, talking to them, but there was just one question I hadn't answered. "Oh," I said, "what was that?" "You didn't tell them whether you were going to die," she said. It simply hadn't occurred to me; we knew I wasn't about to die and we hadn't thought of mentioning it.'

Teachers may be concerned to offer their best to the child but not to get too deeply involved in a situation where they feel relatively helpless and untrained.

Intellectual work may be very difficult at times for children whose parents are ill. Where they are too scared to allow themselves to know facts about their parents' health or about the future they may be unable to allow themselves to know any facts at all or to think about anything. Upsetting thoughts may interrupt their concentration, or they may simply 'go blank'. Seeing other children happy and working contentedly may at times cause terrible rage or quiet despair. Recognising that a child cannot work for a time may be relatively easy for a teacher. Helping a child to catch up is much harder work and may be forgotten or put on one side unless the teacher is reminded, perhaps repeatedly, and perhaps helped. If the child is reluctant or unable to put in much extra time or effort, or wants to remain unnoticed, their schooling may be seriously affected for several years after a missed time. A missed stage in mathematics teaching can make following stages incomprehensible and have a serious cumulative effect. Missing some teaching of spelling in the early years may have a comparable effect in the teaching of English particularly if it means that a child's level of intelligence is wrongly assessed.

> Two young women told us how they used to stay at home sometimes to keep their severely disabled mothers company and no-one at school made any fuss about it. A young man said social workers had arranged for him to take time off school to look after his mother. All three ultimately felt quite angry with the schools and their parents for letting it happen. It was as if the schools too felt that a child's education should take second place to the mother's needs. Nobody suggested seeking other help for the mothers in order to protect the children's future.

One experienced teacher (a Head of Year with her own room) said that parents or other members of the family, or even other children, sometimes alerted her to a child having to cope with illness at home. She would call the child into her room discreetly and say that she knew, and that if the child wanted to use her room as an escape, he or she could. She would be there, although the child did not have to talk to her. She felt strongly that counselling should only be offered by specially trained counsellors, but she could provide a sanctuary. She also found that children often would not go for counselling even if it was available. With older children, it seemed the best she could do was enable them to continue coming to school: for a time, teaching had to take a back seat. Later, she would do what she could to help them catch up.

Sometimes a child does not appear to be affected immediately but there is a displaced reaction later. A child may be very good and quiet both at school and at home while their parent is ill, but suddenly burst into tears for no good reason or show uncharacteristic, demanding behaviour when the parent recovers and the child feels safe enough to make demands again. This can be irritating if it is not understood, particularly as there may seem no good reason for such behaviour, and no obvious remedy. In a new class the child may simply be labelled as attention-seeking. A new, supportive teacher may release behaviour which draws attention to a child who previously kept anxieties under control out of fear or despair.

It can be difficult to recognise that certain behaviour is a delayed reaction to an earlier problem. The child may be upset and disturbed by their own behaviour without having any idea that it might be connected with an illness which was over a year or even two earlier, while the child was in a different class or even school. The teacher too may not know. However, some teachers may be in a position to help such a child understand what is happening and to offer some sense of acceptance within firm boundaries.

Young Minds is a charity which works to promote the mental health of children, young people and their families, and has written a booklet for teachers which may be of help. The booklet suggests that teachers need to be clear about their own boundaries; about what they can and cannot do, and about the limits to the time they can give the child. Within this, 'it is often sufficient to listen to the child, conveying sympathy or concern, and reflecting back or summarising what is on the child's mind. It may be necessary to follow up with one or two further talks, but it is generally inadvisable to go beyond this on an individual basis' (Young Minds 1996). The booklet also suggests that it is important 'to help the child share his or her problem with other people in the family or school. The teacher needs to be clear about matters of confidentiality and parental involvement...'

Young Minds is also clear that teachers need support in such circumstances. Confidentiality does not mean the teacher cannot discuss what has been said with anyone, but it does mean that the context, purpose and boundaries of the discussion need to be considered. It may be very important to talk over what the child has said with someone else who can be trusted to keep a confidence. It may be only in such discussion that the teacher becomes aware that a problem is in fact serious and needs action. There are other people who may be a source of support in such circumstances.

A school counsellor, if there is one, may help the teacher decide how best to help the child: so too may a Special Needs Co-ordinator (SENCO) or Head of Year. *Childline* (0800 1111) or *Youth Access* (01509 219420) are sources of help which can be suggested to a child or young person. Teachers can ring the *Young Minds* (0345 626376) or *NSPCC* (0800 800500) helplines. *Young Minds* also has a national database of statutory and voluntary agencies which can help children and those involved in taking care of them. Social Services or the local Child Guidance Clinic can advise teachers if there is concern about whether a child is at risk.

The Carer's National Association (0171 490 8818) may also be helpful: they have a designated Young Carers Officer who may be able to help even if children are not actually carers. As of June 1996 they are focussing on the needs of teachers in connection with young carers. In the USA some schools run group discussions for children who need support: this seems to be less common in the UK. What evidence there is suggests children value one-to-one support most highly: groups may enable them to obtain this.

It seems to us that more systematic help could usefully be available to children and teachers in many schools. Many schools do not even have a counsellor, yet this would be one way children with ill parents could obtain support without being singled out: many children have reason to wish to talk with a counsellor, for many reasons. Some schools have a pastoral system which ensures that children's home circumstances are known and continue to be known as the child progresses throughout the school. Others do not. Unfortunately, there is no guarantee that teachers will respond well if they do know a child's circumstances. Some teachers may believe that ignoring it is the best they can do – and they may be right. However, children may be more likely to feel supported and safe with those teachers who can convey some sense of awareness of difficult emotions without being obtrusive.

Conclusion

In this chapter we have tried to describe some of the ways in which adults such as relatives, friends, neighbours, teachers and other professionals can be of help to children who have parents who are ill or disabled. We have also looked at some of the difficulties that can arise when care of children is shared between adults.

CHAPTER 11

Help With Thoughts and Feelings

'The children know all about my illness...'

'I don't know what she thinks about it, she won't say.'

'My son won't talk about it, he just clams up, but my daughter will.'

Why do adults need to listen to children?

- Children need to communicate with themselves; they need to know what they think, feel and fear. Talking to someone else can be a very important way in which children learn about themselves.

- Just knowing that a trusted adult knows what they think can comfort children. The problem has been handed over to someone who can handle it.

- Through talking, children learn to distinguish fact from fantasy, reality from imagination, hope from pretence, and fears from knowledge.

- Parent's worries about their children's feelings and thoughts are often quite unrealistic. Hearing what the children have to say can change their parent's views of the ways the children are being affected.

- Children often have worries which can easily be dispelled by an adult. Discovering this can be very reassuring to parents.

- Children often seem to have difficulty feeling that they count as much as an ill parent. Listening to them and helping them to put their thoughts into words can help to counteract their belief that they and their lives do not matter to anyone – including themselves.

- Talking about events brings them to mind and allows feelings to be located and felt in a safe context. In distressing circumstances the ability to feel at all may be lost if painful feelings cannot be shared by an understanding adult.

- Children who are trying too hard to be good may be enormously reassured and allowed to live a little more if they can share their beliefs about their badness.

- Children who are not encouraged to think about their parent's ill-health may not allow themselves to think at all.

Some children have had to deal with a sudden, unexpected event, such as a parent's accident or stay in hospital. Others have to cope with the insidious onset of an illness in their parent, perhaps very gradually bringing changes in the parent's behaviour and capacities. There are some guidelines for helping children with their feelings and thoughts in different situations.

Putting words to thoughts, ideas and feelings

Children have thoughts and ideas which may be very disturbing. They can be much less disturbing when spoken than they were when they were kept hidden. They often also turn out to be untrue in a way which is obvious even to the child (or adult) whose thoughts they were. If a child's fears remain secret, the child has to bear them alone. If an adult listens carefully, children give hints about their fears which can be picked up and acknowledged without adding to them. In our experience, if an idea about a child's fear has come into the adult's mind while talking with a child, the chances are it has already come into the child's mind, probably long ago. It has to be put to the child carefully, so that if the child has not thought of it it becomes a possibility for the child to explore if they wish. Sometimes the adult may be able to say it in such a way that the child realises it cannot be true.

A fear that has been put into words has lost some of the terror it had when it was unnamed. Sometimes fears that are named become the subject of grief that can be shared, where previously they had to be suffered alone and in silence. In this case the sense of loneliness and abandonment can be reduced even if some of the content of a thought remains. Acknowledgement of fears or anxieties which are felt as 'unworthy' or 'bad' may also reduce the sense of shame or horror attached to them: putting them into words is a necessary first stage to acceptance.

There is also, it seems, a sense of relief in uncovering bad thoughts that are felt to be true, which results from no longer having to make the effort required to hide them, perhaps from the self as well as from others. Unfortunately, children can also feel threatened, invaded and resentful at the idea of a parent or someone close knowing their secret thoughts; the difficulty is to know when it will help and when it will make matters worse.

There is a particular difficulty in putting names to fears, because adults can be afraid they will frighten the child or give it something to be anxious about which was not a problem for the child before. There is also a fear of being intrusive. This risk is real: adults have to beware of invading the child's privacy. A distressed adult's own anxieties and fears can easily be added to the child's: a child is sometimes expected to share too much of the adult's concerns, leaving its own unrecognised.

Sometimes adults are afraid they cannot help children with their feelings because they feel inadequate themselves.

> Darren lived alone with a mother who had been seriously ill for a long time and he had recently begun to miss school. He sat in the school nurse's room looking pale and hopeless, saying little. For the school nurse the feelings of despair, hopelessness and above all, inadequacy which he evoked in her were extremely uncomfortable. She felt she was not capable of the task before her and took him to see a specialist counsellor. The counsellor recognised these feelings which Darren also aroused in her: such feelings of hopeless inadequacy were ones she often had with children who had been left to look after an ill parent single-handed.
>
> This enabled both the nurse and the counsellor to recognise that these feelings were not caused simply by their personal inadequacy, but by the unbearable situation Darren had to bear. Darren was probably feeling like this beneath his unresponsive exterior. The nurse regained confidence that she could work with with Darren.
>
> It turned out that Darren had managed with his mother ill until his grandfather died. It was then that he collapsed, afraid to go to school and leave her for fear she too would die.

It was true that the nurse and the counsellor were inadequate to change much of Darren's situation. However, behind Darren's apathetic exterior it emerged that he was feeling totally inadequate himself about looking after his mother and stopping her from dying too. When the counsellor and the nurse recognised that their feelings of inadequacy were perhaps reflecting feelings that Darren had but could not bear to expose directly, they were able to ask Darren if this was what he felt: the response was dramatic as he emerged from his listlessness and talked animatedly for the first time. It became possible to help him to think and to grieve for his huge losses.

Acceptance of feelings as they are

In Chapters 2–4 we looked at some of the feelings that children have towards their parents and their situation. We observed anger and sadness, guilt and rejection, shame and misery, jealousy and triumph, hatred, resentment and a sense of unfairness, as well as a strong sense of responsibility and a powerful desire to make their parent better or keep them safe, even at great cost to themselves. Many of these feelings leave children feeling guilty *for feeling the way they do*. One of the important roles of an adult in helping children work through upsetting reactions is to reassure the children that their feelings are bearable and are not monstrous even if they are hateful and horrifying.

One normal response to bad news is a sense of triumph: 'it has happened to him/her, not me!' Laughter or giggling may break out as a result of this, or in an attempt to deny the message and to insist that it doesn't matter, that it is not true. These reactions may cover for a while all sense of sorrow, sadness, guilt or misery, all of which require more recognition of a very unwelcome reality. If children feel guilty because they laughed when they were told something terrible they may try to stop themselves laughing ever again.

Children may have strong beliefs about how self-sacrificing or considerate they ought to be, which their actual feelings or thoughts contradict. They then have a serious problem. Either they must deny their feelings or they have to change their beliefs about what is and is not possible or reasonable. An adult may help children to change their attitude to their feelings by helping them accept that people do have feelings they do not want. The alternative of denying the feelings is a common one, which many of us may have experienced: it can leave children with a 'false self', trying to be good but, in fact, losing touch with the reality of their own impulses. The conflict between their inner reality and their beliefs about how things ought to be may play itself out in many ways. Sometimes children develop physical symptoms, such as a pain (a physical feeling), to symbolise and replace a thought or emotional feeling; they may become very judgemental of others and themselves; they may keep a tight control on their feelings and their behaviour, losing spontaneity.

Accepting feelings does not mean condoning any kind of behaviour. Adults as well as children can have difficulty recognising the difference between thoughts, feelings and actions. It is perfectly reasonable to be extremely angry at a parent having a serious illness, and even not to distinguish carefully between being angry with the illness and being angry with the parent; it may not be permissible to act upon this anger, by, for example, kicking the parent.

Distinguishing between 'understandable' and 'justifiable' and 'reason' and 'excuse' can be useful. There may be a good *reason* why a child hit a parent, but whether it is considered an *excuse* or not may depend on the child's age and on family beliefs about physical attacks. Adults need to react firmly and with full authority to control children's behaviour. A kind of 'understanding' that allows children to get away with too much leaves them in trouble, lacking external support against their own destructive impulses. (This has been called 'repressive tolerance': if the adults are too tolerant the child may become very inhibited. If external controls are too weak children have to increase their own internal controls. A certain amount of internal control is vital; too much is very restrictive.)

Cultural differences are important here, as different kinds of behaviour and different feelings are condoned or rejected by different cultures and sub-cultures. Adults, whatever their relationship with the children, show children what they will or will not accept. Grandparents may have different expectations from parents. A teacher and pupil or doctor and patient may come from widely diverging cultures or sub-cultures and may sometimes need to make explicit differences in their beliefs about what it is and is not permissible to say or do. They may need to recognise that each may find different feelings hard or easy to accept. Differences between men and women can also be a problem; 'different' can often be understood to mean 'wrong'. Children may learn to express different feelings in different ways with different adults.

FEELINGS AFTER A TRAUMA

After a really traumatic event (such as the Hillsborough disaster, for example) the feelings of those involved seem to be extremely disturbing indeed. They may take some time to be felt at all. With a few of the more emotionally deprived children we saw we had the feeling that the cumulative effect of their experiences added up to a similar kind of psychic disaster.

A sense of unreality and of being cut off from others who do not know about a disturbing experience is commonly described by people who have suffered traumas. Describing and sharing their experiences may help them begin to re-establish the sense of living in a shared world.

Another feeling that is common is that of anger with the rest of the world: 'How can they just carry on when the world has changed so much for me?' It may be the child's external world that has changed; it may simply be the child's perception of itself and life, the child's internal world. These feelings can be enormously strong for a child if a parent has suddenly been seriously injured. They increase the feeling of being alone. Where fury and hatred are too overwhelming, and the sense of adult support too weak, anger cannot be felt, but may be experienced as a total mess inside, spilling out in behaviour, perhaps as dirtying or swearing; expressed in some form of 'shit'. These feelings may pass quite quickly after a minor event; but they may last for days or weeks or years after a major one or as a result of an on-going disaster.

When people have been involved in disasters in which other people have died, many shameful and difficult feelings are aroused. The sudden, shocking discovery that their feelings and behaviour are not as they imagined them to be can be totally shattering. There may be a feeling of no longer deserving to belong to the human race, of being outcast, fit only for the company of other outcasts who share a terrible secret. A sense of being 'marked' by a traumatic event may remain for a long time.

There is also an incredible excitement in being involved in making history, feelings of being 'high' and very alive at the time may be felt as shameful and hard to live with afterwards. Guilt at continuing to live when others are dead is common. The feeling that there must have been something more the survivor could have done needs to be taken seriously and examined. Real helplessness and awareness of being at the mercy of others or of inanimate forces can give rise to terrifying feelings which may be feared more than the guilt of feeling responsible.

There are bad feelings attached even to saving others; the feelings attached to attempts to save one's own skin, perhaps at the expense of someone else, may be terrible. Children who fight with or abandon an ill parent can feel they have saved themselves at the expense of the parent. It can be helpful to know that these feelings are shared with others.

Adults need to know that they are likely to have disturbing reactions themselves when talking with a child about such a disturbing situation. Revulsion, anger, exhausted helplessness, despair, impotent fury or even sexual feelings may be aroused in such situations as well as pity and sorrow. If the adult can hold these feelings and think about them without simply reacting to them, he or she is helping to 'contain' some of the child's distress. This is likely to be impossible for an involved adult in the immediate aftermath of an event.

The fact that it is normal to feel something does not mean it should not be challenged; some normal reactions imply that help needs to be sought. It is normal for people to refuse to talk about traumatic events, but if this state of affairs is allowed to continue for too long, the long-term effect may be disastrous. Where a traumatic event is pushed out of thought in its raw state, the sense of being damaged and partially dead inside may remain constantly on the edge of awareness; many years later the most horrifying aspects may be triggered and relived.

USING PROFESSIONAL HELP

Where memories or feelings are too shocking, this work needs to be done with a professional, in a room which is separate from daily life, if normal relationships are not to be threatened. Professional help may also be necessary if a child is withdrawing or becoming violent or refusing to play.

In less terrible situations parents or other close adults may be able to do all or some of this work with the child, and may even find it a relief themselves. Parents may sometimes be able to do this with the guidance of a professional. Parents sometimes do what they can and then ask someone else to check up that they have not missed anything. One woman talked with her daughter about her MS at great length and was worried about the things her daughter said. She then rang a counsellor and repeated the conversation, asking what the counsellor thought about it. Together they were able to think about the child's reaction. Another woman asked a social worker to have a word with her daughter; another asked the child's teacher.

Difficulties for adults

Talking with children in painful situations can be difficult in many ways for the adults concerned. There are many reasons for avoiding telling children facts about a parent's condition. Sometimes these reasons are not questioned because the parents think the child already knows. They may have actually told a child who has forgotten or distorted the information, or they may have told an older child and have forgotten a younger one has not been told. Many of the parents we met thought their children knew more about the parent's illness than they did.

We look now at some of the reasons why people have difficulty talking with children.

Upsetting the adult

Many children's worries are of a nature that is not disturbing to adults. Children may keep the conversation at a level which they know the adult can bear, and hide or disguise their more disturbing worries. However, many adults fear that talking and listening to children may give the children a chance to say things that will upset the adult.

> 'When daddy dies, mummy, we are going to be very sad. We will have to take it in turns to cry. We will go and put flowers on his grave every Sunday.'

Different families have different attitudes to crying and being upset in general. Tears can also have different meanings, and this will affect how a child reacts to them. They may not be simply a sign of sorrow or misery but exaggerated and hysterical, manipulative, a sign of anger or frustration, or 'socially correct behaviour'. If a parent is suicidal, children may be extremely frightened of their crying because they may be afraid it means the parent is about to kill him or herself, whether this has been acknowledged or not. Quiet crying is different from out-of-control sobs. Children can be very frightened if parents seem to lose control, of their anger, their sorrow or any other feeling.

Sometimes an adult's crying may draw attention to the adult and away from the child's distress; an adult may use it like this in order to avoid staying with the child's misery. In some situations it may be a relief for parent and child to cry together. This can be both reassuring and disturbing for a child. A child can be afraid a 'carer' parent has no feelings, or does not love the ill parent; seeing them upset can be a reassurance. However, parents' distress can frighten children, and some parents prefer to allow their children to know they are upset and to know that they cry in private, but not actually to cry with them.

Children often seem to feel it is wrong to be upset even if their parents do not think this. If parents keep their grief entirely hidden, children may believe their parents are never upset or that they disapprove of it. They may believe it is better to have no feelings. Unfortunately, avoiding sorrowful and painful feelings means, ultimately, that loving and caring feelings may also be lost.

The question of upsetting adults is relevant when considering whether to 'keep it in the family' or seek outside help. Children are likely to worry differently about upsetting different people, and may be able to bring up different worries in different situations. Children may be able to talk more freely to their parents in the presence of some other adult who makes it clear that their parents can 'take it'.

For many adults their own lonely sufferings as children were too powerful and painful, and they closed the door on many feelings many years ago. They may have no memory of feeling desperately lonely or despairing, but they may have a strong fear of 'opening cans of worms'. Many adults react to children's feelings with denial, distraction, forgetting or joking. Such reactions also have their time and place: it can be a relief not to be serious at times and to be allowed to hide feelings. Talking and understanding is by no means the only aspect of parenting that counts. A justifiable reason to be angry with a parent who refuses to understand can also itself be a relief, allowing anger to be felt in a way which is not guilt-provoking.

Upsetting the child

We have given many reasons why it can be important to allow children to be upset by information or events around them, but adults can find it almost impossible to do this. Sometimes adults worry about upsetting children because as children they were upset by some illness-related event in a way that was unbearable, without an adult to support them.

When a child gets upset because a parent refuses to buy it something, the parent has memories of its own parents refusing and knows that this is the right way to behave with children. The parent knows that the upset is short and that it teaches the child something important. The fact that the child may feel punished may not worry the parent who feels that greed should perhaps be punished, or should be kept firmly under control. However, when an adult has to upset a child by telling it something about an ill parent, there is no such support. The memories of being told upsetting facts in a loving and supportive way may not be there. The child's grief is likely to be lasting. The adult may not realise that grieving is very important. And it seems so very unfair that the child, who has done nothing wrong, should have such terrible feelings inflicted on it.

Parents can also worry that their own lack of knowledge and control will upset the child. Children's questions about religious faith may be feared when the parent's own faith is shaken by events and they cannot give the children satisfactory answers because they cannot see any. Some parents are worried about spoiling the illusion that parents know everything: others think it important to help children recognise this.

Just listening

Telling children anything may lead them to ask questions which are difficult to answer. Some people are afraid that they have to have answers: they have to be able to reassure children and answer all their questions or worries, from 'Why can't I come to the hospital?' or 'Why can my sister go and not me?' to 'Why won't God make mummy better?'

Children can often feel more understood if their own answers are explored. 'Why do you think you can't come?' or 'Why do you think God doesn't make mummy better?' allows children to put into words their precise fear and have this relieved. An adult's answer may easily miss the relevant point.

Simply holding onto what the child has said, thinking about it, imagining what it would be like to feel or think that, may be helpful. Children need time to think about what they have said. They are often surprised by what they hear themselves saying and will sometimes say afterwards 'I didn't know I thought that.' An adult responding with words too quickly may prevent them from thinking or working out what follows. Sometimes it is enough to repeat back to a child what it has said, not to elicit more information, but to ensure that the child knew or meant what it said, and to allow both child and adult time to think about how much truth was in it.

Uncomfortable realities

Parents can be afraid of the child raising uncomfortable realities. They may fear accusations that they have in their own head: 'It's all your fault you are ill and I am deprived of a mother'. 'You made dad ill.' If parents are to tell a child that it may inherit an illness the parents may feel that their genes are their own fault, as if they had some control over them. Adults may also fear that children will say things later to other people who will disapprove of their having been told.

If a child has raised some uncomfortable issue, it is tempting to say something like 'Don't worry, it will be all right'; or 'Don't say that!' or 'Don't think about it!' which implies that the adult cannot bear to think about it. Quick reassurance closes the conversation and may make the adult feel temporarily less uncomfortable; for the child it leaves vital questions unanswered. These remain a continual source of anxiety which the child must then bear alone.

Sometimes parents will need professional help themselves to think about very uncomfortable issues before they can help their children.

> One of the issues between Megan and her mother seemed to be the question of which of them was in control. It was hard for Megan's mother to admit she was in control and had to take responsibility for uncomfortable decisions that left Megan without some of the attention her mother felt she should have. Eventually Megan and her mother grieved together for this loss, whereas previously Megan had blamed herself unconsciously and her mother consciously. Her mother had simply felt guilty.

Many of the children we met made it clear that they felt their 'healthy' parent was not looking after their 'ill' parent properly. This was a very uncomfortable thought for all concerned, particularly when the adults felt that the child may have been right. Even this thought is bearable and can be shared with a child who believes it. After having shared the initial horror, it becomes clear that the child's view of the situation is not entirely realistic. The reality of the parent's care and the reality of any neglect or lack of care can be discussed with a child, as we showed in Chapter 3, describing Martin.

The shortcomings of adults in general and parents in particular are difficult for children and adults to bear, but they are a fact of life and have to be borne, if not verbally, then silently. Having them in the open can reduce them to realistic proportions, leaving the child with a better sense of what the parents really can and cannot do.

Talking will make it real

Children and adults can be afraid that talking makes things real, whereas covering them up leaves them uncertain and maintains an illusion of hope. It is important that adults recognise the dangers in this belief, many of which we have already discussed. Feelings that are covered up emerge in less appropriate situations; thoughts that are covered up remain unrealistic and more frightening and damaging than they need to be. Realistic hopes may not be discovered.

People sometimes assume that children are very stupid indeed. They tell them 'The doctors are going to give me this treatment, and it might work...' and just hope they do not think 'What if it does not?' It is very hard to think that the child may well have asked such a question silently. Sometimes people do not want to be the one who raises the painful question. They hope that the other person, child or adult, has not thought about it, when, in fact, they must have. Waiting for the other person to raise it first, the opportunity may be lost forever.

Some people seem to fear the power of 'suggestion' enormously. Should adults tell the children that the children of people with multiple sclerosis have a slightly greater chance of getting it? Should they tell children that they might develop cancer or AIDS or heart disease themselves like their mother or father? Or should they not tell the children and hope they will not find out?

If they do not tell the children, they leave open the chance that the children will find out on their own and will be unable to be comforted by their parents. Children may think their parents do not know things like this which they have found out. Both young and older children may not want to tell their parents they know, for the same reasons the parents do not want to tell them.

If we tell them, will they imagine they have it?

Some people think they have illnesses when they do not. Children also develop symptoms their parents have. It is possible to talk with children about these things, including the possibility of developing symptoms by identification, as described in Chapter 4. Not talking about these issues may leave children developing the symptoms through identification, not telling their parents 'in order not to worry them' and not realising they do *not* have the condition.

How do adults tell the children of people with a directly inheritable condition that the children would be advised not to have children, or that their children are very likely to get the condition, or that their own lives may be cut short or be seriously affected by it? These issues and others like them may well be put off by parents and by doctors in the hope that someone else will handle them or that the children will never need to be told. The children's need to know, to plan their lives in the light of such knowledge, may be overlooked in the fear that talking about these things will make them real.

It may also be very difficult to be truthful about such issues partly because we cannot tell what medical advances will be made, and partly because we may find it unbearable not to leave children with some hope. People sometimes feel that the only alternative to despair is belief in miracles or maintaining illusions. The idea that children might learn to live well and realistically with the knowledge of a serious future loss of their own health or of their fertility, for example, may be difficult to imagine. It may be vital to let the children (and parents) know that it is possible.

'Have I really understood?'

This is one of the few anxieties we suspect people should have more than they do. It is very difficult for one person really to understand another, however close they are to each other. As children grow up, they gradually come to realise that their all-seeing parents do not know what is in their minds; this is a painful discovery.

Rather than imagine that they know just how a child (or adult) feels, it may be better for adults to admit to the child that they do not; though they may have some idea from their own experiences, these will not be exactly the same. Bearing the fact of the differences and the separateness between people is part of the difficulty of growing up, harder but just as important when 'different' means 'much worse', as it may when an illness is involved.

Guesses that adults make about what children are thinking or feeling have assumptions built into them that may not be correct. Even the general, neutral formulations such as 'That must have been difficult for you', or 'I wonder what you felt then' have assumptions built in: the assumption that something was difficult, when it might not have felt that way; or the assumption that something was felt at all, when there may have been a complete deadening of all feeling. Children can feel very misused if assumptions are made about them.

A natural way of talking with children or young adults in an informal or parental relationship is for adults to tell the children of their own experience, or how they think they would have felt in a similar situation. Some children resent this, feeling that the adults are pushing themselves forward for attention while hypocritically pretending that they are offering it to the child. They may listen politely but, in fact, withdraw from the hope of being really listened to themselves. They may feel a need to point out how different they are themselves, and dislike the implication that they and the adult, the past and the present, are similar. However, some children may respond more positively.

'Have I handled it the right way?'

Because every situation is different we do not feel in general that there is a right way and a wrong way to help children to deal with their feelings and thoughts. Parents and other adults have to behave in the way which seems right for them at the time; some later regrets may be unavoidable. Some of their decisions may relieve children; some may cause them trouble at the time; some may cause them trouble later. Life is risky and people cannot be sure they are behaving in the best possible way. In the situation where a parent is ill, there is no way to make everything better. We are all inadequate and we need to accept this without denying how painful it is.

Bearing the anger directed at the bringer of bad news is not easy and few people would willingly choose this role. Information given may also make children more openly anxious. But an adult may need to know about these anxieties and either share or modify them rather than pretend they are not there. This is not impossible: we have already shown how many of the children's anxieties are unrealistic, and how easily parents or other adults could remove some of them. The knowledge that a trusted adult knows and cares about what a child thinks and feels is a comfort to a child, even if no other comfort is available. Without correct information, worse anxieties will develop, but hidden where an adult may not be able to relieve them. A child being upset or even angry for a time may be a sign that an adult has handled things well.

Through counselling or psychotherapy, or sometimes with partners, many adults are able to deal satisfactorily with painful difficulties that began many years earlier. There may be a chance for children to find help later as adults if we cannot help them now.

Conclusion

In this chapter we have looked at some of the reasons for making the effort to listen to children, and some of the concerns that arise when adults try to listen and to talk with them about their ideas and feelings. We have looked at the importance and difficulty of dealing openly with uncomfortable realities and at helping children to accept their thoughts and feelings, including the 'bad' ones. We have also looked at some of the difficulties involved when adults themselves are upset.

CHAPTER 12

How Can Adults Talk to Children?

Children can be helped by being given information of the right kind.

- ° Information gives a sense of control. It may give time to prepare for an unwanted event. Even if the information is 'We don't know' children can feel the adults are more in control than if they say nothing.

- ° Without information, children's imagination about what is wrong and who is responsible runs riot.

- ° Without information children feel left out and cut off; they may cut themselves off further.

- ° Hiding vital facts can be felt by children to be the same as lying to them.

- ° Children need to know what is happening in order to make informed decisions about what they want to do, both in the present and the future.

One of the difficulties adults have in talking with children about the health of their parent is the fear that they do not know how to do it. Parents often have had no experience themselves of being told upsetting facts in a way which was truthful, sensitive and well-timed. They may not know how to help children cope with desperate feelings except by forgetting and distraction. They may also feel incapable because they cannot make their partner better, and this feeling then may spill over into other areas of their lives. Teachers, doctors and other professionals may also feel inadequately trained for emotional conversations.

In this chapter we look at the kinds of words to use, at ways of overcoming a child's reluctance to listen or talk, at the use of play for communicating with younger children. Giving children information involves finding out what they know already, and checking to see what they have understood of anything we have told them; we discuss some of the practical ways of doing this here. We also list many of the common worries children have. Knowing these can make it easier to notice them and to dispel them; this in itself may open up communication.

Talking with children

Parents or other adults talk to children in different situations. They may sit down 'for a serious talk' but much talking goes on when members of the family are doing something else, such as travelling in a car or on a bus or walking to school. Parents also communicate with small children through stories, songs and play.

Sitting down for a serious talk may be extremely difficult. Parents and children may be embarrassed; it may be very hard to persuade children to stay to talk; even at bedtime they may insist on a ritual which prevents the parent from saying anything the child fears it does not want to hear. However, some children do allow such conversations. Older children may wander into the kitchen late at night; younger ones may be forthcoming at bedtime or immediately after school. A teenager may talk seriously and confidingly with the parent of a friend. Some parents make up stories or songs for young children that give information and put words to feelings.

> 'Sam was walking along the road with his dad one day, when all of sudden his dad fell to the ground in a heap. Sam was very frightened and didn't know what to do...'

The child may join in or correct the adult's version of the story.

More often, parents will be in a position to pick up remarks or statements made by children in passing or during their games. Very often children throw out hints for their parents or others. For example, a child might say 'When mum gets better...' when they have been told that their mother is not going to get better. It is very tempting to allow this kind of remark to pass without correction, and sometimes this might be appropriate. However, it does not help children to allow them to live in a world of fantasy, and may leave them feeling the adult has not listened to them or taken notice of what they have said. Allowing such remarks to pass and not taking them up later may confirm to the child that the adult is pretending to themselves and cannot face the truth. Often a statement like this can be seen as the child's *wish*. The adult could say 'It would be good if she were going to get better again wouldn't it, and it is hard to think that she won't...' A younger child may need to be cuddled while this is said.

A teenager whose father had recently died told his aunt he wanted to buy a racing car and drive it 'to destruction'. The aunt was afraid he was feeling suicidal but she said nothing. She said she did not want to put the idea into his mind.

In our view, the nephew was telling his aunt because he wanted her to know that he was feeling like destroying something which might have included himself. Her lack of response meant that she missed an opportunity to help him think clearly about his conflicting and dangerous feelings.

How to give children information: Practical suggestions

Clear, correct, truthful words are the best. It is surprising how difficult it can be to find and to use them. Children can get very muddled if adults use the wrong words.

Peter at six said he knew what was wrong with his father, who had MS: 'He's got bugs biting his legs.'

They also get muddled if adults say something is 'like' something else. Particularly under stress they are likely to take words literally, like the child who for years was terrified of the potato peeler because her grandmother used to say 'I'll skin you alive!'. If you say 'it's like...' then you also need to say 'but it's not the same as...'.

Older children need more simple explanations as well as ones appropriate to their age.

A young child is learning the meaning of words; whatever names adults use to describe a condition, the symptoms of the parent will colour those particular words. If a child is not to be told the name of an illness because parents want to conceal it from others, some other correct, specific name should be used, such as 'mum's illness'. There is difficulty with even this, because 'illness' then takes on this meaning for the child and it may mean that other illnesses take on meaning from the mother's. Children should never be asked or expected to keep family secrets: because of their magical beliefs, children find secrets a far greater burden than adults in general imagine.

If possible, the name of the illness or condition should be used, rather than simply saying 'mum's legs don't work properly', for example. Saying at some point that 'Mum's legs don't work properly because she has got multiple sclerosis' or 'motor neurone disease' or arthritis or some other ailment gives children the chance to sort out the difference between their own legs not working (if they are tired, for example) and their mother's legs 'not working'. They may not be able to do this when they are very young, but as they grow, they will need this information.

General, vague statements may also make difficulties for the children. 'Something is wrong up here' (in the head) may mean many different things, and the child will need help to sort out some of the things it does not mean.

Parents also may need to think about their use of the word 'bad', as in 'My legs are really bad today', or 'I was feeling bad last night' or 'I've got a bad head'. For a child, 'bad' may mean naughty, wicked or hurtful and frightening. There is good reason, of course, why 'bad' has different uses: a 'bad head' may mean a bad temper as well as a headache, but this does not mean that a smack on the head will make it better.

Too much cannot be taken in all at once. The adult needs to decide what to tell first, and what can wait. It can be reassuring for a child if an adult says 'That's enough for now; now you can go out and play (or go and watch television, or whatever) and we'll talk more another time'. The adult is making it clear that the child needs time to play and to laugh as well as time to think, and that laughing is still 'all right'.

Children need time and space to take in what they are being told. If the information is uncomfortable, they need time to say 'no' first, and then to react to this 'no'. They will need time to think during a serious conversation, so the adult should not talk all the time even if a child is saying nothing.

It can also be important to just share the child's feelings, particularly bad ones; talking can sometimes prevent children or adults from becoming aware of their feelings. Taking time to be silent together can be valuable. Children will also need time in between conversations. One serious talk is not enough.

Checking what a child has understood is essential. Even adults usually replace what they have been told with their own words and understanding; it is very likely that children will totally distort what they have heard. (A child heard the words 'I believe in God the Father...' as 'Ivy leaves in God the father...') Children who have been given important information should always be asked *what*, not *if*, they have understood. Raising the subject later is important in order to reinforce information, to ensure that it has been understood correctly, and to check whether it has raised questions or anxieties in a child's mind.

> 'You remember what I said the other day?... I wondered if you had been worrying about it?... What do you remember? I wondered if I had told you properly...'

> 'I don't know if you want to talk about it, but we do have to; sometimes you have to talk about things you don't like talking about.'

> 'Look, I've found the pictures we drew the other day...do you remember what you said then? Would you draw them the same now?'

If the child wants to hide them, tear them up, throw them out: 'I know you don't want to think about it, it would be lovely if we could get rid of it all just like that wouldn't it? I would like to as well, but we can't.'

Once a conversation has started it may be easy to pick up cues from the child about how it is feeling or what it is thinking. The adult's words may be less significant than the child's own thoughts. It is the child's own feelings and thoughts which will stay with the child and affect its reaction over the next few days or years: it is these that will determine how the adult's words are interpreted.

The child's thoughts or ideas are likely to be unrealistic and need to be taken literally by the adult, even if the child then says they did not mean them. It is important to acknowledge that adults and children can believe and feel several quite contradictory things at once. Love and anger in particular do not cancel each other out but exist side by side.

Younger children may need to be held on a lap or in arms while told some painful information. Older ones too may be offered a cuddle. However, listening and sympathetic understanding can give a child a very strong sense of being held; for some children this may be more reassuring and less disturbing than physical holding. Children often have strong feelings towards the adults close to them and may find physical contact frightening, embarrassing, distracting or repulsive rather than comforting. They may want an adult who is not their parent to keep his or her distance in order to show that he or she is not trying to replace the parent.

Play

Anxieties and fears about a parent's illness may be expressed quite directly in play. For example, children may act out 'mummy going to hospital', or they make their toys play out events they have experienced. Through their play children can tell adults a lot about the way they see the world as well as using it to handle the feelings they have to bear.

An adult who sits with a small child at play may be able to understand some of the feelings and fears the child needs to communicate. Sometimes the adult may join in. This may be an opportunity to find out what the child thinks or to give it information.

Melanie Klein described how a seven-year-old girl she saw in analysis wanted her to pretend to be a doctor.

> 'When I asked her what was supposed to be the matter with her she answered: "Oh, that makes no difference." I then began to have a proper consultation with her like a doctor, and said "Now, Mrs —, you really must tell me exactly where you feel the pain." From this there arose further questions – why she had fallen ill, when the illness had begun,

etc. Since she played the part of the patient several times in succession I obtained abundant and deeply-buried material in this way. And when the situation was reversed and she was the doctor and I the patient, the medical advice she gave me supplied me with further information.' (Klein 1975, p.73)

Play may also be a means of checking what a child has understood from a conversation. A child who has just been told 'mummy is in hospital' may say nothing. However, the adult may be able to begin to play saying: 'Teddy is worried because his mummy is in hospital...'

An adult may also sit down with a small child and suggest 'Let's play what happened when mummy went to the doctor...' or 'when daddy had his accident' for example. The child may join in immediately or may hang back and watch the adult. Toys to represent the parents, the child, other members of the family, doctors and nurses may be picked out, preferably by the child themselves but otherwise by the adult. The adult can use the toys to show the child what happened and to talk about how people felt at the time. The adult's view may be quite new to the child.

Once the child joins in, such play can help the child to show the adult what it is thinking, or may help an adult to guess. The child may express worries clearly in words: 'The baby is crying because there isn't any food'. The adult has several choices here. He or she can play someone bringing food to the baby or the baby to the food, for example, or help the child work out what to do for the baby. The adult could also directly ask 'Do you think we'd leave you hungry?' for example. These direct worries may hide more symbolic ones: does the child feel it would be 'hungry for love' perhaps?

Other worries may be expressed, for example, by a child getting angry with a toy and breaking it. Broken toys may express children's feelings of being broken themselves; they may feel an adult can or should be able to mend the toy (and therefore, them or their parent perhaps) or they may be quite hopeless about it. Allowing children to be sad and angry about having broken a toy may be as important as trying to mend it or admitting it cannot be mended. These situations may lead to a conversation about whether mummy or daddy can be 'mended' or not, and whose fault it was that they were damaged.

If a parent has been to hospital it may be a good idea to encourage the child to play 'hospitals' or 'doctors and nurses' with their toys. An adult joining in may be able to correct some of the wilder ideas children have about what goes on in hospitals. Some of children's most disturbing feelings and ideas may be attached to hospitals; they are a place where birth and death take place and where a child may imagine all kinds of disturbing physical contact (often both cruel and sexual) between adults. Playing with a sensitive adult may help a child who imagines a parent being involved in these activities.

If a child will not play, or simply repeats stereotyped actions, professional advice should be sought.

Music, writing and drawing

Older children may communicate with themselves and with an adult by music, writing or drawing. 'Mum's accident'; 'Jo's book about multiple sclerosis'; 'The day mum fell over in the street' 'The nervous system'; 'My family'; 'Dad'; 'Dad in hospital' are all possible titles for home-made books or pictures that might help children to talk and to hear and keep information they need.

An adult who sits and watches while a child draws, or who actually draws or writes to a child's instructions, may be given plenty of information about the way the child sees the world. At the same time, the adult may be able to add and correct facts and ideas, or enable the child to correct them him- or herself.

Depending on the child (and the adult) such books and drawings can be very factual or full of feelings.

> Tom, nine, drew several very revealing pictures when asked to draw his family. Finally he drew one which showed his father with a big black arrow through his heart. Asked what it was, he said it was death. He was then able to talk about how he saw death, and whether it was like this really, for his father or for him.

> 'Let's draw you and me going to visit dad in hospital the first time. Were you smiling or looking sad? You hadn't been to a hospital before and you didn't know what it was going to be like...'

Children may express considerable feeling in such pictures. They may end up by scribbling all over them or tearing them up. Some feelings can be expressed in words or pictures; others cannot. Children may be expressing frustration and fury with their failure to communicate on paper. This may be because the adult is not understanding well enough but is trying to impose his or her own ideas. It may also be because the child feels the adult does understand, and can understand the frustration expressed in the scribbling or the tearing.

Books about a condition may be helpful, particularly if the adult reads them with the child. Older children may be helped to read the book by the parent asking them what they think of it. Some children might be interested to think about what they would like to add to such a book, or to write or draw for younger children, perhaps in their own family.

'I don't want to know'

Children may make it clear that they do not want to be told anything. They may hide in their rooms, insist on watching television all the time; put on earphones whenever their parents try to talk with them, or make sure that there is never a quiet moment. The adult then has to decide whether to try to talk to them or whether to leave them alone and wait. If the waiting goes on for several months without the children allowing any talk about a parent's illness or new disability, firmness may be needed. It may also be needed if a parent is getting worse and children are resisting being told this. Someone outside the immediate family may be able to talk with the children or the parents can try some of the following suggestions.

> 'I know you don't want to be told things, and I don't want to have to tell you either. We just don't want it to be true...'

> 'You may be very frightened of being told something which is *much worse* than the truth: that is why you need to be told the truth... Once we've talked about it it will feel a bit different... It will still be there but you won't be quite so frightened...'

The adult cannot *know* this of course, and it needs to be said in a way which allows the adult to admit to being wrong, but it usually does turn out to be the case. It may be a challenge to the child to then prove the adult wrong; in this way the child has to put its fears into words, and if (very unusually) they do turn out to be a completely true and realistic, the adult can share them with the child.

Sometimes it helps to say that *'part of you'* doesn't want to know, while perhaps another part does.

The adult may try to guess why the child doesn't want to know. Possible guesses are:

> 'If I don't know it won't happen / it won't be true.'

> 'What they are going to tell me is totally, unbelievably unbearable.'

> 'I don't want to know *now*. If I can put it off for long enough it will go away.'

> 'They can tell my brother then I needn't worry about it, he can. He's clever and big and can worry about things: I'm too stupid, I'm only small, I don't have to know things I don't want to know.'

'If someone says "Daddy is going to die" it will kill him and me.'

'Talking about it makes it worse.' This often means: 'Talking about it means it is true: as long as we don't talk I can pretend it isn't.'

These would need to be put into the adult's own language, using the words the child uses if possible.

A child may also refuse to talk because they do not want to say something that will hurt a parent. They may be afraid of saying the wrong thing and making the parent worse. They may be afraid of being told off or afraid of the accusation they want to make. They may not want to betray one or other parent. This may make them unable to listen to the parent or other adult concerned. If such worries are suspected, it may be a good idea to find another person to talk with the children in a setting that is confidential.

Common worries

Many worries children have prevent them from talking with adults and make them hide their own difficulties. If an adult thinks a child might possibly not be talking to him or her because of such a worry it can be helpful to say 'Some children think...' or 'Some children worry...' or 'Some children feel...'. It might also be a good idea to follow this with '...I don't know if you feel like that or not...' The child themselves may not know either: it is possible to worry without knowing it (just as it is possible to be in love without knowing it). The worries we have listed below are ones which adults have not known their children had. Even if the child does seem open and prepared to talk, these particular worries may not be voiced until the adult raises them.

It may be helpful for adults to add their own list of the thoughts they think they might have if they were in the same position as the child, and to write these down before checking with the child.

Older children may worry about all the things on the list; younger ones may not worry about the later ones, though if they can understand the idea at all, they may have the worry.

What will happen to me? (It will be the end of me and my life.)

What will happen to mum if anything happens to dad? (or vice versa). I can't cope with looking after mum on my own.

What will happen to me if something happens to both my parents? It will be the end of everything if both my parents die or leave me.

It's something I've done or not done. I caused it; I am being punished for something.

They're going to die and leave me, but they're not telling me.

I will have to do all the looking after. I will have to comfort mum/dad and keep them alive on my own; how will we live without mum's/dad's money? I will have to make decisions about which school to go to; I will have to do the cooking/be mum/be dad.

My big sister will take over and she will think she's my mum: she'll boss me and she doesn't like me like mum does... I will be left out of everything...

Does it mean I can't be in the school play/get my GCSEs/go to college? How can I do these things when my mother or father is ill or dying? How can they do this to me? I won't be able to do things for me.

I must stay and keep an eye on mum/dad or something terrible will happen while I'm away.

I'm selfish to think about myself instead of them.

Children *have* to think about themselves if their mother or father is not there or able to think about them: this is one of the ways in which children actually suffer from the loss.

When the news is that a parent is ill or disabled and unable to do some of the things they could do before a child may think:

'You/she/he won't be able to do *anything.*'

'I won't have a mum/dad any more.'

'No-one can love me/look after me like my mum did and she won't love me/look after me any more.'

Adult and child need to talk through what the parent will be able to do: 'I'll still be your mum, I just won't be able to do everything I could before.' 'I'll still be able to take you to school, but we'll have to go by car, not walk.' Losses also need to be acknowledged as losses. 'We're all sad I can't take you swimming any more.'

Existing knowledge getting in the way

A child may not be able to take in new information if they already believe they know it, or if they have other knowledge, true or false, which seems to contradict or make irrelevant the new information. We have given many examples of this. One was Alice's idea that 'Mummy is just defending daddy; daddy really just hates me, she is only *saying* it's his MS that makes him behave like that; it's not true'. Another one is 'I know what is wrong with mum, she's like (someone with a more serious condition); they are pretending it's different because they can't face the truth or they don't want to tell me.'

Some of these ideas can be discovered by parents; but not all of them can be corrected by parents, since they work, like Alice's, to counteract everything a parent says. Alice could not be told about her father's condition by her parents and had to hear it from an outsider.

Checklist: Giving children painful information

If adults give children disturbing information they have to be prepared to

- allow time and space for the children to react while the adults are with them

- try to find out what the children already know and think before giving them information

- allow time if a child withdraws; perhaps put up with temper tantrums when the subject is raised

- hold a younger child while he or she cries, perhaps considerably later; sit with a distressed older child in comforting silence. Perhaps give explicit permission to cry in company

- make time to discuss it further later and repeatedly

- look out for decisions the children make as a result of distorting the information or drawing false conclusions from it.

Timing

Handling feelings

There are times when children are better left alone to handle their feelings in their own way. Immediately after an event, for example, anyone else's feelings may seem like an intrusion, bringing the outside world in when it is not wanted.

There are also times when it is better to accept having to cause some kind of disruption in order to bring about necessary changes. Timing of any intervention depends very much on the relationships concerned, and on the issues involved. There are times when one person can help, but not another: this can cause jealousy and competitiveness.

Adults and older children have to be allowed to make their own choices about whether they talk or remain silent, and who they talk to, though discussion of the importance and difficulty of talking may be helpful.

With younger children we suspect that encouragement to talk is essential. Sometimes they will naturally talk about what has happened or what they see going on. We suspect that often they cannot get adults to listen or take them seriously, or they are picking up strong messages about the adults not being in a state to listen. The timing of any intervention for them may not be decided on their needs and the signals they give, but on the needs of the adults around them and the willingness of the adults to acknowledge their signals.

With children under twelve, it may be appropriate for adults to take the initiative and decide for them that they need to be given the opportunity to talk to someone about some family difficulty shortly after it has happened, or within a few months, or later if the child begins to show cause for concern, even if the child says they do not want to talk. A child who is in obvious distress and cannot discuss it may need considerable support before admitting a need for help, but may, in the long term, recognise and value the help received.

Giving information

Some information follows on the events and is part of an attempt to help a child cope with something that has happened. Here timing depends on the age of the child, and knowledge may have to be reviewed as the child grows.

Parents often want to put off giving children upsetting information about an illness until they are sure that bad news is definite. Doctors do this to adult patients too. There are several problems with this, some of which have already been discussed. Children need time to prepare themselves for unpleasant events. Part of the horror of a parent's accident or illness can be the unexpectedness of it: children who have no warning are likely to feel completely disoriented and that their world is disintegrating. If it is possible to give warning, not only do the children feel more in control of the situation, but they can feel that the adults are in some control and have not lost their own minds.

Without information, children are left in a family where the adults are seriously worried but the children have been told nothing. The children make their own explanation for the feelings they can sense, and this explanation may be very distressing. Children may feel abandoned and unloved by the adults; forgotten and neglected as well as entirely responsible for this state of affairs.

If children are told when the news is not definite, the worst possibility can be taken in and then rejected, with the children taking refuge in the fact that it hasn't happened yet. The child has time to try out the thought and return to a more comforting present. The worst possibility can be assimilated gradually, in small doses, with parents who are themselves more likely to be emotionally available to the children than parents facing imminent disaster.

When the information is given only at the last minute children have no realistic possibility of escape from the worst reality. Since thought, feelings and reality all seem unbearable, the child may be forced into attempting to destroy all of them. This makes it more likely that they will feel their world has fallen entirely to pieces and that they are completely unsupported and unloved. It may also disturb their more general ability to think or feel, possibly for many years.

Parents sometimes worry about 'upsetting children unnecessarily' if they warn them about something which may then not happen. We look at it differently. First, we do not think that it is terrible to upset children, though we do not like doing it. Thinking upsetting thoughts may be preferable to having to pretend that there is nothing wrong. Upset is linked with grief and mourning: with recognition of reality and with salvaging goodness out of loss. Helping children to think on their own level about things which are troubling the adults in a family allows the children to feel less excluded as well as giving them a chance to prepare for a possible future grief.

Second, we think that all children at some point in their childhood think about the possibility of their parents leaving them, or becoming ill, or helpless or even dying. Children can sometimes surprise parents by talking quite matter-of-factly about the death or illness of their parents, sometimes quite out of the blue. When they are very young they may even say 'I wish mum was dead then I could marry you, dad', for example. Older children may not share these ideas with their parents, but they still have similar ones particularly when they have felt angry or jealous towards one parent. Such thoughts may not be particularly upsetting to the children, since they may split off the sense of loss and simply feel triumphant, though older children may feel guilty about them. Many children's stories incorporate ill or absent parents. If a disaster or illness does occur, the child will have ready-made ideas to fall back on. If a parent has talked about these fantasies with the child, they are likely to be more realistic and perhaps less guilt-provoking than they would be otherwise.

Children need to be prepared to deal with the fact that other people, such as teachers or other pupils, may have wrong information about their parent's condition.

People also put off giving children information because they do not know what it means. If there may be a long time between being told the diagnosis and discovering what this means, children can be told: 'We know dad has got (...) but we don't yet know what it means. We're trying to find out and we'll let you know when we know anything...' It may be necessary to add: '...We are anxious and worried, but we don't yet know how bad it is; it may not be as bad as we are afraid it is...' or: 'We do know it means he's not going to die of it...' It is important to ask the children something along the lines of: 'What does it make you think of?'

Trying to find out what a child understands at this point is important. Even the name of the condition may have a meaning to the child which the adult cannot imagine. The child may have some experience of another child's parent with a very different condition and be thinking 'It'll be like so-and-so's dad'.

In general, our feeling is that it is best to give children information as soon as possible. However, delay can be advisable. Parents' initial reaction to a serious diagnosis, for example, may be very frightening and possibly excessive. Obtaining more information before discussing it with the children may be a good idea. So too may the parents allowing themselves some time to think and discuss what they know and fear with someone else. Time to overcome their own first reactions may help parents to avoid telling the children in a way that is more frightening than it needs to be.

It is not sufficient to leave all discussion until the child is older, since then only more mature ideas may be expressed. Nor is it sufficient to wait until a child asks: the most frightening questions are the least likely to be asked. Ideas formed when the child was younger need to be caught at the time if they are not to live on, buried but powerfully effective. However, delay may be advisable even if the news is urgent for adults when children are of an age where next week seems a very long time indeed. For children aged one or two, every week increases their understanding and the possibility of giving them information they can grasp without confusing them with ideas or facts they cannot understand.

A child of any age needs time to get used to a new idea. How long it needs will depend on the child, but the younger the child, the shorter the time. For an adult, time to get used to the idea of moving home, for example, might quite reasonably be one year; for a teenager, a few months seems a long time; for a child of ten, a few weeks can seem long, and for a child of two or three two weeks may be an unimaginably long time.

How do we tell them what might happen?

An adult may have to explain what it means that something 'might' happen. This will depend both on age and the way the family use language: some children are taught the use of such words early on, others not. Both possibilities need to be discussed; what if it does happen, and what if it does not? Both good and bad outcomes need discussion. Children sometimes join in with wild possibilities as a way of establishing the meaning of 'it might...' It can be reassuring if the worst possibility has been discussed in a way that acknowledged the real feelings and made it clear that life would go on for some of the family and would be worth having. Both child and adult can feel 'If we could cope with that one, we can cope with anything.' Reminding children of present reality may be a good end for the conversation.

It may be important to think far enough into the future until after a terrible crisis would be over. It is not possible to cry for ever and children need to know that their and the adult's grief would eventually be worked through. We do not ever forget people we loved but have lost, but grief does not stop everything for ever. The sense of the love of a parent stays with people throughout their lives.

Conclusion

In this chapter we have looked at ways of talking with children about their parent's illness, and at some of the issues involved in timing.

CHAPTER 13

What Should Adults Tell Children?

Here we list things children need to know. Many of them have been discussed elsewhere in this book; we put them here to give a reference list that can be used to check what has been discussed with the child.

Truthful facts

Children need truthful facts about an illness or a disability. These need to be explained in such a way that the child can understand them without being overwhelmed. News of a diagnosis may be a shocking event, though it may not. The diagnosis needs to be understood: what it means (in terms of events and feelings) for the children and for the adults, as far as can be known.

Children may also observe frightening or disturbing behaviour; wounds, machinery, nurses and doctors coming and going; hushed voices, all of which they will interpret in their own way. In addition, certain events connected with a parent's illness may be frightening for a child. A parent's fall; a visit to the doctor; an accident; a fit; a short stay in hospital; or the development of a strange symptom may arouse disturbing feelings and thoughts in children. Adults' views and children's views of the relative importance of events may be very different and it is important first to discover which events or situations trouble the child. It is unlikely that a significant event can be sufficiently dealt with at the time.

In the case of both major and minor events, a description of exactly what happened, when, how, and if possible, why, may be important for the child to enable them to come to terms with it. However, sensitivity is required here. The wrong sort of detail may disturb children. Young children, for example, do not need all the details about a parent's operation, though their questions do need to be answered at a level that makes sense to them. With many events, such as a father falling over, it may be important to reach the ending and to move on to a discussion of a time when it was over or will be over. The situation before

174

the event may also need to be included; for example, if a parent was injured by an accident. The feelings that go with these descriptions are very important, and we look at this aspect later.

'Going over the past' may be very painful, but we now know it is extremely important if the child is not to remain 'traumatised'. It cannot take place all at once but it should not be neglected nor put off indefinitely. The child understands events differently at different ages and may need to go over significant events again and again as they grow up, with different feelings coming out each time. Very young children may be totally unable to believe an event or situation was not their fault or their parents' fault: it may not be until they are much older that they can fully grasp how little control people have. Adults need to look for the time when children can understand this if the children are not secretly to blame their parents or themselves all their lives for something nobody could alter.

Reality

Children are not helped if adults try to protect them by allowing them to falsify events or to pretend that people behaved better than they did. The pain of reality may be hard to bear, but the complications and disadvantages of distorting the truth are much greater in the long run. It is very important not only to tell children the truth about what has happened to their parents, but to make sure they understand what it means in the present and the future. It may be tempting to cover up some of the more disturbing facts or thoughts. Children may continue to deny knowledge they have, but this tendency needs to be gently and sensitively corrected.

The reality of real kinds of recovery and real hopes also need to be acknowledged. Past events do not change, but feelings about them do. Pleasure and fun are possible even after and even during appalling situations. Idealising the situation as it was before an illness or event is not a good idea: the child needs to remember the bad things as well as the good from the past if the present and future are not to seem terrible by comparison. Talking with children of how they were before the diagnosis or the onset of the condition can also prevent them losing whole sections of their personal history and both idealising and denigrating themselves.

Beliefs about the parent's feelings also need realistic discussion. Children may, for example, restrict their lives because they fear their parent will envy them their fun and their health. Discussing whether their parent is really envious is possible: it may be the children's own envy seen in the parent, or it may not. People have contradictory feelings, and parents who do want to spoil their children's happiness may also want them to be happy. It makes a difference if children know that at least one adult approves of them having a life for themselves.

Full information

The information needs to be as full as possible within the child's level of understanding. It is neither possible nor desirable to tell young children every symptom that a parent with a deteriorating illness might get but if a child is warned in some way about the possible or expected course of a disease they feel their parents are more in control. This kind of full information is not urgent, but it does need to be discussed at some time. It should include realistic hopes.

In Chapter 12 we listed common worries children have and which probably need to be addressed, whether the children talk easily or not. In addition, children need answers to the following questions:

- Will dad/mum leave because of it?

- What happens to the parent who has it? Do they have pain? Do they get tired? Do their muscles stop working? Are their minds affected in any way? Are they frightened by what happens to them?

- Why or how do symptoms happen?

- How long will a symptom last? Will it get better or not? If it might get worse, what does this mean? How soon will it happen?

- Will I get it?

Parents will be unable to answer some of these questions, but it may be very important to state where there is lack of knowledge in order that the children know enough, for example, to challenge someone else who makes a false statement about their parent's condition.

Will you die of it?

A parent's illness or accident may raise thoughts in the child of the parent dying. Children may also be asked by others how long their ill parent has to live. If their parent is not about to die they need to be told explicitly. Sometimes children find out that their parent's condition will cause their death 'eventually' or 'in ten years', for example. They may not dare to raise this with either parent, and not be sure if their parents know or not. Thoughts of one parent dying provoke thoughts of the other parent dying too.

Talking with a child about thoughts of parents dying may be difficult, but it is important. Children can be helped to see that they will be older, that they will feel differently then, that they will not be expected to look after themselves, or that they will be old enough to look after themselves 'even though this is difficult to imagine when you are small'.

I've got it too

Children can be told that they might develop some of their parent's symptoms and that this does not necessarily mean that they have the condition. If there is a possibility that the child does have the condition, this needs to be discussed seriously. Hasty reassurance may simply increase the child's belief that the situation is too frightening for the adults to think about, without stopping the child from inventing much worse scenarios for itself.

It is confusing to tell a child that symptoms are 'imaginary'. Symptoms that arise as a result of conversion of an (unconscious) idea or emotion into a physical feeling are real, even though they are not caused by illness. The fact that the idea or emotion is quite unconscious means that the child cannot simply decide to lose the symptom when it wants to: a totally unwanted and unrecognised idea, probably extremely painful, has to become thinkable first.

It is possible to explain to children that when a parent is ill, children (and adults) often try to look after the parent by *being* the parent or by trying to keep him or her safe inside themselves. The symptoms may be a part of this; they can be caused by trying to *be* their mother or father. When people do this they are not pretending to have their symptoms; they are trying to convince themselves either that they *are* their mother or father or that they have that parent safe inside them. It is different from ordinary pretending partly because they are pretending to themselves and they do not even know they are doing it, and partly because they cannot easily choose to do it or to stop it. (This may sound a little far-fetched, but children may find it less crazy than adults do.)

Playing at being mum/dad

Small children need to know that they can play at being a parent without becoming that parent: that they can try out a symptom (such as difficulty walking) without risking 'getting stuck'.

> Jody's mother talked with her about the difference between being 'like' mummy and 'being mummy'. When Jody was older she also talked with her about ways she wanted to be like her mother and ways she did not.

Parents often know they need to remind their young children who they are: 'You are my baby'; 'You are my little girl'; particularly at bedtime or after acting play. They may need to add: ' – and you don't have a bad leg.'

'You don't want to be like me' may be a mother's natural response if she sees her child copying her disability or illness: but for the child 'being like mummy' includes not only the illness but also all the creative and good aspects of being a mother which the child wants and needs to keep throughout their own lifetime. Children need to know that it is all right to want to be like a parent even if that parent is ill or disabled in some way. They may need help to distinguish between the illness or disability and other aspects of the parents.

'The doctors don't know'

The fact that parents and doctors do not know everything may need to be discussed. Some children simply do not believe this, and think that when parents say they do not know they are simply hiding something from the children.

Information about treatment

Children may need to know something about their parent's treatment. If the parents differ on what treatment is best, the child may need to have more of an explanation including a discussion of the fact that parents can differ. Younger children, particularly, may look on treatments as magic and be very worried if their parents do not follow them exactly.

Information about their parent's behaviour

A common problem with any illness is that tiredness, pain, worry and a constantly exacerbated sense of their own losses brought on by the illness may preoccupy parents, making them snappy or unresponsive to the child's need for care. The child may interpret this as a lack of caring, however much the parent is doing for the child and worrying about it. Children do not always know what events mean to their parents, and may need to be told even if it seems obvious to the adult.

> A small boy asked his mother anxiously why she was so gloomy. She said, 'My father has just died, you know'. The boy's grandfather had died a few days before but he had not connected his mother's mood with this fact.

Adults who want to talk with children about their parents' behaviour need to think about the realities of the situation: illnesses do make people more self-centred, and it may be that children have in fact lost the caring attention of one parent. This needs to be handled sensitively, recognising that the child may feel:

- it is their fault the parent no longer cares for them
- the other parent (or everyone else they care for) will also stop loving them

- ° that their own ability to care for others is not good enough

- ° very angry with one or both parents

- ° angry with brothers or sisters or other people who do not care enough.

Children and both parents may need help in recognising this situation, exploring how true it is that an ill parent no longer cares for anyone other than him- or herself, and discovering perhaps that the whole family needs to grieve for a very real loss.

Children also may need to be told, and shown, that parents have to be allowed to get angry and upset sometimes if they are to go on being parents. Trying to protect their parents from 'stress' is not necessary and may even take away a role their parents could still perform well.

'It is your parents' decision'

Children need to know that it is for their parents to decide on treatment, not the children. They also need to know that parents or other adults will continue to take decisions for them while they are children and that they will not be expected or allowed to grow up too quickly and 'step into their parent's shoes' when that parent is absent or incapacitated. They need to know their opinions may be considered, but the adults are in charge.

If children have been left in a situation where adults have not taken charge the children may need considerable help later. Child carers may have considerable difficulty both at the time and later if they have been allowed to take on too much responsibility. Adults themselves often do not notice how much they are allowing children to take on.

Causes

Information about causes is helpful. Children's own ideas should be checked.

Whose fault was it?

If someone was at fault it is probably best if this is discussed openly. It is important to make sure that children realise, for example, that just because one doctor (or hospital or car driver or whoever) made a serious mistake, not all will do the same. Good examples of doctors, hospitals or car drivers need to be pointed out.

The child's own lack of fault needs to pointed out. If another member of the family is accused, rightly or wrongly, of making a condition worse (for example, in a quarrel), the extent and limits of this need to be discussed with the child.

Some things will not change

Children need information about what will remain the same. Any information that means a big change in their lives will need to include explicit discussion of what will not change. Will the child need to move house, change school, lose their friends, for example?

Children of any age need to be told that they will go on being looked after. They also may need to be told that they will not entirely forget parents who have left them for any reason: even if they do forget some things, the love and care they had from the lost parent will stay with them throughout their lives. Bad feelings will change as the child grows.

Some things will change

Children need to know what changes will happen. Will a parent lose his or her job, for example, and what will this mean? Will it mean the family has no money? Will it mean no more presents, clothes, shoes or food? Will they lose a pet? Their ideas about parents being out of work or losing the house may be unrealistic.

If there are to be changes in where the child will live or who will look after them, the children need to know as soon as possible who that person is and where they will be. If possible these people and places should to be introduced in such a way as to make them familiar before the change. It is best if a parent or other familiar person introduces children to a new person or place where they are to stay. Children should never be left without warning. They should be allowed to say goodbye and to cry and cling for a while to the person who leaves them.

What can I do? What can't I do?

Children need to know what they can do for their parents and what they cannot do. They need to know the difference between making their parents happy and making them better; between making them cross, bad-tempered or in pain and making their illness or condition worse. They need to know that their bad feelings are not dangerous. They need to know if anything they do or do not do could cause their parent real damage. If there is anything, they need to know that they will not be left alone with the parent at risk of this happening, and what to do if the worst happens.

Children need to know the difference between what they want to do for their parents and what they can do. They need to know that their parents do not expect them to be perfect carers and that they cannot expect themselves to be perfect, however much it matters.

What can my parents do? What can they not do?

Children need to know what their parents can and want to carry on doing for them, including for example, listening to their worries (if they do).

They need to know that it is not dangerous for even ill parents to cry or be upset.

Reactions to expect

Children need facts about some of the emotional reactions they can expect, in themselves or in others, and about how long these can be expected to last. They need to know that people have emotional reactions and thoughts they do not want or like, but that these are important and cannot be avoided. They need to know it is normal to be upset, to cry, be angry and frustrated, unable to think clearly, be bad-tempered or generally miserable if a parent is ill, as well as to want to laugh and joke or forget it sometimes. They need to know the reactions listed under 'Common worries' (Chapter 12).

They may need to know that people learn to live with disabilities and losses (such as loss of the ability to walk), and that life with a parent in a wheelchair or after some other serious loss is not simply the end of all life and all happiness for the whole family. (Getting used to such losses may take two years or more but this does not mean two years of unremitting misery.)

They also need to know that sometimes they may be happy, they may go out with friends, forget their own and their parents' troubles; that sometimes they will be miserable and sometimes they will forget, and that this is normal.

How long will it go on for?

Adults need to help children separate out in their minds what will last from what will not last. A parent's loss of a leg will last: a father who leaves home may be gone forever though the child may continue to see him; a parent's frequent weeping or bad temper associated with a loss is likely to gradually reduce over a period of two years, as everyone adjusts to a new normality. Some feelings will last; others will not.

Permission to seek help outside the family

Children sometimes worry about themselves. They need to know that they can seek help from a counsellor, a doctor, a sympathetic teacher, a social worker; that it is their circumstances that may make this necessary, not some serious fault in themselves. They need to know they are not betraying their parents by seeking such help outside the family; that there are issues that are better discussed with people other than their parents. They need to know if their parents agree with this or not.

✠   ✠   ✠   ✠

Reading through this list it is clear that children are not going to be told everything on it. For some children and some situations, not all of these issues are relevant: there will be others we have missed out that are relevant only for certain conditions. We expect people to be creative with the list and add to it as they think best.

Much of the information will be given to children in passing remarks rather than in serious conversations. We do recommend checking that children have this information; younger children particularly may grow up with quite serious misunderstandings in several of the areas listed. Raising the subject periodically as the child grows and their understanding changes is also important.

CHAPTER 14

The Death of a Parent

Introduction

In this chapter we look at some of the ways in which adults can help children who have to live through the most difficult and damaging of all losses: the loss of a parent's life. Even thinking about these issues can be distressing.

Thinking about a death before it happens

Some parents know that they are going to die while their children are young, as a result of an illness or other condition. These parents and their partners have the opportunity to help their children themselves, though they may be unable to do so.

Children (and adults) who have had some warning about a death suffer less than those for whom it is totally out of the blue. The opportunity to think with their parents about life without them can help children after their parents' death. Some of the fantasies which children have when their parents are alive include fantasies about a parent dying and the child taking over their possessions or their partner.

> Peter, aged three, was listening to a New Guinea folk tale, in which a mother ran from her husband with her small son. The father was killed and Peter looked up at his mother with delight. 'So then she could marry her son!' he exclaimed.

Such fantasies may seriously disturb the children if the parent actually dies. They may well be afraid that their thoughts caused the death. If the parents have talked with their children about what will happen when their parent dies the children have some reassurance that such fantasies will not come true.

However, many parents will not broach such subjects with their children. If they are ill, they may be unable to think clearly about anything because of their own pain, physical or emotional. Parents often do not clearly distinguish their children from themselves in their own minds and they may have very unrealistic views of the ways the children will be affected.

> A mother and father were discussing with a social worker their feelings about the father dying. Both were saying how they had come to terms with it and had accepted it. Their nine-year-old daughter indicated her brother and said 'What about us?' There was a shocked silence.

Some parents do manage to tell their children what is happening, and do manage to talk with them about the child's present situation and about their future. One mother dying of cancer not only talked to the children about her impending death, but also wrote a series of letters to her children, for them to open on each birthday until they were grown up.

When children do not have parents who can talk to them about their own death they may have closely involved parent-substitutes such as grandparents or childminders or step-parents who know them well and love them and who are better able to talk with them. If cancer is involved, Macmillan nurses, who are trained to help families with these issues, may be available.

What do we say?

Chapters 11–13 are relevant here, but there are extra anxieties when death is involved.

Children need clear and truthful information, and the opportunity to cry about it, think about it, play and talk about it with an understanding adult. Telling a child that their parent is going on holiday, sleeping, or 'gone away' simply makes the child anxious about holidays, going to sleep or other people going away. It also means they cannot trust adults.

> One woman said that when she was two her father told her that her mother had gone away. When he remarried two years later he pretended her mother had come back. She knew he was wrong but was totally bewildered and very disturbed.

'Gone to heaven' can leave children feeling left behind, abandoned and unloved. They may also be tempted to join the parent or be very scared of their watchful presence. They may worry that if they are not always totally good, they will never join the parent there.

A popular children's book describes dying as 'the body getting tired' and 'going down the long tunnel' without using the word dying or death; these phrases risk raising small children's fears about getting tired themselves and going into tunnels.

Children need help to understand the meaning of death. William drew a black arrow through his father's heart and angel's wings. Children's feelings about death are based on being alive. They often think dead people can go on feeling or breathing or can 'get up again'. They also think people can choose when or if they will die. Stories they have read, television programmes and experience of the death of a pet or with other children who have lost a parent will all influence their ideas. It can help children if adults talk to them about the way they remember people who have died, and how the deceased go on being important to them and to other people for the rest of their lives.

Children need to know if a parent is about to die 'soon' or not. If it seems likely but no-one can tell when, they need to know this too. They can understand or be taught what 'we don't know', or 'might' means, though they may resist believing it. If a parent is very unlikely to die within a time span that for the child is long, it is important to tell the child this too.

A very young child may be told that 'mummy is very ill and she is going to die'. This needs to be followed by 'She isn't going to die today or tomorrow, or next week', provided this is true. 'You will be bigger then' and 'We will tell you when it will be, so you will know in time' may also be important pieces of information: young children change a lot even in a few weeks. Younger children may need to have 'next week' explained (in terms of going to bed and waking up, repeated seven times, for example); older children may be given some idea of the time involved by reference to what they will be doing at school, or how old they will be. If they know a child of this age it may help them to realise that they will have changed by then and may be more able to bear it and to feel more grown up than they do now.

WHO WILL LOOK AFTER ME?

Children worry that they will have to look after themselves: they may find it hard to believe that adults will go on looking after them. If they are to be cared for by someone they do not know well, they need to be encouraged to talk about their feelings about this, even if they are negative ones. It may hurt or upset the parent to know that children are not happy to go to their grandparents, perhaps, or that they are, but it may be important for children that their parents know how they feel even if they can do nothing more about it.

> A six-year-old boy asked his mother spontaneously what would happen to him if both his parents died. She said he'd go to certain friends, whereupon he said 'I don't want to live with them, they'd make me eat meat!' The mother had to discuss it with the friends in front of the child in order to convince him it was untrue.

SPECIFIC WORRIES

Many simple, specific worries can be uncovered and dealt with. Children worry about where they will live, who will look after their father or mother, who will feed the cat, who will take them to school, and so on. All these concerns will have their actual meaning and a symbolic meaning for the child too. Adults do not need to know the symbolic meaning but it may be important to know that how they talk about the cat, for example, may have deep significance for children. A cat may stand for a non-verbal, scratchy, needy yet independent part of the child, a combination of mother and baby self, which the child is quite unsure will be cared for, for example. Dismissing worries about the cat may mean to the child that this part of itself is to be dismissed: taking the worries seriously may mean to the child that this part of the child will be cared for and will not be forgotten.

The list of 'anxieties' we give later in this chapter may help adults to guess or find out some of their children's actual worries where the children have not put them into words.

REASONS AND EXPLANATIONS

Children work out their own ideas about why people die, and may pick up wrong ideas from adult conversations or from stories or magazines. Death in children's minds may be associated with punishment and guilt. Their thoughts about what they can do or could have done to stop the death need to be heard before they can be challenged: less conscious ones may need to be guessed.

> A child afraid for her and her families' life on a sinking ship was reported as saying 'I've never told any lies…'

Children may think that a parent simply needed to eat the right food, or to be loved sufficiently, or that he or she 'caught their death of cold', or was 'worried to death' for example. They may think the parent wanted to go to heaven and did not care enough about the children left behind. Giving a child true reasons or explanations (as far as they can be known) will not be enough on their own to counteract these ideas, though it may help.

SHARING FEELINGS WITHOUT TALKING

Giving information and talking is a way an adult can feel they are doing something. More painful but perhaps of greater importance for the children, may be the moments when adults can do nothing except wordlessly share the children's feelings: the sense of loss and grief or anger or confusion at the way things are. There are times when words are a distraction and prevent more important communications.

One of the aspects of mothering that seems significant for children's long-term well-being is the belief that the mother understands the child, 'warts and all'. Her recognition and acceptance of 'bad' as well as 'good' aspects of their character affects children's acceptance or non-acceptance of themselves, and the kind of treatment they expect from a partner and from their own children later. The sense of being understood and accepted may not always require words. A look, a touch, a smile, a small gift or an acknowledgement in any other way, may convey important and lasting meaning to a child of any age. Many parents, ill or not, find it hard to accept their children as human beings and ignore certain aspects of their character while exaggerating others: this is something children have to deal with as they grow up.

Timing

We have discussed the general issues concerning timing in Chapter 12. How much warning children need must depend partly on their age, but it is probably better to tell children too soon rather than too late unless there is very good reason for delay. Children benefit from time to get used to an idea before it actually happens. They can be reassured by the fact that the death has not happened yet without having to deny reality entirely. They also need to be given a chance to say goodbye if at all possible, after the death if not before.

Children who know their parent is dying may begin to separate themselves from the parent, and it may be partly this that parents dread. There is a risk that children will withdraw into themselves and deprive themselves of parenting they could have, as a result of knowing they are about to lose the parent. This needs to be watched. If it seems to be happening the children can be asked if they are trying to make themselves independent now, before they need to be, to reassure themselves that they will be able to manage without their parent when the time comes. If they do this too much they will actually miss out on the benefits of a relationship they could have.

If children know they are to lose a parent, they may begin to seek other people to take that parent's place. Beginning this process while they still have their parents to fall back on may help them to attach themselves to people who will be able to support them well. Children or teenagers who turn to a friend or friend's parent because their own parent is dying will be influenced in their choice of person by the experience with the dying parent. If the experience seemed cruel and arbitrary, leaving the children feeling desperate, abandoned and hopeless, they may find friends who will leave them in this way, or they may treat friends very badly themselves. If the experience was more loving and understanding, with a relationship capable of bearing very sad and angry feelings, the friend or adult who fills the gap is more likely to be like this.

Adults and children need to know that the pain of parting and grief cannot be avoided without much more serious damage being done. Too much cutting off of feelings can lead to cruel and destructive behaviour later in life: feeling the pain hurts more, but is less damaging.

There are times perhaps when it is better to delay giving a child news about the dying or death of a parent. If very young children are to be looked after by someone other than their parent, it may be possible to wait until they have got to know this person before they are told. For a child of less than two, a few days is a long time. In this time they can get to know someone and to feel fairly comfortable with them. For a child of three or four, the time needed to get to know someone is longer and they need to know why they are being left with that person.

Clearly parents have to consider their own and their child's situation and decide accordingly. It is very difficult to make these decisions, and parents are likely to feel they have done the wrong thing whatever they do.

Teenagers may understand better than younger children if there is a very good reason to keep information from them. They may be more aware of their own independent existence. They may be aware how precarious this is and want to avoid too much involvement with their parents. A parent's death, amongst everything else, is a disruption in the process of separation from the family and the development of the teenager's own life.

Teenagers are likely to feel angry and resentful about a delay, but at the same time may also be grateful if bad news is not given to them just before important examinations when it could be kept until afterwards. It is not easy to predict how they will react and how seriously they will be affected: there is really no good time to tell children that their parent is dying or is dead. However they feel, it may be important for young adults that their parents consider that their exams, their careers and their independent lives should take priority over caring for an ill parent. Parents have to accept that their children may not thank them for making decisions the parents consider to be in the children's best interests.

Adults may not want to tell children that a parent is about to die or even has died in order to prevent the children from restricting their life sooner than they need to. This may be sensible up to a point, but the delay should not be too long. Children sense it when the family is disrupted by grief and they make their own interpretations. They may fear something worse or different, and may change their own behaviour according to their own interpretations. For example, if they know another child whose parents have divorced, they may think that it is this that is about to happen. In this case they could blame one or other parent, and perhaps begin to behave differently towards them in the light of this belief – with serious consequences when they discover the truth.

Some children are not told until after a death even when the adults knew it was imminent. If parents do decide to keep such knowledge from children, however good the reason, they should expect children to react badly when they find out; children are likely to feel betrayed and as if something vitally important has been taken away from them.

Including the child in

Sending children away 'on holiday' because their mother or father is about to die is not a good idea. The children need to know what is going on, to be allowed to see the dying parent, to be included in the events. They need to be left alone with the parent sometimes if that is what they want.

> A seventeen-year-old boy sat by his father's bedside for three hours after his father died, talking to him and crying.

Can I do anything?

Most children seem to want to do something for their ill parents. They may hope that their actions could make the parent better; they may fear they could make them worse. Children are very unclear about what adults can and cannot do, and need time to work out what they think could be done, and then to talk about it.

> A sixteen-year-old boy was convinced the doctors had made his mother ill, because she had gone into hospital walking and had come out in a wheelchair.

> A woman of sixty-five said she didn't want her father to go into hospital: they were dangerous places where 'you go to die'. She felt he would be much *safer* at home, not just more comfortable, even though she knew he was dying.

If a child could actually cause a parent's death by doing something or failing to do something, and parents cannot simply prevent this happening, it needs to be discussed very carefully with the child. This could happen, for example, in some circumstances if a parent is in the last stages of Motor Neurone Disease, or if a parent has severe asthma or epilepsy. The fact of the illness itself being the prime cause of death, not the child's behaviour, needs to be emphasised.

Real pleasures a child can give a dying parent can be sought and brought to the child's attention. The value of 'making Mum/Dad happy' even if Mum or Dad cannot be made *better* may need to be made explicit.

Home nursing

The presence of a mother or father is important to children. The small girl who told the social worker how much she loved her daddy, how he got cross with her, laughed at and with her, and loved her did not mention the fact that he could not speak. The studies on maternal deprivation in animals make it clear that the simple presence of the mother may be vital in protecting the young from fear and anxiety; in allowing them to eat, explore and later parent their own children.

The presence of a parent in the house, even if they are severely ill, may be very important to the children even if they are embarrassed by it at times. There can be reassurance and comfort in knowing that the parent is there; in knowing that they are still alive; in knowing what they are doing and how they are being looked after; in being able to contribute to their care in small ways. The decision whether to keep an ill parent at home or to arrange for them to be looked after in hospital or in residential care is not an easy one. Many factors have to be taken into account, and each situation is different. The amount of help available may be crucial. The children may have their own views on what should happen.

> Matthew, nine, thought his father should stay in hospital rather than be brought home because he was afraid he would die at home in bed and that his mother would be frightened to wake up with a corpse beside her.

> Matthew's father's condition improved enormously after he came home from hospital and he did not die as had been expected. His mother had been under considerable pressure to keep her husband in hospital, and people kept telling her it was bad for her and the boys to have him home. She continually worried if this was right, but on balance it seemed to her that it was not worse than having him in the hospital. The children loved him even though he took little notice of them, and when she asked them, neither of them wanted him to go back in.

> He eventually died peacefully at home and none of the family seemed to have any regrets about the way he was able to live at home until the end.

A mother who is there but is not speaking or doing anything may still provide comfort for her children. The same may be true for a very ill or disabled father. The fact that a parent is really there plays a part in helping children to develop realistic views, phantasies, beliefs and assumptions about parents. When they are not there, when they are dead or absent entirely, children develop beliefs about them which are based more on the child's own unconscious fantasies.

In addition, parents, whether they do anything or not, represent important aspects of the child. They may represent part of the child that says 'don't do it' or the part that says 'go on, you can do it', for example.

If a parent is sent away from home, the child may understand that something about the parent's neediness or behaviour was intolerable. This may be true: ill parents do sometimes behave in an intolerable way. Whether it is true or not, children may need help to understand why the parent has really gone and what this means for them. Their own anger or sense of being rejected or failing may need to be explored if they are not simply to take it out on other members of the family or themselves. They may also feel very powerful and triumphant against such a parent; this too has its problems.

When children can participate in an appropriate way in caring for an ill parent, it may be helpful in reassuring the children about their own ability to love and be loved.

There may also be real and realistic anxieties about the quality of the care given in hospital. Children will pick up the nurses' attitudes when they visit.

In our experience it is extremely difficult to decide if it is in children's or parents' interests to nurse a parent at home or elsewhere. Parents may feel the children's lives would be more 'normal' if there was no sick room, though having an ill parent elsewhere can, in some ways, be more embarrassing and distressing for the children. It may be a real relief to have a seriously ill or badly behaved parent out of the house for a time in spite of the disadvantages, particularly if good help at home is unavailable. Good home nursing by professionals, on the other hand, means the nurses themselves are a potential source of emotional support for the family.

Parents may need to take a long time exploring the full implications of the choices available. Professionals sometimes have strong views of their own and may try to impose them. It seems that guilt may be unavoidable, whatever is decided. It may be helpful to remember that what is most fundamentally *wrong* is the illness and potential death itself, not the ill parent, the children, the partner or the professionals.

Talking about a death afterwards

The death of a parent is always sudden when it happens, however much it has been expected and however well prepared the children and adults have been. Some deaths are completely unexpected and there is no chance to prepare the children beforehand. Much of the discussion in Chapters 8–13 is relevant here. What children know about the circumstances of the parent's death will stay with them for the rest of their lives. Unfortunately, it seems that children often know when something very disturbing is being kept from them. For example, if a parent commits suicide, children may detect this in the behaviour and words (and silences) of the adults around. Feelings towards a suicide are very different from feelings towards an accident; children need to know what they and the adults are grieving. Some children in therapy have shown that such knowledge can be all the more powerful and dangerous for being hidden. However bad, reality can be a relief compared with the hidden anxieties.

> One morning in primary school, the teacher said that Gary's father had died. Ahmed and Gary were not close friends (Gary had none in school) but they were supposed to be making a rock garden together. Guessing that Gary would not want to be in class, Ahmed asked Gary if he would

like to come and work on it, and they went out together. Ahmed did not know what to say, and to begin with he talked about the rock garden and how they had missed Gary working on it. Eventually he said 'Did you get on with your father?' Gary looked at him with a look of 'mind your own business'. After a pause he said 'My dad was all right' and went to the toilet to cry.

We have the impression that in this context, this simple question is seldom asked by either adult or child.

During the last period of the day Gary started talking to Ahmed about his father. He said that his father was often away working, and that he was always out playing football when his father was there because they didn't really get on. He said how he wished now he hadn't, and if he could have his father back he wouldn't. He wondered if his father had killed himself because his parents had been talking of living apart for a while. He talked for a long time, and describing it some years later, Ahmed said he ended up feeling really 'bad' – not guilty, because it was natural to cry, just bad for Gary.

At the end Gary said rather spitefully, words to the effect that 'If you hadn't asked me I wouldn't be feeling all this.' A teacher said something implying that Ahmed had been tactless, but Gary said no, it was all right.

We wonder if any adult was told of Gary's fear that his father committed suicide, and what the consequences for Gary were.

If a parent died as a result of an attack (self-inflicted or otherwise), or in prison, or as a result of an avoidable accident (for example by a drunken driver), children are likely to feel particularly destructive and violent. These feelings will be directed at somebody; perhaps at authority figures; perhaps at the child itself; perhaps at someone who is directly accountable. Violent behaviour at school or delinquent acts out of school, either of which bring down punishment on the child, may result. Such children may need considerable help if they are not to be destructive towards themselves and others in the long term.

If a parent died in circumstances that do not bear imagining, children may be left feeling the parent is still and always will be at the point of dying; because thought of the death itself is unmanageable, it remains for ever frozen and uncompleted, at the point of most anguish. Hard work may be needed to help such children allow their parent actually to die in the imagination. Similarly, if children have witnessed events connected with the death which were too frightening to think about and talk about, they may re-experience traumatic experiences in nightmares or in frightening 'absences' during the day. We know from work with adults that without becoming able to translate their frightening

THE DEATH OF A PARENT

experiences into words or symbols in some way, these children may never find peace. Knowledge of their parents' death is an important source of ideas, fantasies and feelings for adults faced with their own death. Fear of death can make an old person very anxious; fear of dying can seriously inhibit living.

In children's imagination their parents go on thinking the thoughts and having the feelings towards the child that the child thought they had at the time of their death. These may well include children's own feelings of anger, revenge and punishment attributed to the parent; this is one reason why it is important to remind the child of earlier, different feelings and to encourage children to think about the death when they are older and have different feelings towards the dead parent themselves.

If a parent died in hospital there may be a question about whether to take the children to see the dead body or not. Seeing the body may help children to realise what death actually means and may help the grieving process to begin. Some children find it very reassuring and not at all frightening; others may be frightened but, later, glad they went. They need to be accompanied by someone who cares for them.

What about me? Children's anxieties

Here we list some of the anxieties children have in connection with the death of a parent. Some we have already discussed.

- I must stop it happening.

- I will have to look after myself.

- I will have to be mum/dad and look after dad/mum/the other children.

- No one will love me like mum/dad did. No-one will be able to cope with me.

- Mum/dad didn't love me; they died because I was not good enough.

- Did mum/dad think badly of me? They remember me like *this*. I mustn't change or I'll lose them.

- I am a bad person because I was not thinking about them.

- I could have kept them alive by thinking about them, being them, dying or taking on the illness myself.

- I have to sacrifice myself for them/for my remaining parent.

- Can I keep my senses (and know what has happened) or do I go crazy (and not have to know)?

- ° I shouldn't go on living: I'm too bad, it hurts too much, it is a betrayal; I want to go to heaven too.

- ° Do I have to wait for mum/dad to die before I can start my life?

- ° I was doing something bad at the moment when my mother/father died...

There are many works of fiction and art that can help both adults and children to acknowledge, recognise and work with the feelings involved when a parent dies. Shakespeare's *Hamlet* illuminates many of the conflicts of a son facing the death of his father. It demonstrates the belief that it is possible to talk with and be given instructions by the father's ghost; the son's conflicts towards his mother; the questions of sanity and suicide; the disruption of the son's own sexual relationships and the loss of friends; and the risk that the son's whole world/country will fall apart and be vulnerable to ancient enemies (Fortinbras, who was defeated at the time of Hamlet's birth). As with all Shakespeare's work, close study of *Hamlet* offers subtle insights into the fantasies involved in human relationships.

Long-term effects of the death of a parent

There are many practical issues that affect children after the loss of a parent. They may lose not only mothering or fathering but their home, their school, their town, their social class (a move up or down is a loss), and family income. They may move to another part of the country or have to learn a new language and new behaviour. They may find themselves surrounded by people who speak differently and see them quite differently. Adults relate to children partly by unconsciously identifying them with the child part of themselves. They also identify them with (loved or hated) people from their past. This means that the child's sense of themselves may be severely shaken when they are looked after by totally new people. Their dislocation and confusion may be both in the external world and in their inner selves, as they struggle to hold onto the person they were and to cope with the new demands upon them to be someone else.

For children, keeping contact with people from their past is important, especially at first, but may not be easy. It can give children enormous reassurance; they can check their new perceptions with their old ones; they can discover that they have not been forgotten; that their old self is still liked and still exists for the people they have left. Shared memories of the past create a strong and important bond; talking about these allows new views of the world as it was and now is. We feel strongly that at least one return visit within the first year is advisable.

When children have to move to people outside the family, other issues are raised. Children find it difficult to believe that anyone who is not 'family' could really want them and love them for themselves. They may hide their real feelings and develop a placatory 'false self' to cover the self they fear and fear adults cannot bear. They are likely to have a very strong sense of not belonging and being dislocated, which may be covered up. Cultural differences exacerbate this, but in reality there is no matching any child's exact cultural background since each family has their own culture.

The long-term emotional difficulties for a child who has lost a parent may be considerable. A study of women in Camberwell by Brown and Harris (1978) showed that the death of her mother before the age of twelve was statistically likely to increase a woman's chances of a seriously depressive reaction to later difficulties. However, not all women had such a reaction. Having a 'confiding relationship' with contact at least once a week seemed to have a protective effect on these women. Loss of their father in childhood, however, did not seem to affect women's chances of becoming seriously depressed in adulthood.

We do not know exactly what, in the loss of a mother, caused some of these women to become depressed. We do not know exactly what in the loss of mothering may cause young children later problems. Not all children deprived of their mothers react in the same way. We suspect that a firm, loving, long-term relationship with an adult who can tolerate aggression, rejection and punishment from a child may be significant. A confiding relationship with contact at least weekly may help to protect vulnerable children in stressful circumstances from depression.

If a parent's illness or death has anything to do with sex, the children's fears about their own sexual identity and sex-life, their own ability to have children, lovers or partners need to be particularly considered. The anxieties for a child whose parent has AIDS or syphillis or cancer of the womb, for example, may well include very powerful fears about sex and about having babies. They may fear infecting their partner even if the parent's condition was not infectious. Children whose mothers have multiple sclerosis may attribute her illness to their birth and may fear having children themselves. Some of these anxieties may be too deep and too powerful for parents to deal with alone and professional help may be needed. However, the long-term effects of loss of a parent in childhood are not all negative.

Loss and Creativity

In the long-term, after the initial shock is over, loss of any kind can be a spur to creative activity. For many adults, past losses, including childhood ones, provide the motive force (often on an unconscious level) for creative activities, including work of all kinds as well as art.

C S Lewis, author of *The Lion, the Witch and the Wardrobe*, lost his mother when he was twelve. A lonely child with little contact with his father, he invented a world of his own which he later developed into the world of Narnia. He also wrote movingly about the loss of his sick wife in adulthood. Much of his writing can be seen as his way of coming to terms with the losses in his life, primarily that of his mother. *The Lion, the Witch and the Wardrobe* as a whole illustrates many of the conflicts facing children who lose a parent: the sense of time standing still, of it being 'always winter, never Christmas'; the need for some super-human sacrifice; a child's greed threatening the existence of a wonderful world; a dangerous, seductive witch-woman who brings freezing and death and a warm combined mother–father figure who loves and brings life but who has to be allowed to choose death.

J R R Tolkien lost both parents when he was child; his books, too, evoke a lost world in a powerfully moving way.

Creative work can be a way of overcoming loss. Children may find painting, drama, schoolwork, music or any other activity helps them in many different ways to cope with the loss of a parent. When they grow up, children may be able to find ways to work with their losses that give something to the world.

Loss of a parent before his or her death

Martin's mother (see Chapter 3) had not died, but many of the issues raised by Martin's situation are also raised by a death. Sometimes the loss of the parent seems to have happened long before the actual death, particularly if the parent's mind has been affected or if the death has been expected for many years.

> Sophie was twenty-nine and her mother had recently died of Motor Neurone Disease. She said 'It doesn't feel as if she has just died: I'd already lost her as a mother years ago'.

Her immediate worry in fact was the fear of losing her father next.

Risk of suicide in children after a parent's death

> William, nine, said 'If my dad could not do things any more he might as well be dead, and then I would be dead too'.

Some children try to kill themselves after a parent dies. It can be very difficult for parents to believe that their child might really be attempting to damage or kill themselves, but it may be important to consider this possibility seriously. They may also have accidents which are actually a result of gambling with death: of not taking a normal amount of care, but 'testing fate' or 'testing God' to see if they will be killed or not, and by implication, whether God thinks they should die.

Often children, like William, will have feelings or thoughts about dying which they do not attempt to put into practice in any way. When children can have such thoughts consciously they can test the idea against different thoughts and feelings: where the idea is totally unconscious they are more likely to act upon it without thinking.

There are circumstances when adults need to be prepared to ask bereaved children if they have thought of dying themselves. If they have not, the child will simply say so; if they have, they may find it a great relief to be able to discuss it. The child might express totally unrealistic ideas and feelings about the death of their parent which the adult can easily challenge. It is possible that the child simply needs the loving attention of the remaining parent, needs to know they are loved and to know that they are not going to be abandoned. It may be that this itself will be enough to remove a suicidal impulse.

If not, it might be appropriate to seek help, either for the child or for the parent. Identification with the parent, guilt and desires to punish the self and/or the other parent are possible sources of such impulses. The description of Martin shows how such feelings might arise. Where these feelings are not conscious it may be difficult to help the child with them.

Care of children after a parent's death

We know that the quality of care that children receive after the death of a parent is crucial: adults who are firmly and lovingly attached to a child may make a difference to the child's survival, though whatever they do, the loss cannot be taken away. With the loss of a parent, children may lose something to do with their fundamental identity; some potential for building on their own past in a coherent and natural way. The sense of discontinuity, of a break, may remain in their personality throughout their lives.

If a mother has been involved in decisions about the care of the child after her death, letting the child know this may help to reduce some of the sense of discontinuity. When this is not possible, children's views about the dying mother's feelings towards their continuing care are likely to be quite unrealistic: these beliefs may actively work against their accepting care.

Adults may recognise the need for a young child to continue being mothered and may provide this mothering. They may overlook the need for an older child to be mothered, and not offer it. It is not unusual for one or more members of the family to collapse at the time of a death and for one to remain in control. This may be a child.

> Rachel was thirteen when her mother died. She looked like her mother, and her sister, who was fourteen, looked liked their father. She remembered that relatives who were staying with the family were very concerned about her father. They tried to mother him, but they all said to Rachel and her sister 'You have to be strong now for your father'. On the day of the death Rachel's father and sister cried but Rachel worried

about where they were going to get enough money to live, since her mother had earned the money, and she did not cry. She felt that someone had to carry on. At the time she did not think anything of this, but later as a young adult she often cried for no reason. She then began to feel angry that nobody had thought of her and her sister's need to be mothered and what they had lost. She still felt a responsibility to look after her father.

Husbands often feel like a bereaved child themselves in the crucial time after the death of their wife. Eventually, even so, some can offer their bereaved children a motherly, 'confiding' relationship. Some fathers seek a new wife to mother their children, and may be disappointed when it does not work out in this way.

Children who are given adult responsibilities may be quite unaware that there is any loss to them in this, and it may be the parent who has to keep this in mind. Some parents feel that there is no loss, and it is good for children to grow up in this way. However, if a child can be convinced that they are not expected to take the place of the lost parent, they will not lose their child status and child self but can grow up without leaving part of themselves behind. A child who has not been allowed to be a child may later have many difficulties related to ways of dealing with this child self. We looked at some of these in Chapter 5.

Some disturbed mothers actually set out to destroy the happiness and health of their children while dying themselves. Sometimes children think that this is happening when it is not. Since children identify with their mothers this is very damaging whether it is talked about or not: such children may become very self-destructive or violent to others. If it can be discussed realistically and the feelings held, in a setting where children are safe and know they are secure, they may be helped to react differently. The fact that parents can hate and be cruel and can bury their loving feelings is very hard to deal with; however, living in a state of knowing this with only a child's understanding is even harder.

When a single parent remarries, the child may feel, as well as the obvious jealousies and fears, a great sense of relief at having responsibility for the parent taken off their shoulders. Bad behaviour at this time may be a reflection of a regained belief in the parent's ability to cope with the child's bad feelings which previously had to be hidden. However, relations between step-parents and step-children are amongst the most difficult to handle.

In Chapter 10 we looked at some of the conflicts for families when parents have to share the care of their children with others. Many of the issues raised there are relevant here. Conflicts between parents and other people who care for their child may go on in the child's mind even after the death of the parent.

Feelings after a death

'When my dad told me my mum had died under the anaesthetic I thought "Now I can have her jewels!" I've got them now but I don't like having them.' – young woman who was six at the time her mother died unexpectedly.

There are many feelings around after a death. Some of these are implicit in the anxieties we have listed. Often people, including children, seem to feel they do not have the 'right' feelings after a death, and this may worry them very much. Children sometimes need to be told that their initial feelings will not go on for ever. It does not help to tell them not to be sad 'because mummy is happy now (that she is dead)...' for whatever reason, even if the adult truly believes this.

The painfulness of grief reactions when they come may be unexpected. The fact that these feelings last as long as they do may be very unwelcome; the way in which the lost person goes on being 'seen' or 'heard' or 'felt' may be frightening as well as, at times, comforting. Children, like adults in similar situations, can feel totally isolated, abandoned and afraid of falling apart. Life may seem to have lost all meaning. Feelings of numbness, and having lost the ability to feel at all, can be very distressing.

Some distressing reactions may be buried, perhaps for a long while. Some of the more disturbing feelings about the loss of a parent may first emerge with the loss of a lover or a pet, or an exam failure, for example, many years later. Feelings which can be made conscious at the time do not re-emerge in such a disturbing way: they are remembered rather than re-enacted.

Feelings that are not felt and given words at the time of the death are particularly likely to be re-enacted with other children at school or within the family, both in childhood and in later life, perhaps isolating the child socially. Adults may have some power to affect this by ensuring that the child has space to feel their own feelings, not just those acceptable to a particular adult, and to talk.

Anger is a common reaction to feelings of loss and grief. Adults are often angry that it takes them a long time to recover from a death: children may not be aware of their own grief, sadness or guilt except as anger and bad temper. They may fight with adults or other children as a means of making contact with them when more loving contact seems for a while impossible.

Losing their parents may leave some children afraid to use the powerful, demanding, angry aspects of their own personality. They may be afraid that these feelings are dangerous and caused the loss. Physical contact with adults, including playful fights, wrestling or even smacking may at times help children to re-establish a sense of the power of adults to control them in a way that is not damaging. Chapter 7 is relevant here.

Children sometimes develop symptoms which were their parent's before the parent died. They may well be afraid they are going to die, and just telling them they are 'imagining' it is wrong: imagining is different. It may help to explain to children that they may be trying to 'be' their lost parent in order not to feel the loss. It is a common reaction; a way of trying to show themselves: 'I haven't lost her, I am her' or 'she is inside me'. The symptoms are a very real part of this attempt, but it does not mean they are getting the illness. Of course, if there is a chance that a child might be getting the illness, this too needs to be discussed and taken seriously. After a time such an identification with the parent generally becomes unmanageable and the painful grieving process begins.

The process of allowing someone else to leave, whether by death or other means, involves separating. Children are often not at all clear what is them and what is their parent; in unconscious fantasy they may believe that they live inside their parent's body or space, and/or their parent is inside them. The identification with the lost parent may be part of the process of sorting out what is the parent and what is the self. For example, a bossy, controlling mother may represent to her daughter the daughter's own bossy, controlling aspects. While her mother is around to do the ordering about, the daughter may never boss others about but always take orders meekly. If her mother dies, however, the daughter may become temporarily bossy and controlling as her mother was. It may take some time before she settles down to a new kind of behaviour, and is neither as bossy as her mother was nor as meek as she was herself.

Full separation does not always take place. Some signs of a continuing identification may remain. A woman who lost her father when she was small may choose masculine-looking clothes, or behave towards her mother as if she was her husband rather than her daughter, for example. These traits may be harmless, or they may be a sign of some inner difficulty in accepting herself, which make life harder than it could be.

When these children grow up, if they have children themselves, they may have a sense of their parents coming back to life in their children. This can be a source of very loving feelings as well as more complex and less pleasant ones.

Memories

Memories are a very important aspect of children's development of a sense of themselves in relation to others. Helping children to remember or piece together a coherent picture of the events in their life may help them to establish a coherent sense of their own identity. An adult who shares the memories can remind the child of the past; an adult who does not may encourage the child to think and talk and ask questions about it. Losing the memories may seem to the child the same as losing the parent for ever: regaining them may feel like regaining the parent for ever.

Adults generally have a strong sense of 'the mother in their head', whether she is dead or alive. Memories can establish this mother as good and loving or rejecting, punitive and hateful; supportive or undermining or a mixture of the two. Mothers are usually seen in many different ways. Understanding can work on memories, influencing the picture that lives on with children, influencing their behaviour and expectations towards others and themselves as they grow into adults.

Memories and fantasies about lost parents may be important in the children's development.

> Dylan, born in 1970, was the son of a young man who was heavily into drugs and 'being free'. His mother eventually moved away from the alternative culture, settled down and married a much more stable man. During his teenage years Dylan experimented with drugs in a way which made it very clear he was idealising his lost father's way of life. He wanted to reject his mother's 'boring' lifestyle and live like his father had. He also wanted to be like his mother's new husband who combined some of the elements of both his parents.

> Shirley lost her father during the war when she was three. Her mother remarried. Shirley had a picture of a glamorous, exciting, rather wild father and a staid but loving and respectable father. Her choice of men quite clearly reflected the two fathers. She found it difficult to settle with the one kind without craving for the other.

Shirley, like Dylan, found it helpful as an adult to seek out more information about her dead father and to correct some of her ideas about him.

Social difficulties

Children may appreciate help coping with the social difficulties of losing a parent. Their teachers as well as other children may not know what to say to them and may avoid them or be awkward. Children may need to be told that it is all right to be upset at school, but it may be necessary to clear this with the teacher too. The teacher may be asked to encourage children in the class to talk about the loss rather than discourage them. (See chapter 10 and References and Further Reading.)

Children often avoid telling people that they have lost a parent; they may behave as if it is a guilty secret. To some extent this may be simply a reaction to the difficulty of constantly explaining: too much instant sympathy from strangers becomes wearing. The conflict between telling the truth and avoiding difficulties is always a problem. Discussing it with an understanding adult may help.

Such a cover-up may involve a desire to be treated 'just like anyone else'. Children sometimes seem to feel as if all the things that have happened to them should not make any difference to them or anyone else. There is anger involved in recognising the way events disrupt lives, but living as if the event could just be 'put behind you' and ignored is likely to cause problems. The difficulties of growing up without a mother or a father are real and do affect children, however unpalatable both children and adults find this.

Children also sometimes feel and behave as if they should be exempt from all the troubles and restraints of everyday life because of their past difficulties, which made them 'special'. There can be relief as well as anger when they are expected to behave like everyone else.

Conclusion

There is much evidence that the death of a parent at any age affects children. However, we also know that they can be helped to live through it. Acknowledgement, recognition and understanding of their thoughts, feelings and fears can free them from some of the worst effects of such a loss.

CHAPTER 15

Issues for Professionals and Other Workers

Introduction

This chapter raises some of the issues which affect those whose work, paid or unpaid, involves trying to help people with disabilities or chronic illnesses. For many years we have been facilitating discussion sessions for such people, in which the focus has been on their emotional reactions to disability. Counsellors, social workers, doctors, home helps, home care workers, personal assistants, nurses, occupational therapists, Crossroads volunteers, day care workers, residential home staff, managers of services and many others have all contributed. We use the word 'worker' to cover all of these, and 'client' or 'patient' to refer to the person at the receiving end of the services.

People with disabilities and their children may have to cope with more than their fair share of workers of one kind or another. In one session we were told of a family which had 22 people coming into their house on a Tuesday. Some of these people are in high status jobs, others are among the worst paid and least trained in the economy. Some have considerable control over their working conditions; others have to do as they are told, perhaps by untrained and over-controlling managers. Some have considerable experience of working with people who are ill or disabled; others may have very limited experience of either illness or disability or both. Some have experience of parenting children themselves, others do not. Some may like children, and others dislike all children, or some children in particular. Some are as young as 18; others have been doing their job for forty years or more.

The potential in these relationships is considerable. Both worker and client family can potentially enjoy each other's company and give support, validation, sometimes affection, to each other. A young personal assistant might have a lot to learn from a civil servant retired through ill-health, or from an older woman with a lifetime's experience of men, work and children. She may get on well

203

with the woman's adult son or enjoy the company of smaller children. An experienced social worker or nurse may still enjoy the discoveries involved in making a relationship with a new client, particularly perhaps if the client has a new baby. Bonds of friendship can develop over time, even with 'difficult' people, whether they are in the role of helper or helped, client or close relation. But in order for this to happen, each has to see the others as people capable of giving something worth having, and be able to appreciate them for what they are. In our experience, most workers can describe some very good relationships with clients or patients. Most can also, however, describe some relationships which are far from satisfactory. Certain clients or members of their families become known within a team as 'difficult'; this may help a worker to feel a little less responsible for what is going on, but it still leaves a discomfort. If it is the children who are perceived as difficult, the client may be blamed for 'making a rod for her own back' or may be seen as a victim and the children blamed. Action to address the problem may or may not be seen as necessary. Equally, people who have to use the services of others are sometimes happy with what they are given, and sometimes extremely dissatisfied. They may or may not be able to complain or to have one worker replaced with another. Members of a family may or may not be in a position to obtain relief through talking with others about their frustration with 'difficult' workers.

Some of the difficulties in these relationships are easily recognised. For example, a professional or other worker may fail to recognise how much a perfectly competent client or family member knows about the care required. Children's knowledge about their parent's needs, in particular, may be ignored or discounted rather than checked. Or perhaps the client would rather manage without help and the worker would rather be doing another job. Sometimes an illness or disability has given rise to feelings of being worthless or useless which can all too easily be passed on to those most closely involved in offering care, professional or family. Equally, some workers feel powerless for reasons to do with their job or with their life outside, and may pass on a sense of frustrated powerlessness to those in their care – or to their children.

Less easily recognised, perhaps, are personality disorders in either client or worker which may be misdiagnosed as normal reactions. One woman talked repeatedly of how she was deliberately making her children hate her so that when she died they would not miss her: her social worker was very worried about this but did not see it as requiring the intervention of the mental health team because she thought (wrongly, as she later realised) it must be a normal reaction to fears of dying of multiple sclerosis. Similarly, an experienced nursing assistant in a mental hospital told a junior colleague who questioned his sadistic behaviour that it was no different from the doctors' and was normal behaviour in the health service.

Helpers may get on very well with parents but dislike or be irritated by the children. The situation may also be reversed, with a helper liking the children and perhaps getting attached to them. If the helper disapproves of the behaviour of the parents in some way, the children may become involved in a covert or open battle between helper and parent. The potential for difficulty is enormous. The emotions which can become involved can run very deep. A worker's rivalry with the children or rivalry with the parents for the affection of the children can raise tensions in the household.

Children who dislike a worker for any reason can make their life and their parents' life more difficult, as well as suffering terribly themselves. Their dislike may be well-founded, or may be based on a misunderstanding or rivalry.

> One girl got very upset because her mother's care worker ate all the biscuits, leaving none for her when she got in from school. As well as being physically hungry, she may well have felt that the helper and her mother were having a good, emotionally nourishing relationship while she was out, leaving her with an empty, emotionally exhausted mother like an empty biscuit tin. She felt bitterly that her mother had someone to talk to, but she had nobody; she couldn't complain to her mother openly about the worker because she knew her mother needed her. All she could do was make a token protest about the biscuits and then cry in her room.

Professionals in the home may observe behaviour towards children which disturbs them. It can be very difficult to assess whether someone else's treatment of their children is within safe bounds or not. At what level does teasing become emotional cruelty? If a threat of violence could not be carried out, is it a reason for calling in social workers? Is a mother who holds a knife behind her back while shouting at her children just behaving normally for her culture, or is she seriously at risk of killing one of them? If she says she wants them dead and would be prepared to go to prison for some peace herself, what should the worker do? Workers may fear for the lives of the children, perhaps realistically, perhaps quite unrealistically. A home care worker who calls in the Child Protection Team may feel she or he has betrayed the parent they were sent to assist and care for.

Children can also be a danger to their parents, and this also raises anxieties in workers involved.

> A boy of seven threw china ornaments at his mother and kicked her while she lay where she had fallen on the living room floor, unable to get up or stop him or even to defend herself properly. Clearly intervention was needed, but the mother was terribly afraid the child would be taken away. Eventually this mother was able to accept help for herself and for the child.

Parents may have serious concerns about workers' relations with their children. Workers may bully or tease children; they may make what the parent thinks are unreasonable demands on them, or they may simply ignore the children's feelings. Distressing as these situations may be, there is a bigger danger. One young man who was employed to help disabled men used his position within several families to sexually abuse their young sons. The parents of several boys concerned were in fact unaware of this until another told; they had been glad he was so attentive to the boys and happy he was prepared to pay them some attention.

Culture, attitudes and splitting

We want now to look in some detail at a particular mental mechanism which can be responsible for many difficulties between client and worker, where the client is a parent with an illness or impairment of some kind which may cause a disability. We briefly examine some of the thoughts and attitudes which can come between workers and disabled clients. Finally, we give two examples of working with difficulties arising from the worker/client relationship; one an example of working on an emotional level, and one a practical list of considerations in assessing risk.

Illness, impairment and disability have powerful meanings attached to them. For example, Shakespeare in *Richard III* uses the idea of being hunchbacked to heighten a sense of envy and murderous rivalry; the Romantic notion of a beautiful invalid dying of consumption was connected with feelings of tenderness; and in Hitler's Germany 'a healthy mind in a healthy body' was used to justify mass murder of people with disabilities, mental or physical. Currently, the words 'sick' and 'unhealthy' have metaphorical meanings as in a 'sick joke' or 'unhealthy interest': 'spastic' was (and perhaps is still?) an insult used by teenagers to mock each other. 'Disabled' may mean incompetent and valueless in a society which overvalues *doing* (as in earning money, for example) and undervalues *being* (as in being there, or being a father, a partner, a dependent child).

The cultural meaning attributed to illness and impairment or disability may be shared by worker and client or it may differ. For example, a person who believes in the evil eye or possession by evil spirits may give a different meaning to blindness or epilepsy from someone who does not. Attitudes to HIV infection may depend on the individual's attitude towards sexuality and homosexuality. Cultural meanings attached to children and childhood also differ. They may be seen as a 'blessing' or a 'curse'. Children and young people may be seen as a natural support for their parents, and as 'strong' and able to withstand whatever life throws at them. Another culture may emphasise children's need for care and protection by strong adults. The meanings available within a culture may be contradictory and opposite ones used by adults in different circumstances. In some societies and subcultures too, parents and parenting are more valued than others.

Personal meanings may also be shared or differ: for example, direct experience can endow a particular illness or impairment with meaning taken from the personality of the individual who had it. Meaning will also be affected by the level of personal threat attached. The question of whether the condition is actually contagious or infectious is important, but so too is a more symbolic level, for example, whether a condition runs in the person's family or not. There are also more primitive meanings attached to illnesses and disabilities, arising from childhood fantasies; for example, the idea that blindness may be a punishment for looking at something which should not be seen; or that paralysis is a bewitchment perhaps connected with forbidden movement of some kind. After all, witches can turn people who have offended them to stone. The fantasy that children can cause their parents illness or dangerous stress, exhausting or perhaps even killing them, is not uncommon. Such meanings may have more power for being unrecognised and therefore unspoken.

Asking a group of workers to free associate to the words *healthy* on the one hand, and *ill or disabled* on the other, can demonstrate a very clear split between them. Ideas of goodness, beauty, love, loving strength and understanding may be quickly attributed to good health; and badness, ugliness, hatred, envy, ignorance and both weakness and paradoxically, malevolent strength, to illness or disability. Truth versus dissembling or pretence cause more trouble, since it is the able-bodied who are generally seen as lying to the ill. The ability to give is commonly attributed solely to the able-bodied, and the need to take to those who are ill or disabled or impaired in some way. Dependence and neediness go with illness; independence and the ability to satisfy needs is associated with health. Workers are commonly located on the 'healthy' side, regardless of their actual state of mental or physical health, and clients on the 'unhealthy', needy side, regardless of their strengths.

Being a parent oneself is likely to be located on the 'healthy' side, though many people actually see their own parents as ill or disabled in some way, not necessarily simply because they are old. Having a baby has such strong associations with good health that it may be a very powerful source of support for a disabled or ill mother: 'at least my body can do something right'. If the baby has anything wrong with it, not only is this support taken away, but it can be replaced by very disturbing and undermining feelings which threaten the parents' sexual relationships as well as life in general.

Looking at meanings attached to 'healthy' and 'ill or disabled' as an exercise it becomes more and more clear that the divisions are to a considerable extent arbitrary; that professionals are sometimes needy, sometimes impaired and sometimes bad; that clients can often give to other people including to workers of all kinds; that nobody is totally independent and nobody totally dependent for all their needs; that understanding is by no means only the province of the physically healthy. Once gradations begin to be examined, the splits, and the 'them' and 'us' attitude which accompanies them, may be at least partially dismantled.

If this exercise is undertaken individually, each person produces their own list and the 'bad' side is likely to include all the aspects of the self which are felt to be disabling. These may include hatred, envy, destructiveness, intolerance, selfishness, jealousy, self-deluding and manipulative behaviour, for example: the common scourges of human beings.

> A very caring and concerned doctor knew she found one disabled patient overwhelming and suffocating. She felt guilty for not attending as often as she should, but pushed the thoughts to the back of her mind and allowed her busy schedule to provide the excuse. Seeking help for the patient, she spoke to a counsellor whose normal response to professionals in this situation was to ask first about the professionals' own involvement with their patient. The doctor became interested in her own response, aware that it might be shared by others. Thinking about it with the counsellor she was able to recognise her identification of the client with a fantasy of herself which was fat, slug-like, immobile, and suffocating; which wanted to be waited on and did not care about anyone else's life; the opposite of the way she normally behaved. Having talked this through she was able to visit the patient and found her quite unlike the fantasy. She no longer feared talking to her and visiting her, and the patient no longer seemed so needy.

This is sometimes called projective identification: this means that instead of owning parts of herself she did not like, the doctor was seeing them only in the client and was unable to see the client as having her own characteristics at all. It is natural to try to understand other people by 'putting oneself in their shoes', but projective identification goes further than this when it is used to deny ownership of parts of the self. Rather than enhancing the similarities between people it exaggerates their differences and prevents perception of the other person as anything other than a split off part of the self. Undoing it, as in this case, can feel liberating as both the self and the other person are freed to be themselves.

Professionals and other workers, paid and unpaid, are vulnerable to this kind of splitting and projective identification. Without realising it or even consciously feeling it, workers can often behave towards disabled people as if the worker had only 'healthy' characteristics and the client only 'unhealthy' ones. Where there is agreement as to what characteristic belongs where, the pressure on both may be very strong. A worker may feel a strong pressure to be a superhuman carer, with no 'bad' or 'ill' characteristics; the client may not be expected or allowed to be any kind of carer towards anyone.

Clients too, of course, make such splits, and sometimes a disabled adult will talk as if all they have left now and for the future is the 'bad' disabled part of themselves, believing that they have lost the 'good', non-disabled part. This may play a strong part in suicidal thoughts, particularly if their own good, loving aspects are attributed to someone else. The idea of being a burden to others is strongly linked to such splitting, and may also include a hidden resentment towards those who are left to be the carers, supposedly with all the virtues which go with this role, but who manifestly fail to perform as angels. The complaint is often that they fail to behave as the disabled person feels they would themselves, if they were carers. This is a sign that such projective identification is taking place; the carer has been loaded with the ill person's own 'good' aspects and is expected to demonstrate them.

It is only with more considered thought that it becomes clear that both client and worker can be perceived as less split or idealised and therefore more human. It may take some work before people recognise that a particular disabled client might not be more emotionally disabled, for example, by envy, than a particular worker; that a client might be capable of love, of loyalty, of understanding, for example, and that any individual worker might be deficient in these virtues.

It is not surprising that in these circumstances people may have to make a conscious effort to tolerate even the idea of an ill or disabled person being a parent. Sometimes an ill or disabled parent may begin to talk of themselves as a child within the family; as if ill-health, dependence and childhood are all the same. Other family members may join in this, and professionals too can be drawn in. The common practice of calling all patients in hospital by their first name encourages such infantilism: workers who come into the home seem less likely to speak disrespectfully of their clients, though it can happen.

The effect on children of hearing their parents spoken to as children has to be considered. It may undermine the relations between parent and child. It may give the child the idea that it is adult or correct to relate to their ill parent as if the parent carried all the child's own split off and unwanted childishness and dependence. It may even validate some children's physical attacks on their parents: they may see themselves as punishing a naughty child/parent. An older child may be desperately embarrassed; feeling as if they had caught their parent undressed – which workers may also subject them to thoughtlessly. Children do not feel safe with the boundaries between themselves and their parents broken down. Their security somehow depends on knowing that their parents and other adults can maintain boundaries. This includes knowing the difference between being an ill or disabled adult and being a child.

Don't get too close

It is also not surprising that many people avoid too close contact with people with disabilities, even while working with them. Children may also avoid their parents, for much the same reasons as workers do. There are many reasons for this avoidance and each may need to be tackled separately. The interrelation between children's avoidance and worker's avoidance also needs to be considered.

There may be a fear of catching the condition, even if it is not contagious; particularly when an illness is not properly understood there is scope for fears to run wild. Such fears need to be specified and dealt with individually before they can lose their power. If a worker has such a fear they may pass it to the children in the family, or they may use the children in the process of avoiding the cause of their fear. A child who is afraid of catching their parent's condition may be helped by a worker who can discuss it, but may be made worse by a worker who shares the fear without realising it.

There may be a fear of the demands that might be made, for example, for extra consideration, or for certain kinds of behaviour which transgresses normal boundaries, such as giving an arm or helping someone in the lavatory. Children, particularly at adolescence, often fear the imagined or real demands of their parents: illness complicates this fear considerably. The issue of boundaries and distance can be a problem in any professional or work situation, but an illness or disability raises questions about which normal boundaries have to be kept, which should be kept, and which cannot or should not be kept. The significance of breaching such normal boundaries, for the client, their children and the worker needs to be addressed and acknowledged. The worker may be involved in a discussion with the client about what demands are reasonable and what are not; this may well take place in reference to the children as well as to the worker. Where projective identification is involved there may be excessive fear of the demands which might be made and of the superhuman strength required to deal with them. If the fear is too strong, the need may be ignored and completely overlooked, and the children left to provide by default. The worker may have to make a conscious effort to think about the demands made on the children and the effect of their own policy on this.

Fear of the emotional state accompanying illness or deformity can be another cause of avoidance.

> A nurse said she was scared to talk with a patient with multiple sclerosis because the patient was depressed and she was afraid she would catch it.

Even without this fear, depression and grief are hard to watch. Sometimes the difficulty is that they remind the worker of a time in their own past when a loved relative became depressed, perhaps with significant consequences for the worker themselves. A worker who avoids eye contact with a client, and never talks to them properly may be giving strong messages to their children. Equally, a worker who is always cheerful or encouraging but does not allow tears or 'negative thoughts' can leave the client to cope with their misery and depression alone – or with their children. Some parents will only cry with their children: it is very painful to watch a parent upset and be unable to do anything about it. On the other hand, a worker may be able to involve children in less threatening but meaningful conversations with their parent. Such a worker may be able to reduce the child's fear of the parent's emotional state.

A fear that external appearances reflect inner reality can also cause avoidance, particularly if someone has a grotesque appearance. What is experienced as grotesque depends not only on objective criteria but also on the significance of a particular condition to the worker concerned. People working with clients with disabilities have told of their fears of dementia, incontinence, dribbling, walking in such a way that they appear drunk, all of which seemed to the individuals concerned to be completely horrifying or disgusting. For some people, deformity is equivalent to evil or the punishment of God. A child who witnesses this reaction towards their parent may be very distressed indeed. If they are taught it in church their relation with their parent may be seriously damaged. Alternatively, they may become disillusioned with the church, and deprived of a potential source of support.

Generally, getting to know someone over a period of time reduces the sense of alienation aroused by appearance, but a worker may have insufficient dealings with a family for this to happen. Children in the family are likely to be very sensitive to even covert expressions of disgust towards their parent. If their own feelings of disgust are feared and denied they may react very angrily to a worker's feelings. Their sense of loneliness may be increased too, as they sense the rejection of the worker towards a parent with whom they identify, and they know that the rest of the world shares this rejection.

If the worker receives no help with their fears, these fears may simply be covered up, leaving a relationship scarred by pretence and falseness. Children are generally credited with seeing through such falseness: adults do too, of course, but may choose to keep more quiet about it. However, if fears and feelings which lead to avoidance can be explored in a safe setting they can sometimes change. If they do not change it may be appropriate to move to a different kind of work, or to pass on a particular client to a colleague. A worker of any kind who is scared to get too close to a client may not be seeing them realistically and may be unable to think clearly about the situation of the client or their children.

Miscellany of attitudes

I know what is wrong and how to put it right

Many illnesses and disabilities arise from poorly-understood conditions. One of the problems of having such a condition is that people often react by giving advice. It seems that it can be very difficult to tolerate 'not knowing' and it is generally much more comfortable to invent some spurious 'knowledge'. Any worker may find themselves tempted to give advice on how to live with or overcome a disability or illness about which they know very little.

> A home help was quite determined that her client should go for counselling because she said it had cured her own illness. Her client had a condition which would not be cured by counselling.

Such convictions may make it very hard for the worker to take seriously the client's own preoccupations and their own experience of attempted cures or other supposed solutions to their problems. This may then quite reasonably appear to the client as lack of respect and failure to recognise that the client has a knowledge of their own condition which nobody else has.

Children can be seriously disturbed by such pieces of advice. They may believe the worker and nag their parent to try the cure, feeling desperate if the parent cannot or does not explain well enough why it is that they do not consider it worth trying. They may interpret the parent's reluctance to obey as 'not wanting to get better', perhaps thinking the parent does not care sufficiently about living. The idea that a parent does not really want to live threatens the child's whole existence. Children (as well as many adults) do believe in magic, and may pin their hopes on all kinds of supposed cures, however irrational, if encouraged to do so by an over-enthusiastic worker.

I can't put it right

It may seem that unless a professional or worker can offer a solution, they can do nothing. The worker may know intellectually that it can be important simply to be there so the client is not always alone while they suffer or while they work out for themselves what to do in a difficult situation, but this knowledge may disappear temporarily under pressure. In order to tolerate a client's or patient's sense of impotence, a worker has first to tolerate their own, and this may be difficult. Hearing a client going over and over unrealistic beliefs and anxieties may feel like a waste of time; it may be hard to offer understanding and patient listening while a client grieves.

Doctors in particular may suffer from this. The whole focus of their training tends to be on curing and making things better; few have been trained in the value of suffering alongside a patient.

This is one area where children may be left to care alone for their parents. They may be the only people around while the parent feels free to grieve. This is likely to have consequences for the rest of their lives. They may develop an exaggerated sense of their own importance and strength, triumphing over the parent in the process of denying their own vulnerability and fear. They may develop a sense of a broken-down mother inside them, unable to support them throughout their life. They may become intolerant of other people's misery, or more able to survive it, or even attracted to it. They may learn to always offer support to others while denying their own need for it; perhaps successfully, or perhaps breaking down later in life and suddenly behaving like the grieving parent themselves. Their own children may pay a price as they in turn expect their children to give them support. The effect will depend on the pre-existing personality of parent and child, on circumstances (both in childhood and later in adulthood), and on the outcome for the grieving parent.

You have to be particularly nice to them

People in general can find it hard to relate 'normally' to someone who is ill or disabled. Where an immediate reaction to the person's condition is judged unworthy or unprofessional and to be hidden, it can be difficult to recognise ordinary feelings of anger or irritation with the person. It can be very difficult to know what is reasonable sensitivity to another's difficulties and what is being patronising and making too many allowances.

Sometimes 'being nice' means assuming that because someone is ill they cannot bear bad news. In some situations this is reasonable, but if it means that important information is withheld over a long period of time it can be seriously damaging, to the individual, to their emotional development or to their relationships with others. 'They can't take it' may be a product of projective identification, whereby the ability and chance to 'take it' is denied to the 'victim' and used to increase the sense of power and authority of the 'helper'. Deciding whether this is the case or not can be very difficult.

A worker who struggles to be 'nice' to a difficult client may be very aware of the children watching. The temptation to share their more irritated feelings with an older child later may be strong; but this is tantamount to asking the child to keep a secret and is foolish as well as bad for the child. Children should never be asked to keep a secret from their parents, whatever the circumstances. On the other hand, sharing the irritation with the client, if it is possible to do so in a good way, may help the client and their children to handle the conflicts in their own interaction. By making it safe to talk about the irritation, perhaps to joke about it, the worker may enable the child to own their own bad feelings and their own guilt, and enable them to choose whether to act upon them or not.

We must be positive

Workers of all kinds, as much as the rest of the population, can have strong beliefs in the therapeutic importance of 'being positive'. People often try to find positive thoughts to use as means of stopping negative ones; this has similarities to turning to alcohol, drugs, or even violence as a response to terrible grief. All of these can be used as short term 'solutions' to block the feeling and expression of grief or anxiety. Negative thoughts and feelings are buried, hidden from others and often from the self. Such negative thoughts are always in a less realistic state than they would be if openly discussed and allowed to pass in their own time. They are likely to include exaggerated ideas such as 'I have lost everything'; or 'nobody loves me and nobody ever could love me'. Sometimes 'positive' thoughts are insufficiently discussed because both worker and client secretly believe the unspoken, exaggerated negative ideas. Unreal brightness and insincere cheerfulness may cover a sense of terrible insecurity and loss of hope.

Children can be very aware of such underlying feelings and of the fear of disturbing them. In some circumstances they may act out the unspoken fears, perhaps becoming the focus of worries about their own safety (for example, by drug taking or getting involved in road accidents or fights) as a means of both trying to deal with them with their own limited means and trying to take them away from their parents. Children may also learn to show such unconvincing brightness.

> One such young woman saw herself as very strong and positive; her mother had taught her always to put things behind her and move on. She came for help because she had terrifying thoughts of dying which seemed to have no relation to reality. When she was given help to face distressing events in her past rather than to turn away from them she lost these fears.

It is only after a period of distressing emotional work, thinking through the consequences of a disturbing change, that truly realistic and lasting positive thoughts gradually emerge. The very frightening thoughts and feelings have to be taken seriously before anyone can discover, perhaps against the expectation of both worker and client, that they are unrealistic. Positive thoughts which arise early on in the grieving process are often to some extent unrealistic and are vulnerable to being crushed in moments of gloom. Attempts to use positive thoughts to *replace* the work of grieving are thus very likely to fail, often leaving the individual feeling guilty for failing to be positive. Such attempts may seriously delay the completion of the grieving process. Unresolved thoughts may be buried but remain very active; affecting behaviour directly and liable to come to the surface unwanted, either in nightmares or in response to triggers during the day.

A worker's ability to work with negative thoughts may have long-term effects on the children within the family as well as on the adults directly concerned.

Being politically correct

While some workers seem to have no difficulty knowing how to behave, others can be very concerned about showing their ignorance of 'disability etiquette' towards disabled clients. This can be compounded by the fact that there may be disagreements about how one should behave.

Some people having difficulty putting on their coat, for example, want to be left alone to put it on in their own time; some are annoyed at any attempt to help or to offer help. Other people want someone to wait until they are asked for help. Yet others in the same situation would be annoyed at help *not* being offered without being requested; some people can feel one way at one time and differently at another. It can be very difficult to guess what a stranger wants in these circumstances. It is not sufficient to ask 'how would I feel if it were me?' because people differ enormously over how much help they want or can tolerate. In addition, having a temporary disability is very different from having a long-term one; having a new disability is very different from having an old one. This means that any encounter with someone who has a disability may lead to a social gaffe. This has to be tolerated by everyone involved: any watching children in particular may be desperately embarrassed at a perceived insult to their parents, and the worker may be more embarrassed knowing the children saw. There may even be a temptation for the worker to make the children suffer in some way later, in order to re-establish their own superiority. Discussing the situation with children may or may not be either possible or advisable.

In addition, there are many conditions (such as communications disorders and anything which shocks the onlooker or listener) which in a one-to-one situation disable the other person as much as or more than the one who has it. Perhaps the only comfort is that having a disability can itself feel like a social gaffe; the worker who puts their foot in it can know for a moment something of the humiliation and discomfort of having a socially problematical condition. If this can be acknowledged as a shared problem it may be more bearable.

In the long term there is no substitute for discussing the social niceties with the person concerned, and generally people seem to respond well to being asked how they like others to treat them. Unfortunately, the answers may apply only to *this* person, *this* day, in *this* situation.

However, discussion is not always possible. The situation may make talking inappropriate, or it may be blocked by client or worker. Children may prevent talking between adults, particularly if they are afraid of what might be said, or if they feel they are being left out. Some people with disabilities or chronic conditions have good reason to be angry at the treatment they have received in the past and may turn this anger on a new person coming their way, however hard they try to talk. A well-meaning young social worker or nurse may be made to feel the humiliation of being a non-person which a disabled man or woman has been subjected to, perhaps many years earlier as a child, or perhaps the day before. A newly ill or disabled person, discovering at first hand the discrimination to which they are subject, may punish a worker who unconsciously represents a more thoughtless, prejudiced earlier self. A worker whose own mother uses the excuse of (real or imaginary) ill health to exploit her children may get irritated with an ill client who apparently 'won't make an effort': such a worker may be unable to make time to talk seriously about their own behaviour.

Relations between those who are ill or disabled and those who are working with or for them often have an element of power involved, and power games can bring into action behaviour learnt in the playground, or between sadistic adults and children. Either the worker or the person with the disability may find themselves thrust into either a bullying or a victim role by the other. Neither the 'bully' nor the 'victim' may be able to initiate discussion, though an outsider respected by both might. Children within the family may be similarly affected, bullied by or bullying either the parent or the worker. This means that any help which a worker can obtain, whether they feel they are doing the bullying or behaving like a victim, may have an important effect on the behaviour and treatment of the children.

When race issues are also part of the picture, either party may find themselves being treated as the representative of the racial group they appear to belong to, and their personality may have to struggle to make itself known through the assumptions. For a less powerful group, the temptation, of course, is not to bother: to let the other keep his or her prejudices and at the same time to maintain a secret belief in the superiority of one's own culture, but never to try to break through and make real contact. This too, can prevent honest discussion of issues around the way care is offered, delivered or accepted.

Issues around the 'politically correct' areas of disability, race, gender, and sexuality may all be usefully the subject of discussion groups for workers and their clients. So too may issues around the relationship between children and parents, in general and in connection with disabilities. There are good arguments for inviting workers and clients together to such discussions; mixed groups will deal with different issues from those where only workers *or* clients are represented. However, when well run, either kind of group can be extremely moving and bring about significant change. It is important to remember that the quality of the leadership is crucial; if such workshops are badly run they may make relationships and prejudices worse.

It's not fair, how can a disabled person have a child when I can't?

Envy towards others' good fortune is a common source of unhappiness and spoiling of pleasure. It can be found in surprising places: earlier in this book we mentioned the envy a mother can suffer if her child receives more care than she did as a child or in the present. Fathers' envy of the new baby's comfort is sometimes expressed by seeking an affair, which gives the father a special person for himself and in addition serves to threaten the envied security of both the mother and the baby – probably with no awareness that this is involved. In good circumstances, these processes are held in check by love.

People who work with people with disabilities may fail to recognise their own envy of their clients. It is as if it is unbelievable, almost incongruous, and certainly *wrong*, to feel envy towards a disabled woman, even if she does have, for example, a good husband and children when the worker has neither. Envy can be disabling if it gets in the way of enjoyment of the good things of life; it can be destructive if it attacks others' enjoyment.

When the motability scheme started in England there was considerable resentment expressed by some people at the idea that people with disabilities should have access to vehicles which able-bodied people might not be able to afford: it was probably such envy which kept the dangerous three-wheeled invalid cars on the road for so long. There may be times when similar feelings are behind difficulties between workers and their disabled or ill clients.

> A homeworker complained about her disabled client: 'She wants me to pick up her children's things and I don't think I should. They are old enough to pick up their own books: nobody picks up for my children'.

Sex and disability shouldn't be allowed

Sexuality in any context is capable of arousing considerable interest and even more anxiety. This contributes to the complexities of feelings aroused by any issues involving sex and disability. The idea that people with disabilities should not have sex is gradually being challenged in the public arena. In our work we have often come across it in terms which pay lipservice to political correctness: 'I think it is all right for other people, but if it were me I would not expect anyone to want me sexually, certainly not to marry me'. These ideas have complex roots. Many people are secretly afraid of sex or marriage, or afraid no-one would want to marry them anyway: such anxieties can easily be attached to the 'disabled self' – and perhaps, secretly, to the client. There may be a sense that, almost for aesthetic reasons, sex 'belongs' to health and should not be brought into contact with sickness and illness. In literature and film, actual sex (as distinct from the promise of it) is often partnered with violence: there may be a fear that sex is dangerous for the weak or ill or for those partnered with them. The loss of control in sex may be particularly feared if a disability causes loss of control in some way.

Children typically think their parents do not have sex any longer: if a single parent is disabled and considering remarriage, they may simply assume that sex is not involved. The whole issue of single parents making new relationships is of enormous importance to children. On the one hand there may be relief in a new adult sharing care of the parent, whether they are ill or not; on the other hand there are all the issues of rivalry and whether the child's position is threatened. They may also fear that the new adult will be unable to look after the parent well enough, or may need care from the parent which will threaten the parent's health further. Children may well fear their parents having a sexual relationship, for many reasons connected to their health as well as all the other reasons which are always involved.

Sex of course is also connected with pregnancy and childbirth, both of which arouse many complex and disturbing feelings. The risks of pregnancy are real, but perception of them is heightened by feelings of envy, jealousy and rivalry stemming from childhood experience, and particularly, perhaps, for professionals, by adult fears of complications of childbirth. For a doctor, a patient's pregnancy in the best of circumstances may simply mean more work, responsibility and anxiety, both in the present and for the foreseeable future: the doctor does not reap the benefits of the birth. Where a parent is disabled, the fantasy that they may give birth to a monster may lurk in the unconscious of professionals as well as the parents.

Older children may also have fears about their mother giving birth, whatever her state of health. A boy of fifteen whose mother was perfectly healthy was terrified she would die in childbirth. Other people, including professional workers involved with a pregnant woman, may increase or decrease the anxieties of any children involved. A child of even two or three may overhear frightening conversations about the risks involved and draw their own terrifying conclusions. A disabled mother giving birth may also turn upside down her daughter's fantasy of their roles being reversed.

Workers sometimes worry about parading their own sexuality in front of patients; a few workers actually do this. Particularly within an institution of some kind, a fear of arousing envy of sexuality may even sometimes contribute to an atmosphere where staff hide their own liveliness and present only a rather drab appearance to patients or clients, perhaps restricting jokes or laughter as well as discussion of children or marriages to staff interactions, or even banishing them from the work setting entirely. Teenage children may feel themselves particularly out of place and uncomfortable visiting such institutions, and it may discourage them from keeping contact with absent parents. Workers do need to protect their privacy, but protecting disabled patients from discussion of anything remotely connected with sexuality may simply deprive everybody of lively interaction.

Teenagers may also play out anxieties about their own sexuality with workers of either sex. They too may be anxious about letting their parents see their developing sexuality, particularly if the parent is finding it difficult to cope with feeling less sexually attractive as a result of age, illness or disability. How the worker deals with this may be important in opening up or closing down communication between the teenager and their parent. Illness or disability may also sometimes lead to a parent seeking new sexual relationships and ignoring the effect of this on their own children. Adolescent children in particular can be seriously affected by this; again the attitude of workers within the house can make things worse or better for the children. Where a worker and a client fall in love it may be hard to think of the children.

Overtly sexual behaviour of clients or colleagues, within any work context, may arouse considerable anxiety in some situations. Young workers may be shocked to find themselves importuned by disabled clients, and be uncertain how to extricate themselves in a professional manner. They may blame themselves and be too embarrassed and ashamed to seek support or advice from more experienced colleagues. It is not a simple matter to be asked to facilitate a sexual relationship between two disabled people: it is also hard to know that an extra-marital affair is going on within a Day Centre or Residential Home. The issues of privacy, morality and social sanctioning of relationships seem to be heightened if at least one of the partners is disabled, and staff may feel responsible for protecting vulnerable people on 'their' premises. If there is suspicion of sexual relationships between senior members of staff too, anxieties and feelings about these relationships (which may not be discussed openly) may be displaced onto client relationships (which can be discussed).

How this fits with protecting the rights of people with disabilities may be very unclear. What are people's rights when it comes to sexuality? 'Normal' sexual relations often involve an imbalance of power: do staff have a right or a duty to intervene if a younger, weaker client is being seduced by a more experienced, stronger one? Or not? How do the rights of women fit in? What if the more experienced one is a married man with a wife and children who arouse sympathy in the staff? Is a relationship being carried on openly because there is no privacy, or because the couple want someone to intervene? Should a private room be provided, or should a couple be asked to modify their public behaviour? Here, as so often, it is far from easy to decide which rules need to be changed to accommodate a disability, and which should not be; whether the world should change (and tolerate more open displays of sexuality) or whether people with disabilities should quietly accept yet another disadvantage of their state (and be deprived of opportunities for sexual behaviour which an able-bodied person might be able to arrange for themselves). What about the feelings of other clients who are also forced to witness sexual behaviour? Such issues may not be easy to discuss, either within the staff group or between staff and clients. These issues are discussed further in Ramon (1991). The situation of children when their parents have sexual affairs may be ignored by some and be a source of serious concern for others.

Ideas about the effect on society of the birth of children to disabled parents are sometimes nowadays raised in terms of the financial cost to the taxpayer. Even where it is not acceptable to discourage someone from having a child on these grounds, anxieties about the willingness of legislators to provide the finance may contribute to concerns. Many adults, certainly in Britain, do not like children anyway, seeing them as a drain on their parents and a disruption to adult society. Dependence in general, to many British people, from childhood on, is a condition to be avoided, discouraged and sometimes desperately feared, while self-sufficiency is idealised. This strengthens the fact that taxpayers are assumed to have other priorities for their money than helping disabled people to have children, so possibly increasing their dependence on services, if only for a few years.

Everyone would be better off if...

A social worker in a training session confessed to feeling that it would be better for everyone if a certain client were dead. She felt terrible about this thought and had not shared it with anyone. In the discussion the question was raised whether the client himself shared this feeling: the social worker suddenly realised that he probably did, and that he too might be unable to share it. Her whole attitude changed as she realised that it might simply be a communicable thought which could be discussed rather than a deadly action to be avoided at all costs.

The feeling that others would be better off if someone were dead is not uncommon. People sometimes feel it about themselves, whatever their health; children often feel (and may say) it about brothers and sisters, parents or new partners of their parents, even if they also love them. Such feelings may be divided up within the family, with one person expressing one set of feelings and another the opposite set.

> A small boy knew that his mother thought his father would be better off dead. He kept insisting that his father was going to get better.

Relatives, carers, ex-spouses and paid and unpaid workers of all kinds can sometimes feel it about someone who is ill or disabled, ostensibly *because* they are ill or disabled, but perhaps not simply for this reason. Normally such a thought passes rapidly; where it does not, it can provoke terrible feelings of guilt, which themselves can lead to avoidance and more guilt.

Such a thought may not easily or safely be shared. However, if a safe enough setting and the right person can be found, sharing the feeling can help to put it into a context in which other conflicting feelings and thoughts are recognized and given weight too.

> A recently disabled man said he thought everyone would be better off if he were dead. His wife could find another partner and his children would be free of him. In a counselling session it became clear that he was actually angry with his family for not looking after him well enough. His stated desire to relieve them of a burden covered a desire to punish them for their failings. He also recognised that children are never 'free' of a father, whether he is alive or dead, and that *how* he died would affect both them and his wife far more than he first admitted. Once he had recognised this he stopped talking of killing himself.

> A woman with multiple sclerosis said she sometimes had a fleeting thought of killing herself and was then angry that she had children because it meant she could not do it.

If the question of euthanasia or suicide is raised seriously it has to be discussed seriously. Workers may be very uncomfortable with this and unless they have discussed it beforehand with colleagues may not know how to respond, particularly if they have been asked for secrecy. The issues are complex. Death is not a private issue, much as people would sometimes like it to be: it has both long and short-term effects on the lives of those around, especially children, and especially those related. We think it unlikely that children ever forget how their parents died. They may find it difficult to forgive anyone who hastened that death, or even confessed to wanting to hasten it for any reason. If a parent themselves tried to take their own life, a child may feel totally betrayed. Their chances of thinking of killing themselves are likely to be increased enormously, and they may try to put these thoughts into action.

Legally, euthanasia is treated as murder and it is an offence to assist anyone in any way to kill themselves, but it is not always easy in any particular situation to decide whether to take action or what action to take. Different professions and different organisations have their own guidelines for workers faced with dilemmas related to suicide and confidentiality.[1]

A worker who has had a patient or client die while in their care needs debriefing. Someone must offer support and facilitate exploration of the facts,

---

1   For a discussion of the ethical and legal issues involved for counsellors, see Tim Bond (1993) *Standards and Ethics for Counselling in Action.* London: Sage.

the feelings and the issues involved as soon as possible, without reassuring either prematurely or unrealistically. Without this, future patients as well as the worker themselves may suffer; for example, from the worker deciding never to care about a patient again; or never to allow a patient to do anything with any risk attached, so becoming unreasonably restrictive and overcontrolling. Doctors who have lost patients by suicide after a diagnosis of a serious illness sometimes cite this as a reason for withholding information from all their patients. Their reaction might be less extreme if they had an opportunity to discuss the event and its emotional consequences and to place their own actions and their own role in context.

The debriefing needs to include thoughts about any children involved. Workers need to consider whether such children are getting the emotional support they need, or whether it needs to be offered by someone outside the family, or whether no such help can be offered at the present. Families may resist involvement at such a time, but a General Practitioner with long-term contact with the family, or a teacher who is alerted and retains contact with a child over a period of time may be in a position to offer the chance for the child to talk about the loss of their parent, perhaps some years later. These issues are considered in more detail in Chapter 14.

Practical illustrations

Case study; working with feelings

In an in-service training session one group of workers talked of their fear of a particular group of clients being so needy that they would suck the worker dry. In the session several important issues were considered.

First, the client may be aware of the worker's feelings, and afraid that the worker cannot bear to stay with the client for long enough to deal with all their needs; this can heighten the need to demand and to keep the worker there out of anxiety rather than realistic need. A vicious circle can be set up in which the worker's fear is a driving force and the client is left feeling the desperation which the worker is trying to avoid.

Second, the worker's fear could be a reflection of the *client's* fear that they themselves would be sucked dry by the demands of those around them which they did not have the resources to satisfy. Mothers sometimes fear this from their children, for example; men may fear it from their sexual partner.

Discussing these possibilities led to a new assessment of the extent and limits of the client's real needs and seemed to reduce the worker's desire to run away. However, the discussion which seemed to have most impact was when the group considered their own neediness and demands as workers.

At the time, members of the group were faced with reorganisation and new ways of working which they disliked. They felt unsupported and lacking sufficient resources to do their job properly. Listing elements of their experience as workers demonstrated a remarkable similarity between their situation and that of their clients. It seemed that both client and worker had reason to feel a lack of resources; anger with those who controlled resources; abandonment by those who should have been supporting them; resistance to a change which seemed far from desirable. Both had reason to feel their own needs were not being considered, and that their sources of satisfaction in their daily lives were being whittled away. Both had reason to feel frustration at being unable to do their work properly, and a need to grieve for the old while accepting their new, reduced circumstances. The training session itself seemed cruelly to illustrate the way resources were provided 'too little and too late', raising expectations without satisfying them.

Addressing these issues in the group seemed to reduce significantly the workers' sense of being overwhelmed and enabled them to discover a new sense of affinity with clients. Taking care of them in the group, including acknowledging the limits to the care provided in the session, perhaps also reduced their need to split off and project into clients their own desperation. Splitting and alienation seemed to give way to a sense of sharing and an increase in respect for the client and for the self. The experience of having their needs, anger, frustration and sense of deprivation taken seriously, and being allowed to discuss difficult issues without fear of censure, perhaps also provided the workers with a model enabling them to face their clients' emotional state and take this seriously, even where it meant acknowledging the way needs could *not* be satisfied.

Case study: assessing risks: children vs parents

> A young woman with multiple sclerosis attending a specialist clinic spoke with her physiotherapist about difficulties she was having with her children. Her husband had recently left her and she said her son was sometimes very aggressive towards her.

The physiotherapist had to decide whether to pursue this; to try to establish what the mother meant by 'aggressive', and whether the parent or the child was at risk.

She decided that she had to try to find out more, because the child might be at risk either of damaging himself or, equally dangerous to the child, of damaging his mother. The risk to the mother was also a consideration, but as an adult she had the right to put herself at risk and to decline intervention on her own behalf. If the worker felt that the child was at risk she had to inform either the patient's General Practitioner or Social Services: in order to decide this, the physiotherapist had to take into account many complex questions and considerations.

The age of the child was relevant. An aggressive preschool child may be able to cause less damage to an adult than an aggressive child of secondary school age. How isolated the mother and child were, and whether another adult was around to protect child and mother, would affect whether the child was at risk of seriously injuring themselves or someone else.

Aggression in children is normal, particularly at times of extreme jealousy, for example the birth of a new baby or the appearance of a new lover for a parent. Aggression in small children has to be controlled by adults who therefore have to be capable of controlling it.

Aggression in children can also be a sign of severe disturbance, suicidal wishes and future destructive actions. It can also be a sign of disturbance in a parent, necessitating intervention.

Parents who are not in contact with professionals often have to deal with aggression in their children, and may do so badly. The physiotherapist herself felt she sometimes failed to control her own children's aggression and though she would not have minded discussing this with her GP, she knew other people who would hate to have to talk to their GP about such issues.

There is a sense in which it is unfair that parents with disabilities should be more at risk of professional intervention, which may or may not be advantageous to the child or parent. A worker may feel guilty even at the thought that a child might be taken from its mother because of something the worker said. Professional intervention has in the past sometimes made things worse for children rather than better. On the other hand, professional inaction has sometimes left children in danger.

Discussing how to handle difficult behaviour in children is a normal social activity, particularly between mothers. A disabled parent may look on a professional as a friend, particularly if they have little opportunity to meet with other parents to discuss such issues. If the worker responds to such a discussion as a professional rather than a friend they may be accused of betrayal.

However, a friend or relative presented with similar information might also try to find out more, and may also find their loyalties to the parent conflicting with their loyalties to the children. They might also decide to take action if they were sufficiently disturbed by what they found out.

The sense of betrayal may put the relationship at risk, in this case, potentially depriving the client of physiotherapy. Other relations within the same setting may also be put at risk, for example, if the physiotherapist is working within a GP surgery or a specialist hospital clinic with other professionals involved.

In addition, both parent and worker know that the relation between them is not that of a friend, even if this knowledge is both uncomfortable and suppressed. A child may have reason to feel betrayed by professionals who, while knowing that something was wrong, did nothing. The fact that the worker does not know the child, and does know the parent, may make it tempting for the worker to ignore the betrayal of the child.

A patient who has told someone in a professional relationship their worries about their child will be aware that they have done this. The professional's response will be noted. Inaction will be interpreted in the patient's own way: for example, it may be taken as a sign that there is nothing to worry about, or as a sign that the worker is frightened of the parent, or that the parent can blame the worker if the parent is accused later of not taking action themselves. A response which takes the report seriously may enable the parent to take the event more seriously and perhaps to take their own action; on the other hand, it may make the parent decide never to mention such a worry again. An intrusive response will probably alienate the patient, though some people gain pleasure from others being wrong and such a patient may react aggressively but not absent themselves. Either kind of response can leave the patient angry with the worker for not simply offering reassurance.

A child who knows that professionals tried to intervene is in a different situation from one who does not.

There may be no outcome which is comfortable for parent, child and worker. In some circumstances discomfort may move from parent–child to parent–worker, but the parent–worker relationship may be more easily broken. The worker may be relieved of a burden if they antagonise a difficult patient, intentionally or unintentionally and the patient then stops using the worker: this may leave a child to shoulder the huge burden of a difficult parent alone.

The outcome of either action or inaction is not entirely in the hands of the professional. Parents, other relatives, other professionals and existing legislation may all play their part in determining the outcome for the particular child.

> The physiotherapist was worried enough by what she discovered to raise the issue with her senior. The senior said she felt that the client's relationship with the Clinic was a risk if social services were informed directly, but the GP should be informed of the physiotherapist's concern. It would be for him to decide whether to take further action. She felt that, in this particular case, the risk to the child of breaking off the mother's relationship with the Clinic was overriding.

> The next time the physiotherapist saw the patient the patient said that after their discussion she had decided to ask her local Child Guidance Clinic for help for both her children.

What can we do?

In this chapter we have described some of the psychological issues which can influence relationships between families with a parent who is ill or disabled and those who work with them. We have left out consideration of the political and social issues, issues of access and power relations, not because they are not important, but because they are dealt with by others (see, for example, Finkelstein in Oliver 1983; Ramon 1991). Socially, change is required on all fronts, and needs to be tackled on all fronts simultaneously. Political and economic issues as well as psychological ones affect willingness to tackle access problems, including pavement ramps, transport, design of public buildings and poverty, all of which in turn affect public participation and power relations. Julia Segal's interest and experience has been in exploring attitudes and the ways people construct their perception of reality in connection with illness and disability, but we see our work as part of a much bigger endeavour, involving many others.

Many of the issues we have highlighted can be influenced by good training, both before and in-service, and by ongoing support and non-managerial supervision, all of which can provide the opportunity for disturbing issues to be considered seriously, with enough exploration of the facts, feelings and assumptions for a real change to take place in the worker's internal world. If this is undertaken with sufficient respect for the worker it will be reflected in a new respect for the client, their family and for the worker themselves, which allows all concerned to escape the straightjacket of false assumptions about health, sickness, disability and parenting. Unfortunately, it takes political will to provide the finance for such training and supervision, even where it is available.

It is, of course, our hope that reading this book can also bring about change in the ways people understand and perceive their own and others' disabilities and the relationship between illness, disability and parenting. We hope that such understanding leads to improvement in feelings and behaviour towards self and others, whatever the role. We hope that our book may in this way help children with ill or disabled parents, both in childhood and later in life.

Further Reading

For parents and general interest

Aldridge, J. and Becker, S. (1993) *Children who Care: Inside the World of Young Carers*. Young Carers Research Group, Loughborough University: see Useful Addresses below.

Aldridge, J. and Becker, S. (1994) *A Friend Indeed: The Case for Befriending Young Carers*. Young Carers Research Group, Loughborough University: see Useful Addresses below.

Aldridge, J. and Becker, S. (1994) *My Child, My Carer: The Parents' Perspective*. Young Carers Research Group, Loughborough University: see Useful Addresses below.

Anderson, R. and Bury, M. (eds) (1988) *Living with Chronic Illness*. London, Unwin Hyman.

Barnes, C. (1993) *Making Our Own Choices: Independent Living, Personal Assistance and Disabled People*. British Council of Organisations of Disabled People.

Belohorec, A. and Kikuchi, J.F. (1985) 'How do you mother when you are disabled?' *The Canadian Nurse*, March 1985 pp.32–5.

Burnfield, A. (1985) *Multiple Sclerosis: a Personal Exploration*. London, Souvenir Press.

Campion, M.J. (1990) *The Baby Challenge. Handbook on Pregnancy for Women with a Physical Disability*. London, Routledge and Kegan Paul. An informative guide covering the common disabilities.

Campling, J. (ed) (1987) *Images of Ourselves; Women with Disabilities Talking*. London, Routledge and Kegan Paul.

Cattanach, A. (1994) *Play Therapy. Where the Sky Meets the Underworld*. London, Jessica Kingsley. An informative book full of stories and descriptions of therapeutic play with children.

Faber, A. and Mazlish, E. (1980) *How to Talk so Kids Will Listen and Listen so Kids will Talk*. New York, Avon Books.

Forti, A and Segal, J.C. (1986) *MS and Pregnancy*. Available from The Multiple Sclerosis Resources Centre, 4A Chapel Hill Stansted Essex CM24 8AG, tel 01279 817101.

Kohner, N. (1988) *Caring at Home*. National Extension College, 18 Brooklands Ave, Cambridge CB2 2HN, tel 01223 316644.

Lendrum, S. and Syme G. (1992) *Gift of Tears: A Practical Approach to Loss and Bereavement Counselling*. London and New York, Tavistock/Routledge.

Living with MS (1990) London, Kings Fund Centre.

Mace, N. and Rabins, P. with Castleton, B.A., Cloke, C. and McEwen, E. (1985) *The 36 Hour Day*. London, Hodder and Stoughton with Age Concern.

Maddox, B. (1975) *Step-Parenting. How to Live with Other People's Children*. London, Unwin Paperbacks.

Meredith, H. *et al.* (1992) *Report of a Workshop Day on Young Carers in Black and Minority Ethnic Communities*. London, Kings Fund Centre.

Mitchell, A. (1985) *Children in the Middle: Living Through Divorce*. London and New York, Tavistock. Interviews with children and separated parents: describing the differences of view between children and parents.

Morris, J. (ed) (1989) *Able Lives. Women's Experience of Paralysis*. London, The Women's Press Ltd.

Parents with disabilities (1991) Disability Information trust. Available only from Mary Marlborough Lodge, Nuffield Orthopaedic Centre, Headington, Oxford OX3 7LD, tel 0865 741155. £8.50.

Parkin, A.J. (1987) *Memory and Amnesia: An Introduction*. Oxford, Blackwell.

Segal, J. (1992) 'Living with disabled parents or siblings: parents with Multiple Sclerosis.' In P. Leach (ed) *Young Children Under Stress. Starting Points 13 Practical Guides for Early Years Workers*. London, Voluntary Organisations Liaison Council for Under Fives, 77 Holloway Rd, London N7 8JZ.

Segal, J.C. (1986) *Emotional Reactions to MS*. Stansted, Essex: The Multiple Sclerosis Resources Centre, 4A Chapel Hill Stansted Essex CM24 8AG, tel 01279 817101.

Segal, J.C. (1985) *Phantasy in Everyday Life. A Psychoanalytical Approach to Understanding Ourselves*. London, Pelican Books. Reprinted London, Karnac Books 1995.

Skynner, R. and Cleese, J. (1983) *Families and How to Survive Them*. London, Methuen.

Smithers, K. 'Practical problems of mothers who have Multiple Sclerosis.' *Midwife, Health Visitor and Community Nurse 24*, 5, pp.165–168.

Tessman, L.H. (1978) *Children of Parting Parents*. New York, Jason Aronson. A child psychotherapist describes in detail some of the issues which arise for children whose parents separate, some for reasons of mental illness. A relatively positive view of the possibilities of handling the effects of separation.

Dearden, C. and Becker, S. (1995) *Young Carers – The Facts*. Young Carers Research Group, Loughborough University: see Useful Addresses below.

Wessex Regional Library Information Service (1991) *Reflections: Subject Guide to Fiction and Biography on Illness and Disability*. Tabor and Stephenson.

For Children

Althea (1982) *When Uncle Bob Died*. London, Dinosaur. Typical of Althea books: rather wooden in places but perhaps useful.

Ashley, B. (1991) *Seeing off Uncle Jack*. London, Viking. Age 7–11. A family coming to terms with the good and the bad in deceased Uncle Jack. The family black, and to Winnie and her brother it seemed that he had sold out his black identity.

Burlingham, J. (1990) *Grandpa*. London, Picture Puffins. Beautifully illustrated relationship between small girl and grandpa: poignantly wordless when grandpa dies.

MS Society, London (1989) *Has your Mum or Dad got MS?* Available from the MS Society, 25 Effie Rd., London SW6 1EE.

Perkins, G. and Morris, L. (1991) *Remembering Mum*. London, A & C Black. Photographs and simple words describing a father and children remembering. Realistic and moving.

Simmonds, P. (1987) *Fred*. A cat dies. London: Picture Puffins.

Varley, S. (1984) *Badger's Parting Gifts*. Badger is old and his death is described as 'leaving his body behind' and 'going down the long tunnel': otherwise good; focus on friends' memories. London: Collins.

For older children

Booklist for Children of Upper Junior and Lower Secondary School Age. 1991 Available from Cruse Bereavement Care, Cruse House, 126 Sheen Rd. Richmond Surrey, TW9 1UR, tel 0181 940 4818.

Ashley, B. (1981) *Dodgem*. London, Puffin. When his mother dies, Simon has to cope with his father's depression as well as with bullying at school. Taken into care, he is desperate to return to look after his father. HIs escape, with the help of a fairground girl, is exciting and realistic and ultimately leads to his recognition of his own importance and his need to allow his father to look after himself.

Blume, J. (1983) *Tiger Eyes*. London, Piccolo. For 14+ Darney finds her father fatally wounded and realizes she cannot help him. Staying with relatives with the rest of her family, Darney's anger and grief heighten her sense of desolation and isolation.

Carers' National Association. (Constantly updated) Young Carer Information Pack. This pack may also be a useful source of information and support for children whose parents are ill but who are not carers themselves.

Cookson, C. (1991) *Our John Willie*. London, Doubleday. Set in the mining communities of the North East when sheep stealing was punished by transportation, Davy is left with responsibility for his younger brother when his father is killed in a mining accident. Help from other adults enables him to survive. Very readable.

Cookson, C. (1991) *Go Tell It to Mrs Golightly*. London, Doubleday. Nine-year-old Bella, who is blind, is sent to her cold and awkward grandfather to live when her father dies.

Heegaard, M. (1991) What to do when someone very special dies: Children can learn to cope with grief. Woodland Press, Minneapolis. 1991. Mail order Meditec, Medical and Nursing Booksellers, Jackson's Yard, Brewery Hill, Grantham Lincs. NG31 6DW, tel 01476 590505.

Hinton, S.E. (1989) *That was Then, This is Now*. London, Gollancz. Two boys aged 16, good friends, drift apart when Charlie of the pool bar gets killed defending them in a brawl.

Krementz, J. (1984) *How it Feels to be Adopted*. London, Gollancz.

Krementz, J. (1985) *How it Feels when Parents Divorce*. London, Gollancz.

Krementz, J. (1991) *How it Feels when a Parent Dies*. London, Gollancz.

Pilling, A. (1992) *Vote for Baz*. London, Viking. Baz has won a scholarship to a public school and is standing for election as a representative of The Common Man. He struggles to cope with the British class system and with the jealousy and resentment of an old school friend who did not get in. Baz's mother, recently widowed, is striving to make ends meet by doing cleaning jobs. Baz's father has just died in circumstances that Baz finds too difficult to discuss.

Walker, A. (1991) *To Hell with Dying*. Sevenoaks, Hodder and Stoughton. A young woman grows up helping an old man to fight death. Eventually he dies and she has to come to terms with reality. A beautiful picture book for all ages.

Zindel, P. and B. (1991) *A Star for the Latecomer*. London, Red Fox. Brooke's own dreams and her mother's ambitions for her conflict. Brook has to cope with the conflict which gradually recognizing that her mother is dying of cancer.

For mentally handicapped people

The Right to Grieve. A leaflet to help mentally handicapped people who are bereaved. Available from the King's Fund Centre.

For professionals

General

French, S. (1994) On equal terms: working with disabled people. London, Butterworth-Heinemann Ltd.

Robinson, I., Jones, R. and Segal, J.C. (1990) Patients, their families and MS. Chapter 11 in De Souza, L. (ed) *Multiple Sclerosis Approaches to Management*. London, Chapman and Hall.

Young Carers Research Group. c/o Betty Newton, Dept of Social Science, Loughborough University, Leics LE11 3TU tel 01509 228299 Lists projects in the UK exploring various aspects of the situation of children and young people caring for their parents.

Becker, S. (ed) (1995) Young Carers in Europe: An Exploratory Cross-National Study in Britain, France, Sweden and Germany. Young Carers Research Group, Loughborough University: see Useful Addresses below.

Dearden, C. *et al.* (1994) Partners in Caring: A Briefing for Professionals about Young Carers. Young Carers Research Group, Loughborough University: see Useful Addresses below.

For teachers

Carers National Association (1996) Notes for teachers of children with ill parents. See Useful Addresses.

Young Minds (1996) *Mental Health in Your School. A Guide for Teachers and Others Working in Schools.* London, Jessica Kingsley.

Ward, B. and Associates (1995) *Good Grief 1: Exploring Feelings, Loss and Death with Under 11's.* 2nd edition. London, Jessica Kingsley. Comprehensive manual for teachers.

Ward, B. and Associates (1995) *Good Grief 2: Exploring Feelings, Loss and Death with Over 11's and Adults.* London, Jessica Kingsley. Comprehensive manual for teachers.

For Counsellors and Psychotherapists

Bond, T. (1993) *Standards and Ethics for Counselling in Action.* London, Sage.

Brearly, G. and Birchley, P. (1986) *Introducing Counselling Skills and Techniques. With Particular Application for the Paramedical Professions.* London, Faber and Faber. Examples of people with disabilities/chronic illnesses.

Erskine, A. and Judd, D. (1994) *The Imaginative Body: Psychodynamic Therapy in Health Care.* London, Whurr Publishers.

Segal, J.C. (1987) 'Independence and control: issues in the counselling of people with MS.' *Counselling 62*, November 1987.

Segal, J.C. (1989) 'Counselling people with disabilities/chronic illnesses.' In W. Dryden, R. Woolfe and D. Charles-Edwards (eds) *Handbook of Counselling in Britain.* London, Tavistock/Routledge.

Segal, J.C. (1990) *Counselling.* Chapter 7 in L. De Souza (ed) *Multiple Sclerosis Approaches to Management.* London, Chapman and Hall.

Segal, J.C. (1990/91) 'Multiple Sclerosis in the Workplace.' In *Employee Counselling Today 2,* 4, p

Segal, J.C. (1991) 'Counselling people with MS, their families and professionals involved with them.' In L. Fallowfield and H. Davies (eds) *Counselling in Health Care.* Chichester, John Wiley.

Segal, J.C. (1991) 'The professional perspective.' In S. Ramon (ed) *Beyond Community Care: Normalisation and Integration Work.* London, Macmillan Education.

Segal, J.C. (1991) 'Use of the concept of unconscious phantasy in understanding reactions to chronic illness.' *Counselling 2,* 4, Nov 1991 pp.146–149.

Segal, J.C. (1995) 'The stresses of working with clients with disabilities.' Chapter 4. in W. Dryden and V. Varma (eds) *Stresses in Counselling in Action.* London, Sage.

Segal, J.C. (1996) 'Whose disability? counter-transference in work with people with disabilities in psychodynamic counselling.' In *Psychodynamic Counselling.*

Sinason, V. (1992) *Mental Handicap and the Human Condition: New Approaches from the Tavistock.* London, Free Association Books.

For Social Workers

Bilsborrow, S. (1992) '"You grow up fast as well." Young Carers in Merseyside.' Barnados, PSS and Carers National Association.

Mandelstam, M. with Schwer, B. (1995) *Community Care Practice and the Law.* London, Jessica Kingsley.

Oliver, M. (ed) (1995) *Social Work. Disabled People and Disabling Environments. Research Highlights in Social Work 21.* London, Jessica Kingsley.

Oliver, M. (1983) *Social Work with Disabled People.* Basingstoke, Macmillan.

Ramon, S. (ed) (1991) *Beyond Community Care: Normalisation and Integration Work.* London, Macmillan Education.

Sainsbury, E. (1994) *Working with Children in Need. Studies in Complexity and Challenge.* Highly readable detailed reports of face-to-face work with children and families by experienced social workers. London, Jessica Kingsley.

Academic

Baldwin, S. (1993) *The Myth of Community Care: An Alternative Neighbourhood Model of Care.* London, Chapman and Hall.

Banton, M. (1994) *Discrimination.* Buckingham, Open University Press.

Black, D. (1989) 'Family therapy and life-threatening illness in children and parents.'
    Palliative Medicine 3, 113–118.

Brown, G.W. and Harris, T. (1978) *Social Origins of Depression.* London, Tavistock.

Cobb, S.C. (1976) 'Social support as a moderator of life stress.' *Psychosom. Med 38*, 300–314.

Dearden, C. and Becker, S. (1995) *The National Directory of Young Carers Projects and Initiatives.*
    Young Carers Research Group, Loughborough University; also available from the Carers
    National Association: see Useful Addresses below.

Foley, C. and Pratt, S. (1994) *Access Denied: Human Rights and Disabled People.* London,
    National Council for Civil Liberties.

Grimshaw, R. (1991) *Children of Parents with Parkinson's Disease.* London, National Children's
    Bureau.

Honigsbaum, N. (1991) *HIV, AIDS and Children: A Cause for Concern.* London, National
    Children's Bureau.

Hoyes, L., Jeffers, S., Lart, R., Means, R. and Taylor, M. (1993) User empowerment and the
    reform of community care: a study of early implementation in four localities. School for
    Advanced Urban Studies, University of Bristol.

Klein, M. (1975) 'Psychoanalysis of Children.' Volume II of *The Writings of Melanie Klein.*
    London: Hogarth Press and Institute of Psychoanalysis.

Morris, J. (1993) *Independent Lives: Community Care and Disabled People.* London, The
    Macmillan Press.

Morrison, J.M. and Ursprung, A.W. (1987) 'Children's attitudes toward people with
    disabilities: a Review of the literature.' *J.of Rehab. 53*, 1, pp.45–49.

Oliver, M. (1990) *The Politics of Disablement.* London, Macmillan.

Parker, G.(1993) *With This Body. Caring and Disability in Marriage.* Oxford University Press.
    This book has a chapter on parents talking about their children, but nothing from the
    children.

Policy Studies Institute (1993) *Information Enables: Improving Access to Information Services for
    Disabled People.* Papers presented at the National Disability Information Project's 1993
    Conference. London, Policy Studies Institute.

Waterhouse, L. (ed) (1993) *Child Abuse and Child Abusers. Protection and Prevention.* London,
    Jessica Kingsley. Readable reports of research of interest to professionals and others.

Weinshenker, B.G., Hader, W,. Carrier, W., Baskerville, J. and Ebers, G.C. (1989) 'The
    influence of pregnancy on disability from MS: a population-based study in Middlesex
    County, Ontario.' *Neurology 39*, 1438–1440. Found no association between births and
    long-term disability.

Concerning the death of a parent

Abrams, R. (1992) *When Parents Die.* London, Charles Letts.

Black, D. (1987) 'Family intervention with bereaved children.' *Journal of Child Psychology and
    Psychiatry 28*, 457–476.

Furman, E. (1974) *A Child's Parent Dies: Studies in Childhood Bereavement.* New Haven and
    London, Yale University Press. Psychoanalytical: foreword by Anna Freud.

Grollman, E.A. (Updated 1990) *Talking About Death: A Dialogue Between Parent and Child.* Boston, Mass, Beacon Press. Includes notes for situations where parents died from murder, road accidents and suicide. The dialogue itself transposes well from the American.

Hendriks, J.H., Black, D. and Kaplan, T. (1993) *When Father Kills Mother: Guiding Children Through Trauma and Grief.* London, Routledge.

Smith, S.C. and Pennells, Sister M. (eds) (1995) *Interventions with Bereaved Children.* London, Jessica Kingsley. '…gathers together the experience and knowledge of many professionals in the field of childhood grief.' Well written and moving descriptions.

Pennells, Sister M. and Smith, S.C. (1994) *The Forgotten Mourners. Guidelines for Working with Bereaved Children.* London, Jessica Kingsley.

Useful Addresses

The Thomson local directories have a section called **Helplines** which gives local and some national sources of help, advice and support for various situations.

The British Telecom telephone book may have local organisations listed under Disability/disabled...e.g. Disability Law Service; Disability Arts in London etc.

Advice, Advocacy and Representation Service for Children and Young People (ASC). Freepost, Manchester M3 9BA. Freephone: 0800 616101. A confidential service for children and young people who need and receive services from Social Services. An advocate will help a child to make their views known to the relevant authorities.

Alateen. 61 Great Dover St, London SE1 4YF, tel 0171 403 0888 (24 hours). For young people whose lives have been affected by someone else's drinking.

Alzheimer's Disease Society. Gordon House, 10 Greencoat Place, London SW1P 1PH, tel 0171 306 0606.

Arthritis Care. 18 Stephenson Way, London NW1 2HD, tel 0171 916 1500. Helpline 0800 289170 (free of charge weekday afternoons).

British Association for Counselling. 1 Regent Place, Rugby CV21 2PJ, tel 01788 578328.

BACUP (British Association of Cancer United Patients). 3 Bath Rd, Rivington St, London EC2A 3JR, tel 0800 181199. Nurses provide information about cancer for people who have it and their families.

Cancerlink. 17 Britannia St London WC1X 9JN, tel 0171 833 2451. Local contacts with people who have cancer: see Thompson's Directory. Helpline for young people: 0800 591028.

Carers National Association. 20–25 Glasshouse Yard, London EC1A 4JS. Support and information for carers of all ages and for professionals, including teachers as well as social workers. Can put children in touch with Young Carer's Projects which provide support, information and opportunities for young carers in many parts of the country. Some help for children who are not carers too, tel 0171 490 8818; Wales: 01222 880176. CarersLine: 0171 490 8898, Lines open Mon-Fri 1pm-4pm: children can give their number and the Young Carer's Officer will call back.

Centre for the Study of Health, Sickness and Disablement. Brunel University, Uxbridge, Middlesex UB8 3PH, tel 01895 274000 extension 2504.

Childline. Freepost 1111, London N1 OQJ, freephone: 0800 1111.

Crossroads Care. 10 Regent Place, Rugby, CV21 2PN, tel 01788 573653. Local groups provide help at home for carers of people who are ill or disabled.

Cruse Bereavement Care. 126 Sheen Rd, Richmond, Surrey, TW9 1UR. National Bereavement Line: 0181 332 7227. Cruse have counsellors for children as well as for adults, tel 0181 940 4818.

Derbyshire Centre for Integrated Living. Long Close, Ripley, Derbyshire DE5 3HY, tel (Ripley) 01773 740246.

DIAL UK. National Association of Disablement Information and Advice Services. Park Lodge, St Catherine's Hospital, Pickhill Road, Doncaster, S. Yorkshire DN4 8QN tel 01302 310123.

Disabled Living Foundation (including the Association of Continence Advisors). 380/384 Harrow Rd, London W9 2HU, tel 0171 289 6111. Help for Health database including information on different self-help groups. Information and advice on daily living equipment for people with disabilities. Courses for professionals.

Exploring Parenthood. 4 Ivory Place, 20a Treadgold Street, W11, 4BP. National organisation offers professionally-staffed advice line for parents. 0171 221 6681. Other activities include the Moyenda Project which provides parenting support for black and ethnic minority families, and lunchtime workshops for working parents.

Homestart Consultancy. 4 Belmon Street, Swadlincote, Derbyshire DE11 8JU tel 01283 225586. Local groups provide support, friendship and practical help to parents of children under five.

Jessica Kingsley Publishers. 116 Pentonville Rd, London, N1 9JB, tel 0171 833 2307 Fax 0171 837 2917 Also 1900 Frost Rd, Suite 101, Bristol, PA 19007, USA. Source of many useful books for social workers, parents, teachers etc.

The King's Fund Carers' Unit. Kings Fund, 11–13 Cavendish Square, W1M OAN, tel 0171 307 2400.

Mary Marlborough Lodge, Nuffield Orthopaedic Centre, Headington, Oxford OX3 7LD, tel 01865 741155. Problem-solving assessment and advice. Disabled parents may stay at the Lodge with their babies while staff help work out what the difficulties are and sort out individually tailored ways of overcoming them. Leaflets on equipment for disabled people, one specifically for parents; also a book: *Parents with Disabilities*.

Manic Depression Fellowship. 8–10 High St, Kingston upon Thames, Surrey KT1 1EY. Support, advice and information, including a leaflet for young people with a parent who has manic depression, tel 0181 974 6550.

The Maternity Alliance. 15 Britannia St WC1X 9JP, tel 0171 588 8582. Campaigns for better maternity facilities for mothers with disabilities.

Mellow Parenting. c/o Dr Christine Puckering, Department of Psychological Medicine, Gartnavel Royal Hospital, Glasgow G12 0XH. Parents taking part include those who have persistent difficulties relating to their children.

National Children's Bureau. 8 Wakley St, EC1V 7QE, tel 0171 843 6000. Special interest in families with parent who has Parkinson's Disease.

National Council for One Parent Families. 255 Kentish Town Rd, London NW5 2LX, tel 0171 267 1361.

National Schizophrenia Fellowship. 28 Castle St, Kingston upon Thames, Surrey KT1 1SS. Advice line 0181 974 6814.

NSPCC: National Society for Prevention of Cruelty to Children. Tel 0800–800500. Free 24-hour advice service.

National Stepfamilies Association. Chapel House, 18 Hatton Place, London EC1N 8RU, tel 0171 209 2460. Helpline: 0990 168 388 (cheap rate number).

The Network. PO Box 558 London SW1 2EL. Information to young people living with a family member suffering from mental health or emotional problems.

Newpin. The New Parent Infant Network runs 14 family centres offering 'personal development programme' to socially isolated mothers of pre-school children. Women are matched with volunteer befrienders who have already participated in the course, which combines group work with individual therapy. A play therapist works with the children. Fathers groups are also being introduced. Details: Newpin, 35, Sutherland Square, London SE17 3EE.

ParentAbility. Alexandra House, Oldham Terrace, Acton, London W3 6NH, tel 0181 992 8637. National Childbirth Trust Network supporting pregnancy and parenthood for people with disabilities.

Parentline. Endway House, The Endway, Hadleigh SS7 2AN. tel 01702 559900. National office, refers callers to volunteer telephone counsellor within own area. Self-help support network for parents under stress; trained telephone counsellors.

Parentlink/Parent Network. 45 Caversham Rd, NW5, tel 0171 485 8535.

Parents anonymous. 6 Manor Gardens London N7, tel 0171 263 8918. For distressed parents.

Relate (Formerly Marriage Guidance Council). Herbert Gray College, Little Church St. Rugby, Warwickshire CV21 3AP, tel 01788 573241/560811.

Saneline. 2nd Floor, 199–205 Old Marylebone Rd, London NW1 5QP. Telephone helpline for people concerned about mental illness: 0345 678000 calls charged at local rate. 2pm to midnight every day.

Sickle Cell Society. 54 Station Rd, Harlesden, London NW10 4UA, tel 0181 961 7795.

Stroke Association. CHSA House, Whitecross St, London EC1Y 8JJ, tel 0171 490 7999.

Scope – For People with Cerebral Palsy. 12 Park Crescent, London W1N 4EQ, tel 0171 636 5020. Helpline 0800 626 216 For information, advice and initial counselling on anything associated with Cerebral Palsy. Publishes *Disability Now*, newspaper for people with any disabilities; includes 'For Sale and Wanted' and advertisements from dating agencies.

SPOD (Social and Personal Relations of the Disabled). 286 Camden Rd, London N7 OBJ, tel 0171 607 8851. Advice and information on sexual difficulties related to disability or illness.

The Terrence Higgins Trust. 52–54 Grays Inn Rd, London WC1 8JU. Helpline 0171 242 1010 (12am–10pm). Practical support, help, counselling and advice for anyone with or concerned about AIDS and HIV infection.

Westminster Pastoral Foundation. 23 Kensington Square, London W8 5HN, tel 0171 937 6956. Specialist counselling for people with a serious physical illness or disability.

Youth Access. 1a Taylor's Yard, 67 Alderbrooke Road, London SW12 8AD tel 0181 772 9900. A national network of informal youth counselling, information and advice services.

Young Carers Research Group. c/o Betty Newton, Dept of Social Science, Loughborough University, Leics LE11 3TU, tel 01509 228299/223379, Fax 01509 238277; e-mail M.E.Newton@lut.ac.uk. Coordinates projects in the UK exploring the situation of children and young people caring for their parents.

Young Minds. 102–108 Clerkenwell Rd. London, EC1M 55A, tel 0171 336 8445, fax 0171 336 8446. Helpline for teachers, parents and carers: 0345 626376 National database of statutory and voluntary agencies which can help children and those involved in taking care of them. Young Minds will also arrange for a professional advisor to call back to speak personally with parents or professionals to help them to clarify a problem and find a way forward. Leaflets, booklets, reports and a magazine also available.

Subject Index

Author
Index